Disaster AT SEA

John Marriott

HIPPOCRENE BOOKS
New York

This edition published by Hippocrene Books Inc.
171 Madison Avenue
New York, NY 10016

ISBN 0-87052-450-X (hardbound)
ISBN 0-87052-764-9 (paperback)

Printed in the United States of America

M 9 8 7 6 5 4 3 2 1

Front cover:
The *Amoco Cadiz* aground off the coast of Brittany, having broken into three parts soon after grounding. *United States Department of Commerce*

Back cover:
The famous Lutine Bell. *Lloyds*

Acknowledgements
I am indebted to the many organisations which have helped me in the writing of this book, in particular: The Royal Institute of Navigation, the Royal Ocean Racing Club, Lloyds of London, HM Coastguard, The Royal National Lifeboat Institution, the Royal Air Force and the Royal Navy.

I have consulted many books, but principally I have referred to:

Black Tide Rising by David Fairhall & Philip Jordan, published by Andre Deutsch.

The Wreck of the Torrey Canyon by Crispin Gill and others, published by David & Charles.

Without Trace by John Harris, published by Matheson (London).

Some Ship Disasters by K. C. Barnaby, published by Hutchinson of London.

Subsunk by W. O. Shelford, published by George C. Harrap.

An Agony of Collisions by Peter Padfield, published by Hodder & Stoughton.

The Death of the Thresher by Norman Polmar, published by Chilton Books of Philadelphia, USA.

The Wreck of the Memphis by Edward L. Beach, published by Jarrolds.

Fastnet 1979 by L. T. Gardner, published by George Godwin.

The Report of the Fastnet Race 1979 issued by the Royal Yachting Association and the Royal Ocean Racing Club.

John Marriott

Contents

Introduction

This book is a collection of accounts of some of the better known disasters at sea which have occurred over the past 150 years. There have of course been many disasters, but in general I have tried to select those which are of interest to the mariner, because of the questions they raise over navigation and seamanship, and those which are of more interest to the general public because they deal with human lives and the courage shown by men (and women) once the disaster has occurred.

No mention is made of disasters which occurred as a result of enemy action. A large number of ships were lost in the 1914 and the 1939 wars, and in the many other wars in the last 150 years, but more able pens than mine have recorded them for posterity.

Many of the surface warship disasters mentioned occurred whilst carrying out manoeuvres, for the simple reason that when ships are acting in close company there is more chance of collision. Nowadays ships are not often in close company and are dispersed well apart from each other because of the enormous area a nuclear explosion can cover; there is therefore less chance of them colliding. Submarine disasters are usually caused by their inability to surface, perhaps because of some technical fault or because water has entered the boat.

Most surface ship disasters can, in the end, be boiled down to five main causes:

1. Faulty navigation
2. Faulty use of radar
3. Too high a speed in fog
4. Bad weather
5. Downright carelessness

When reading this book it is important for the reader to remember that the words used to direct the helmsman to alter course were changed in 1931. Before this date, steering orders referred to the tiller, a relic of bygone days when ships used to be steered by a tiller. Thus, if it was desired to turn the ship to starboard, the order was given to put the tiller to port; this put the rudder to starboard and thus the ship's head to starboard. Conversely if one desired to turn to port, the tiller was put to starboard. This was obviously undesirable, so by international agreement the system was changed in 1931: all reference to the tiller was dropped, and if a turn to starboard was required the wheel was turned to the right (starboard); this in turn moved the rudder to starboard and the ship's head went to starboard; and vice versa for turns to port. A number of disasters in this book occurred before 1931 and thus the old steering orders were used, but a note to this effect has been included in the text.

Throughout the accounts, the form '00.30' has been used as a standard to indicate the times of events, although the '0030' is the more strictly nautical one.

Two chapters not related to any particular disaster have been included. One is on Insurance, which plays a large part in any marine disaster, and is followed by a description of Lloyds of London, the best known insurance market in the world. The other is on the Air Sea Rescue organisation of Great Britain. Many disasters occur in the crowded waters around the British Isles and this organisation, with its unique bringing together of rescue aircraft, ships, lifeboats and the Coastguards, plays a very significant part in the saving of lives. Other countries have similar organisations and it is fitting that a reference should be made to it in a book on disaster at sea.

Below:
In mountainous seas, a lifeboat takes part in the great search and rescue operation mounted after the 1979 Fastnet Race disaster. *RNAS Culdrose*

1

Lloyds of London

No book on disaster at sea would be complete without a chapter on Lloyds of London, on which the greater part of marine insurance falls. Lloyds started 300 years ago when Edward Lloyd opened his coffee shop in Tower Street, in the City of London, in 1688. Although little is known of the enterprising Welshman, or his establishment, it seems likely that from the outset he encouraged a clientele of merchants, shipowners, sea captains and others with an interest in waterborne trade. In those days, insurance of ships and cargo was a fairly simple matter of hawking a policy round the City for subscription by anyone with sufficient income to take a share in the risk in return for a percentage of the premium. The insurance broker's job was to find men of sufficient financial status to meet their share of the claims to the full extent, if needs be, of their personal fortune. Underwriters were mostly wealthy merchants, signing policies as an addition to their main business.

Lloyd's Coffee House formed a convenient place for all those concerned to meet and discuss their business. They could listen to the latest gossip and Lloyd himself gained a reputation for providing trustworthy shipping news. This was a most important factor in successful underwriting, and perhaps more than anything else ensured that Lloyds, over and above its rivals, gradually became the recognised place to obtain marine insurance.

As far as is known, Lloyd himself took no part in underwriting. He was described in his day mostly as a 'coffee man' and seemed content to provide his patrons with congenial surroundings and the simple facilities they needed to do business with each other. When Lloyd died in 1713 his principal legacy to the future was his name and the establishment bearing it.

Efforts by the Government to restrict speculative investment, after the South Sea Bubble, led to the granting of a Charter to the Royal Exchange Assurance and the London Assurance and prohibited marine insurance by any other company or business partnership. At first sight it looked as if it would put Lloyds Coffee House out of business, but it survived as the Government did not prohibit underwriting by private individuals. Lloyds continued to expand and moved from Tower Street to Lombard Street.

The 18th century saw the first signs of an organised community of interest among underwriters and led rapidly to the establishment of a properly constituted society, out of which developed the business institution that we know today. New Lloyds Coffee House, as it was known, soon proved too small and in 1774 rooms were rented in the Royal Exchange by the previously-formed Committee; Lloyds Coffee House became a registered place of business.

For the next century the society of underwriters at Lloyds evolved and gradually assumed its present day form: membership was regulated and the elected committee given increased authority. The society also saw the birth of

non-marine insurance, but the main marine intelligence side continued to grow, until Lloyds once more found its premises too small and decided to build a new modern building with room for expansion in Lombard Street. It was opened early in 1986.

Briefly then, Lloyds today is a society of underwriters whose members, all private individuals, accept insurance business for personal profit or loss. As Lloyds' members they are all individually liable to the full extent of their personal fortunes to meet their underwriting commitments. They conduct their business in groups or syndicates, managed by an underwriting agent who is responsible for appointing a professional underwriter for each class of business; these specialist underwriters accept risks on behalf of their syndicate members. They do not deal with the public, but their business is brought to them through accredited Lloyds brokers whose widespread contacts, together with their intimate knowledge of the market, enable them to direct their clients' needs quickly to the most appropriate underwriting facility, on the most advantageous terms and in the shortest time.

Lloyds is an international market place for insurance of every description. Almost anything can be insured there. The world's shipping and aircraft fleets, factories, civil engineering projects, oil rigs and refineries are but a few of the many risks placed at Lloyds, which in total earns around £4 billion in annual premium income. Some three-quarters of this business comes from outside the United Kingdom and makes a substantial contribution to the country's balance of payments.

The almost legendary reputation of Lloyds for never failing to settle a valid insurance claim is maintained by a massive chain of security requirements designed to ensure that every underwriting member is at all times fully covered by his personal resources for the proportion of risks he underwrites. In addition to stringent rules for an annual audit of personal solvency and for premium income limits related to his Lloyd's deposit, these requirements cover the safeguarding of premium income for the purpose of meeting claims and deposit of securities with the Corporation of Lloyds.

Marine insurance is one of the oldest surviving commercial practices connected with trade. It may or may not have originated in classical antiquity but it was certainly well established in London during the reign of Elizabeth I, over 100 years before Edward Lloyd opened his coffee house. Although Lloyds handles any sort of insurance business, perhaps its largest interest is still in the marine market. If London is the world's foremost marine insurance market, Lloyds is the axis upon which it turns — Lloyds and marine insurance were synonymous for nearly two centuries. Indeed there were very few other forms of insurance until the 1880s, and even today marine business accounts for nearly half of Lloyds' total premium income.

Modern marine insurance covers not only the traditional areas of hulls and cargoes but the whole field of transport — the carriage of goods of every description by land, sea and air — as well as marine structures such as oil rigs and deep sea exploration platforms. In particular, the marine market gives a lead to world insurers in war risk underwriting and the allied areas of cover against piracy at sea and in the air, as well as insurance against confiscation and expropriation of property.

Membership can only be accepted at Lloyds by elected 'Underwriting Members of Lloyds' who must satisfy the most stringent conditions in order to qualify. They must:

1. Be nominated by one and supported by five other members.
2. Transact business with unlimited and personal liability.
3. Satisfy the Committee of their integrity and financial standing.
4. Furnish security in an approved form, to be held in trust by the Corporation of Lloyds, which, varying according to the volume of business to be transacted, is a minimum of £15,000 for a member not previously connected with Lloyds who is to accept both marine and non-marine business.
4. Pay all premiums into Premium Trust Funds under deeds of trust approved by the Board of Trade and the Committee of Lloyds from which claims, expenses and ascertained profits only may be paid. Every member on election must pay a substantial sum (independent of his deposit) as an initial contribution to his Premium Trust Fund and any part of his Premium Trust Fund Deposit which is used to pay claims, etc, must be reinstated before any future profits are distributed.
6. Furnish a guarantee policy each year in the case of non-marine business for the amount by which their premium income exceeds the deposit lodged with the Committee. The policy must be subscribed by other members of Lloyds according to the conditions set by the Committee.
7. Contribute by means of levy on premium income to a Central Fund intended to meet underwriting liabilities of any member in the unlikely event of his security and personal assets being insufficient to meet his underwriting

commitments. This Fund, amounting to several million pounds, is for the protection of the assured, not of the Underwriter who is still responsible for his liabilities to the extent of his private estate.

As already mentioned, all underwriting members must submit to an annual audit. Each must show that the value of his or her underwriting assets is sufficient to meet their liabilities for all classes of business. The audit is designed to detect any weakness in the underwriter's position at the earliest moment and to ensure that provision is made to remedy any such trend so that the assured's position is always safeguarded.

Today there are over 6,000 underwriting members of Lloyds and they are formed into syndicates of a few to a hundred or more members, each represented at Lloyds by Underwriting agents. There are 146 marine, 86 non-marine, 25 aviation and 29 motor syndicates, and it is underwriting agents who, through appointed underwriters, accept on behalf of 'Names' on their syndicates the risks brought to Lloyds. Thus when a syndicate underwriter accepts (or writes) a risk he can go for a very much larger amount than if he were acting on behalf of himself alone, though the personal and individual liability of the members on whose behalf he accepts business is not altered in any way.

The underwriters for syndicates sit with their staffs in the Underwriting Room at 'boxes', pew-like desks, which, along with features such as a 'Captain's Room' and liveried staff called 'waiters', are hereditary characteristics still to be found in the modern Lloyds. Insurance may only be placed at Lloyds through the medium of the 221 firms of Lloyds Brokers who alone are permitted to place business with Lloyds underwriters in the Underwriting Room. This feature of Lloyds is based upon practical considerations, for as Lloyds is a market it would be impossible for a member of the public, without the specialised knowledge of the Broker, to find the appropriate underwriter with whom to place his business, let alone at the most advantageous terms and rates that Brokers constantly seek on behalf of their clients.

Brokers have associates and contacts all over the world but, as Lloyds underwriters may accept business only in the Underwriting Room at Lloyds, they are the underwriters' only contact with the assured; nevertheless the Broker represents the latter, not the underwriter, and it is his duty to advise his client and obtain for him the most favourable terms available, commensurate with the risk involved. The Lloyds Broker is not restricted to Lloyds and can also place business with the insurance companies.

Those unfamiliar with Lloyds find it surprising that underwriters can be found sitting at the same 'box' and yet competing with each other. However, Lloyds could never have developed without good faith persisting amid the competition, and it is very much part of the strong but intangible 'spirit' of the market. The confidence between broker and underwriter is perhaps exemplified by the 'slip', an unpretentious piece of paper giving the basic details of a risk to be placed and which in the first instance is the only paper evidence of agreement between them. Despite its simplicity the Broker knows that if the slip bears an underwriter's initials a bona fide claim will be honoured, if necessary before time has permitted the issue of a policy.

Initially the slip, relating to a risk, is taken by the Broker to the underwriter who is recognised in the market as being an authority on the particular type of insurance required, and is known as the 'leader'. The Broker will be able to assess the limits within which the underwriter is likely to quote his rate of premium; if after discussion the Broker considers the rate too high, he can and will approach other underwriters for competitive rates.

When a rate for an insurance is agreed and the cover required is large — as is often the case these days — it is usual for the underwriter to accept part of the risk rather than the whole. He then puts the percentage he will accept on the slip and initials it. The Broker then takes the slip to other underwriters, persuading them to take a portion of the risk until he has collected enough to cover 100%. In this way the insurance is spread over numerous individuals or syndicates, so that if there is a loss, the load is spread over a number of people instead of just one syndicate or individual. This principle has enabled Lloyds to withstand the stress of an enormous claim without the dire result that the layman might think is inevitable.

The Lloyds market is administered by a Committee comprising 16 members of Lloyds, elected from and by their fellow members, who serve for four years after

Below:
The Underwriters Room at Lloyds'. *Lloyds*

which they must retire for one year before being eligible for re-election. The Committee members elect their own Chairman and Deputy Chairman annually.

The Committee does not normally dictate the type of business accepted at Lloyds or interfere in the day-to-day conduct of underwriters' business. The Committee is responsible for the election of new members and is vitally concerned with the financial stability of those doing business at Lloyds. It administers the affairs of the Corporation, including the provision of Claims Offices, Shipping Intelligence and Publications, an Aviation Department, the Agency Network, the Policy Signing Office, a central Accounting Office, Foreign Legislation, Membership, Audit and Information Departments and the actual premises themselves. The Corporation employs a permanent staff of over 2,000.

Underwriters are not required to sign each policy. This function is performed by the Lloyds Policy Signing Office, a central department where policies are checked with the slips, signed on behalf of syndicates, and sealed with the seal of the Lloyds Policy Signing Office without which no policy is valid. The office also ensures that underwriters are supplied with details of the business they have done and they are promptly paid what is owed to them.

An important aspect of the marine side of Lloyds is the worldwide shipping intelligence system which is provided by a network of Agents and Sub-Agents throughout the world. Their function is to send to Lloyds the shipping, aviation and other news relating to the ports and areas in which they operate. This is only part of the work, however. The Agents are also called upon to appoint surveyors to report on damage or loss and are authorised to settle claims on behalf of the underwriters for whom they are appointed as claim-settling agents.

The enormous volume of shipping intelligence received at Lloyds from the Agents, coastal radio stations, shipowners and other sources is collated in Lloyds Intelligence Department and distributed in newspapers, radio and television services and throughout the marine and commercial communities in general. The intelligence is also published by Lloyds itself in its many shipping publications, such as *Lloyds List & Shipping Gazette*, and *Lloyds Shipping Index*. *Lloyds Register of Shipping* is a well known document giving details of all the ships in the world. It is not part of Lloyds itself but is a separate organisation, closely affiliated with Lloyds.

A number of documents originating at Lloyds have become standard and are universally used by shipping and insurance circles everywhere. For example, Lloyds Marine Insurance Policy was adopted by Lloyds in 1779, and the wording, only slightly amended, is still used in all marine insurance policies. Lloyds Standard Form of Salvage Agreement, the 'No Cure, No Pay' agreement, features in a number of cases in this book.

Lloyds is a blend of old and new; for with a system based on empirical development it is not always desirable, or indeed possible, completely to replace old and tried methods. Often it is better to improve an established system by modern techniques and in the main this is what has happened at Lloyds. 'Calling', for instance, by which Brokers contact colleagues, dates to Royal Exchange days and in embryo form even earlier to the coffee house days where a boy called the 'Kidney' read notices from a pulpit. The original method at the Royal Exchange of a waiter calling the name of the Broker required through a megaphone is fundamentally unaltered but nowadays a microphone and loudspeakers are used.

11

Once the Broker has heard his name he can signal his whereabouts on screens in the Caller's rostrum and on the gallery by a system which works electronically.

Lloyds is very proud of what is called the Nelson Room. This is a quiet room, off the gallery of the Underwriters Room, to which members may retire to read or rest. There, set out in illuminated cases lined with crimson velvet, are relics of Lloyds' Patriotic Fund. Founded in 1863, the Fund is subscribed to by the Lloyds community, with the addition of charitable gifts dating from the old Lloyds Coffee House and even before that. The Fund is used towards the relief of the families of sailors killed or wounded in action. In addition the Fund occasionally provides presentations, generally of silver plate, to officers who distinguish themselves in battle. The Patriotic Fund still carries out the work for which it was originally formed.

Nelson himself received two presentations of silver plate from the Fund, each valued at £500 in those days. One presentation was for his outstanding efforts at the Battle of the Nile in 1798 and the other was for the Battle of Copenhagen in 1801. The two sets of silver form the nucleus of the museum in the Nelson Room. Most of the remaining exhibits consist of letters written by Nelson, other silver plate, Nelson mementoes and a full length portrait of Nelson by Lemuel Abbett, presented by Lloyds underwriters, Brokers and friends. They form a much-prized collection at Lloyds.

Another relic is the well-known Lutine Bell. The bell originally belonged to the French frigate *La Lutine* which surrendered to the British at Toulon in 1793. She was renamed HMS *Lutine* and was used to carry a cargo of bullion from Yarmouth Roads to Hamburg in 1759. It was her last voyage, for she was wrecked off Terschelling in a violent storm on 10 October 1799, with the loss of all hands and the entire cargo valued at £1,400,000. The insurance was, of course, at Lloyds.

The bell hangs in the Underwriting Room and used to be rung, two strokes for good news and one stroke for bad (such as the loss of a vessel). Nowadays, since the development of modern communications, it is more frequently rung on ceremonial occasions. The last occasion on which it was rung in earnest was to report the recovery of two rogue satellites in November 1984. At the same time the Chairman announced that the five astronauts concerned would be awarded Lloyds Silver Medals for Meritorious Services.

A number of salvage attempts have been made on the *Lutine* over the years, resulting in some £100,000 in bullion being recovered, plus some old relics such as a cannon, the rudder, the Captain's watch and the bell itself, which was raised in 1859. The rudder was made into a chair and table, now in the Writing Room at Lloyds.

Lloyds is a society of underwriters, an international insurance market, a corporation, a publisher, a world centre of marine intelligence and an important City landowner. Every one of these designations is accurate and, in total, they add up to a business institution which, in our modern world, must surely be without parallel. Nowhere else is insurance transacted by a group of individuals having unlimited liability, fiercely competing with one another, and at the same time subscribing to a real if indefinable esprit de corps. This subtle blend of enterprise, competition and co-operation combined with a passionate attachment to the old insurance principle of 'utmost good faith' is what stamps Lloyds as unique.

2

The British Search and Rescue Organisation

Britain has a large search and rescue organisation to deal with all forms of disaster at sea, including oil pollution. It is based on four main disciplines:

(a) The Coastguard
(b) The National Lifeboat Service
(c) The Royal Naval Search and Rescue Service
(d) The Royal Air Force Air Search and Rescue Service

The British Coastguard
The British Coastguard service was first formed in 1824, primarily to prevent smuggling, but at the same time the Coastguard was expected to assist ships in distresses and, in the case of shipwrecks, to do its best to save lives. In 1923 the control of the Coastguards was taken over from the Admiralty by the Board of Trade which established a complete civilian organisation covering the whole of the British coastline. In the 1970s its control was handed over to the Department of Transport which completely reorganised it and formed six major Regions, each headed by a Regional Controller with his headquarters at a Maritime Rescue Co-ordinating Centre (MRCC). The Regions were sub-divided into Districts, each with a Maritime Rescue Sub Centre (MRSC) under a District Controller. Each of the six MRCCs has four Districts (and four MRSCs under it), except for the MRCC at Dover which has only one District under it — Thames, because of the large amount of traffic in the area.

Each MRCC has a fully fitted Operations Room with facilities for the Press, its own staff and storage space for rescue equipment. Vehicles and boats are also kept there. All MRCCs have radar and can also control remote radar sites situated some distance away on high points for increased radar coverage.

Within each District are a number of Auxiliary Coastguard Stations with appropriate rescue vehicles and equipment, grouped into Sectors under the management of Sector Officers. Auxiliary Stations are not necessarily manned all the time but can be set on watch when required at times of risk. Sector Officers train the Auxiliary Coastguards and patrol in Land Rovers, visiting their Auxiliary Stations from time to time, and they also have the use of a boat.

The area covered by the Coastguard is out to 1,000 miles into the North Atlantic and to 30 miles from the entire coastline of the British Isles. It is responsible for all rescues on the actual coast, including cliff top rescues, but offshore its main role is co-ordinating all rescue services including the Lifeboats and the RN and RAF rescue aircraft.

The Coastguard service comprises over 500 officers, all with practical experience at sea, and they are backed by 8,500 Auxiliary Coastguard men.

Coastguard Maritime Rescue Centres

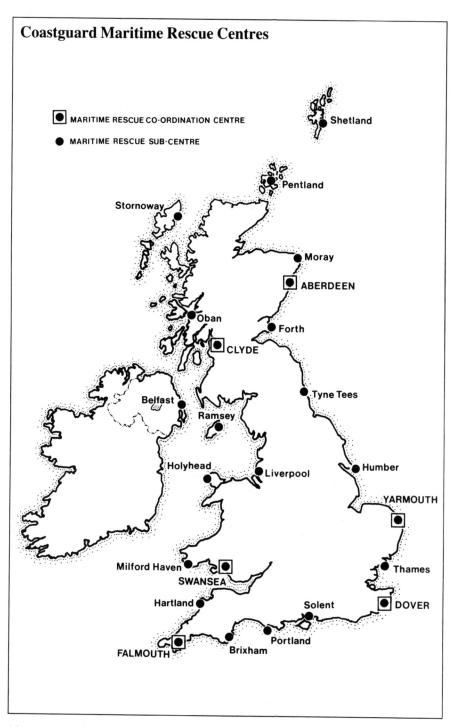

Officers wear a uniform very similar to that worn by Royal Navy officers. The regular Coastguards work in the MRCCs and MRSCs, some also work in the Sectors, and they are probably the first people to arrive at a coastal incident. In addition, there are reporting members whose work place or home is at a vantage point and has a telephone. There are also Auxiliary Afloat Coastguards whose normal activities give them the opportunity of reporting emergencies by radio or telephone to the MRCCs or MRSCs.

Communications

Nearly all rescues depend very largely on adequate communications. In principle, all units taking part in a rescue at sea keep watch on VHF channel 16, 166.8kHz, voice, which is the VHF distress circuit. Lifeboats and warships guard many other circuits, as do the maritime patrol aircraft of the RAF. The Coastguards and Lifeboats have their own VHF channel 6 (156.0MHz), and rescue helicopters may also keep watch on this frequency. The British Telecom coastal radio stations guard the two main distress frequencies (2,180MHz voice and 500MHz morse). Most MRCCs and MRSCs have direct telephone lines to their nearest coastal radio station, but in addition they can communicate direct to a ship in distress by a link call through a coastal radio station. Lifeboats too have VHF and MF voice radio links to their local coastal radio station.

Radar

The majority of Lifeboats and many Coastguard stations are fitted with radar (and with radio direction finding), which plays a large part in rescue operations. Ships (and aircraft) also carry an Emergency Position Indicating Radio Beacon (EPIRB) operating on 121.5MHz and 243MHz. They can be switched on and will automatically transmit to enable rescue craft fitted with VHF DF to home on to them.

There are various ways of indicating distress. The letters SOS followed by the ship's position and transmitted on 500kHz at the distress periods is the best known and all ships keep listening watch, if only on a loudspeaker, at the distress periods, as also do coastal stations. This is probably the first indication a vessel in distress may give. In addition there is the voice frequency of 2,182kHz using the word MAYDAY. It is primarily used by small vessels and yachts within range of a coastal radio station or a Coastguard.

In addition to all this, the British Coastguard is now adopting a more worldwide role by means of communication satellites. It has a UK terminal for Maritime Satellite Distress Communications at the MRCC at Falmouth in Cornwall, which is connected to the UK Coast Earth Station at Goonhilly Down, also in Cornwall. It in turn is part of the INMARSAT global system for merchant ships. Falmouth also has its own Ship Earth station which allows the centre to communicate with other rescue centres similarly fitted around the globe.

Lifeboats

British lifeboats are under the direction of the Royal National Lifeboat Institution (a registered charity). The Institution, the lifeboats, their stations and the crews are all entirely supported by voluntary contributions and they cost £23 million a year to maintain, which is a measure of the great regard the British public has for the work done by the lifeboats.

There are over 130 lifeboats ranging from 33ft to 70ft long, based at the 200 lifeboat stations. In addition there are 126 smaller lifeboats of 16ft to 20ft long, and the RNLI also maintains a relief fleet of 71 lifeboats to replace boats when they are refitting or damaged.

The RNLI's policy is to maintain a lifeboat fleet which can reach a casualty up to 30 miles from the shore within four hours (within two hours for some fast lifeboats). From that point they can continue to search, or stand by a vessel, for a further four hours. Many of the smaller lifeboats are of the inflatable type, but they are primarily used for daylight, offshore operations in the summer, but a few remain on station and can operate at night.

There are 14 different types of lifeboat and all new boats of over 30ft are self-righting. Their speeds vary from 18.6kt to 8kt and there are a few of the sea skimming type with speeds of 20kt or over which are mostly used for close inshore rescues. Many of the older boats are built of wood, but modern boats are now being made of GRP or neoprene.

Apart from the mechanic, the crews are all volunteers and become full-time employees of the RNLI. Many of them are fishermen, but men (and occasionally women) are recruited from other walks of life. Each member of the crew receives a small payment to compensate for loss of earnings when they are on service of £9.50 for the first hour and £1.50 for each hour afterwards. Helpers, who help launch lifeboats, also receive a small payment.

The Lifeboat Station

Lifeboats are kept at stations all round the coast of the British Isles and the stations are divided into seven operational divisions, each under the supervision of an Inspector of Lifeboats. Other non-seagoing staff are distributed to the divisions to look after such things as engines, hulls and electronics. The day-to-day running of each station is the responsibility of a voluntary committee, headed by a Honorary Secretary who is responsible for approving the launching of a lifeboat on receipt of a request from a Coastguard. Stations also have a voluntary doctor who, in addition to giving first aid training to the crews, may also accompany the lifeboat if a doctor is required by the vessel in distress. Outstanding service in lifeboats is marked by the award of medals from the RNLI. The medals are of bronze, silver and, very occasionally, gold. The thanks of the RNLI, on vellum, is used for lower awards.

Funds

Being an entirely voluntary organisation the RNLI has to exist on the generosity of the public. Various fund-raising schemes are in existence, such as a national flag day, regular subscriptions to *Shoreline* — a RNLI membership scheme — sale of catalogues or souvenirs, donations, sale of collections of stamps and coins, and local fund-raising events.

The RAF and RN Search and Rescue Organisation

Currently the RAF has nine detachments of search and rescue (SAR) aircraft stationed at RAF airfields around the coast of the British Isles. The RN has four detachments stationed at naval air stations, mostly in the south of England, but there is one at Prestwick in Scotland.

Above left:
A 'Tyne' class lifeboat with a
maximum speed of 17.5kt
and a length of 47ft. This
type of boat normally lies
afloat, or can be launched
from a slipway. *RNLI*

Left:
An 'Arun' class lifeboat with
a maximum speed of 18.2kt
and a length of 52.54ft. This
type of boat normally lies
afloat. *RNLI*

Below:
A Royal Navy Wessex
helicopter about to rescue
survivors from the sea during
the 1979 Fastnet Race.
RNAS Culdrose

The main function of the RAF and RN SAR services is to assist military and civil aircrews in distress, but the majority of their work involves civil rescue, particularly at sea. Two types of helicopter are operated, the Sea King and the older Wessex, but the latter will shortly be faded out.

Each detachment consists of two aircraft on stand by 24 hours a day, 365 days a year. One aircraft is at 15 minutes notice during daylight hours; or at one hour readiness in the case of the Wessex, and 45 minutes in the case of the Sea King, at night. When the first helicopter is used, the second is brought to 15 minutes readiness.

There are two Rescue Co-ordination Centres (RCCs) jointly manned by the RAF and the Navy, one at Pitreavie Castle, near Dunfermline in Scotland, and the other at Mount Batten near Plymouth. The Centres co-ordinate all Service aircraft used in a rescue attempt. In addition to the helicopters the RAF deploys Nimrod maritime patrol aircraft and Shackleton airborne early warning aircraft to search for survivors, guide rescue craft and helicopters and act as radio links. Nimrods can also drop survival equipment and life rafts, if required, and Hercules aircraft too may be used for this task.

The Helicopters
The Sea King has an all-weather capability and can carry 18 passengers with a radius of action of 200 nautical miles. In addition to its sophisticated navigation and communications equipment, the Sea King has a Flight Control System (FCS) which allows it to home automatically both in foul weather and at night. With the FCS in use, the winch operator can manoeuvre the aircraft by remote control from his position at the cabin doorway, which greatly assists rescues from the sea.

The Wessex has two engines with waterproof flooring and modified racks for equipment required in SAR work. It has an effective radius of 90nm and can carry a maximum of 14 passengers. Whereas Sea Kings have a crew of four — Pilot, Co-Pilot, Radar Operator and Winchman — the Wessex has only three in the crew — Pilot, Navigator and Winchman — and it can fly safely on one engine. In both types of helicopter, survivors can be winched up from a maximum height of 300ft.

Typical Type of Rescue
There are a number of ways in which a disaster at sea can be reported, but let us look at two typical accidents.

● Two ships have been in collision in the Western Approaches to the English Channel. The weather is very rough and one ship sinks and many crew and passengers are in the water. An SOS is transmitted and is picked up by many coastal radio stations on the south and west coasts of the British Isles. The details are telephoned by the coastal radio stations to the Coastguard MRCC at Falmouth, it being the nearest MRCC to the scene of the collision. The duty officer then telephones the lifeboat stations at St Mary in the Scillies and also at Penlee in Cornwall, and they both agree to send their lifeboats. Both lifeboats radio the MRCC to say that the weather is so bad that it will take them some time to reach the scene. Therefore the MRCC at Falmouth decides to ask for air assistance to lift the survivors from the water and telephones the request to the RAF Rescue Co-ordination Centre at Mount Batten, Plymouth. The Centre then

Above left and left:
A small inflatable liferaft, with canopy stowed and raised.   *RFD*

Below:
A typical lifeboat station, including offshore and inshore lifeboats, a tracked towing tractor, patrol Land Rover and, most important of all, the officers, crews, observers and helpers.

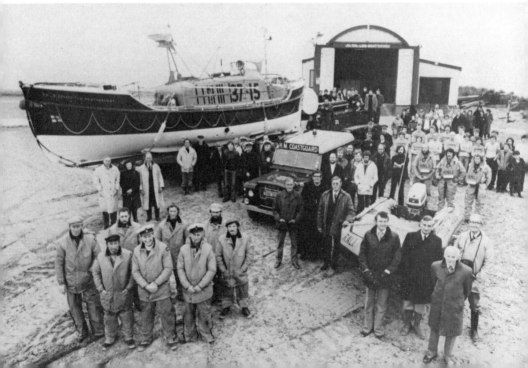

decides to send out two rescue Wessex helicopters, one from the Naval Air Station at Culdrose, and the other from the RAF station at Chivenor. The Navy is also asked to send a warship to act as on the scene co-ordinator, and a Fishery Protection corvette is diverted to the scene.

The two helicopters arrive first and start to look for survivors in the water. These they rescue by winching a man down to the surface who secures the survivor in a harness and has him winched up to the waiting helicopter. Usually only one man can be rescued at a time. However, within an hour the two lifeboats arrive and are able to rescue many others. Finally, the corvette arrives and also starts to rescue survivors, and of course the other ship in the collision is also helping to rescue. Meanwhile the Coastguard is making arrangements with the local hospitals to receive any wounded and Mount Batten is arranging for the reception of the helicopters, and possibly for more helicopters to be sent.

● A small coastal vessel has run ashore in fog off the Humber. It transmits a MAYDAY signal on 2,182kHz and this is picked up by Humber Coastal Radio and is also heard by the MRSC at the Humber. The MRSC, on its own initiative, calls for help from the Humber lifeboat station and at the same time tells the MRCC at Yarmouth what has been done. The MRCC at Yarmouth asks if any air assistance is needed, but the Humber MRSC says that the fog is too thick. The MRSC despatches a mobile patrol in a Land Rover to the point where the ship has run aground. The ship starts operating its EPIRB so that the lifeboats can home on to its position.

These are two relatively simple incidents. The Fastnet Race of 1979 (featured in a later chapter) is a good example of a much more complicated search and rescue operation, involving all available sources of rescue work. In this incident the RAF deployed Nimrod aircraft to act as the scene co-ordinator as many of the yachts were more than 30 miles from the British coast.

Britain is justly proud of its search and rescue organisation, which has saved a tremendous number of lives. For example, in 1985 British lifeboats had 3,813 calls and saved 1,623 lives. The Coastguard handles over 5,000 incidents a year, including more than 3,000 offshore and 500 cliff rescues, and the RAF and RN search and rescue service rescued 1,004 people in 1985.

The worldwide rescue services are constantly being updated by the latest techniques, one of which is the use of American SARSAT (Search & Rescue Satellites) and the Soviet COSPA satellite systems. Both the United States and the Soviet Union have three of each type of satellite in orbit, and the Soviets will shortly put a fourth COSPA into space. The satellites pick up the distress signals from the EPIRBs, both from ships and aircraft, and relay the positions of the beacons to the appropriate mission control centre. They in turn pass the information to the Rescue Co-ordination Centres, the positions so obtained are said to be accurate to within 1½ miles. The two projects work closely together and participating countries are the USA, France, Norway, Sweden and the Soviet Union.

However, it is one thing to be able to ascertain where an accident has occurred, but quite another to be able to effect a satisfactory rescue, particularly if the weather is bad.

HMS Captain

The *Captain* was a 4,000-ton ironclad, over 300ft long and propelled by reciprocating engines with two screws, and also by sails. The vessel had three masts and a considerable area of canvas, through which protruded a funnel. Her maximum speed was 14.2kt under steam and 11kt by sail, and she was commanded by Capt Hugh Talbot Burgoyne VC. The *Captain's* loss was in no way attributable to him, rather to faults in the vessel's design.

Before she was ever built, considerable controversy surrounded her design, not least of which was the fact that the ship was designed by a Royal Naval officer, Capt Cowper Coles, instead of the more usual Naval Constructor. Whilst it was not unusual for naval officers to think that they could design ships, they were generally bitterly opposed by the naval constructors of the day. The opposition to Coles trying to design a ship became bitter and sometimes vituperative, his chief opponent being a Chief Constructor at the Admiralty, Edward James Read, later Sir Edward Read MP.

The story goes back to some years before the *Captain* was built. Coles was a gunnery expert and a great protagonist of the revolving turret method of mounting guns. Hitherto all guns had been fixed and mounted on both sides of the ship, but Coles designed a centre line turret which could be mechanically rotated, thus enabling the total number of guns to be reduced (and, perhaps even more significantly, reducing the overall weight of a ship's armament). The snag of a revolving turret in a sailing ship was that the masts, yards, etc, had braces coming down to the deck and thus prevented all-round fire from a centre line gun to a considerable extent, so Coles tried without much success to reduce the number of masts and rigging. Coles also thought that a ship carrying such armament ought to present the minimum possible target, so he was proposing a low freeboard. In this he was at variance with the Admiralty designers — particularly Read — who maintained that a low freeboard was incompatible with safety, and safety in a ship was all important.

At this time, steam engines were just being introduced into naval ships; however, the sails were retained, making the design of the armament extremely difficult. Coles kept proposing designs which almost as frequently were turned down by professional ship designers.

As time wore on, Coles' ideas, propounded by him in numerous letters to the newspapers, gained the approval of the general public and it was pointed out that similar radical designs of ship were being built in England for foreign navies. With the help of the Admiralty, Coles was allowed to put forward a number of designs; and eventually the Admiralty agreed to the building of a new turreted ship, but designed by Read with Coles' help. The ship was called *Monarch* and was laid down on 1 June 1866.

Coles agreed to Read's involvement with bad grace, and proposed some modifications of the design which infuriated Read and were not adopted. In addition he persisted in trying to get his own design acccepted, receiving considerable help from people in high places, including the Prince Consort. In the end the Admiralty gave way and agreed to finance the construction of a ship built to Coles' design, but insisted that a well-known shipyard should do the actual building. Laird Brothers, which had built many ships for the Royal Navy, including two previous small turreted ships, was chosen. The Admiralty's one other sensible stipulation was that the plans had to be seen by the Admiralty designers. Read agreed, but insisted that they should be marked 'Not objected to' instead of 'Approved'. Thus was the ill-fated *Captain* born.

She was laid down at Birkenhead on 30 January 1867 and was flooded out of a dry dock on 27 March 1869 in the presence of a number of senior Admiralty officers, including Chief Constructor F. K. Barnes, who was deputising for Read who had refused to attend. The First Lord of the Admiralty, Hugh Childers, was also present and was so impressed by Coles and his ship that he arranged for his son, a midshipman, to be transferred from the *Monarch* to the *Captain*, something for which he never forgave himself.

The Chief Constructor, Barnes, noted that the new ship was floating considerably lower in the water than the original design called for, thus reducing the already small freeboard. He reported the matter to Read, and Laird's was told that it was the company's responsibility to ensure that the designed draught was not exceeded, but apparently no steps were taken to ensure that the company did anything about it.

The ship was completed in January 1870, some seven months after the *Monarch*. Laird's was obviously not quite happy about her stability for it had carried out certain additional calculations and had worked out that her maximum righting moment occurred when she reached the point where she had heeled over to 21° from the vertical. This was almost exactly half the figure for the *Monarch*, whose maximum righting moment was reached when the ship had heeled 40°. Furthermore, the *Captain's* overweight had by now risen to 857 tons — the builders blaming it on the additional weight of the guns and equipment — and her freeboard ended up at 6½ft. This latter figure was known to the Captain (Burgoyne) and to Coles, but did not appear to worry them very much.

The ship went to Portsmouth to commission and fit out, and a few days later, in the company of the *Monarch* and the *Volage*, she put to sea for a series of trials before joining the Channel Fleet. The trials were apparently successful for she joined the Fleet shortly afterwards.

On 29 May 1870 the Fleet ran into a heavy gale and the *Captain* apparently stood up to it very well. Both Burgoyne and Coles had been told by the experts that, in view of her low freeboard, they should not hesitate to furl the sails, connect up the engines and turn the ship into the sea. It was considered that as a low-sided ship she might not be able to recover herself if forced over a certain angle by wind pressure. It seems extraordinary that a brand-new ship should have been allowed to go to sea at all with such a threat hanging over its head.

However, Vice-Adm Sir Thomas Symonds was apparently quite satisfied with the *Captain's* and *Monarch's* performance for he wrote that both ships were able to fire the guns in heavy weather, but he thought that in such weather they would be unable to keep up with the Fleet under sail alone, due to the propeller drag.

He made no mention of lack of stability.

The *Captain* made a second voyage, apparently uneventful, to Vigo and back in July that year, proceeding alone. Coles was again onboard as an adviser. The report of the voyage was entirely favourable, perhaps because in mid-summer no strong gales were encountered. The sea did wash over her low weather deck, but it only caused inconvenience and was not considered dangerous. Under steam she achieved 14.25kt, as against *Monarch's* 14.9kt, but the *Captain* had lower powered engines. She proved Adm Symonds wrong by showing a great turn of speed under sail, with the screws disconnected so that they rotated freely. Coles was jubilant and the *Times* preened itself at its foresight in backing Coles against Read. Shortly before the loss of the *Captain* Read resigned and subsequently joined a commercial shipbuilder as a ship designer, became an MP and was subsequently knighted. On his resignation the *Times* declared:

'Mr Read has often been wrong. In his heated advocacy of broadsides as opposed to turrets he has manifested, too strongly for the public interests, a personal antagonism to Captain Coles, and time has pronounced on these two questions in favour of Captain Coles and adversely to Mr Read.'

Read may have spoken out a bit strongly on Coles' design (perhaps with a modicum of the 'not invented here' attitude), but was to be proved entirely right.

The *Captain* sailed on her third and last cruise in August 1870, forming part of a squadron of 11 battleships under Adm A. W. Milne. She foundered in the night of the 6-7 September in a southwesterly gale off Cape Finisterre. The whole sorry story is best told in a despatch from Adm Milne which was received by the Admiralty on Saturday 10 September and published in its entirety in the *Times* on Monday 12 September.

Lord Warden at sea off Cape Finisterre. September 7th 1870.

'Very much regret sending painful news. *Captain* must have foundered in the night. She was close to this ship at 2 this morning. Sudden S.W. gale. Very heavy squalls. Daybreak *Captain* missing. This afternoon her boats and spars found. All have unfortunately perished. *Inconstant* sails tomorrow morning with report. Yesterday morning the 6th inst., I went onboard to inspect the *Captain*, with Captain Brandrith and my flag lieutenant, and visited most minutely every part of her. At 1pm a trial of sailing with the ships of the squadron was commenced and continued until 5pm when the recall was made. The direction of the wind was S by W force about 6. Some of the ships carried their royals during the whole time. At 4 o'clock the breeze had freshened and the speed of the *Captain*, which was at first 9.5 knots, increased to an average of 11 to 13, the sea washing over the lee side of the decks as she met a swell on the lee bow, the lee gunwale being level with the water. I returned to the *Lord Warden* at 5.30pm. Being close to the rendezvous, 20 miles west of Cape Finisterre, the squadron was again formed into three divisions, the *Lord Warden*, *Minotaur* and *Agincourt* leading, the *Captain* being the last astern of the *Lord Warden*. The signal was also made to take in two reefs and send down royal yards, and the ships stood to the west-north-west under double reefed topsails, fore topmast staysail and foresail; top gallant sails furled, steam ready to be used as required. Force of the wind about 6 to 7.

'There was no indication of a heavy gale, although it looked cloudy to the westward. At 11 the breeze began to freshen, with rain. Towards midnight the barometer had fallen, and the wind increased, which rendered it necessary to reef, but before 1am the gale had set in at south-west, and square sails were furled.

'At this time the *Captain* was astern of this ship, apparently closing under steam. The signal 'open order' was made and at once answered; and at 1.15am, she was on the *Lord Warden's* lee quarter, about six points abaft the beam. From that time until about 1.30am I constantly watched her. Her topsails were either close reefed or on the lap, her foresail was close up, the mainsail having been furled at 3.30pm, but I could not see any fore and aft set. She was heeling over a great deal to starboard, with the wind on her port side. Her red bow light was all this time clearly seen. Some minutes after, I again looked for her light, but it was thick with rain and the light was no longer visible. The squalls of wind and rain were very heavy, and the *Lord Warden* was kept, by the aid of the screw and after trysails, with her bow to a heavy cross sea, and at times it was thought that the sea would have broken over the gangway. At 2.15am the gale had somewhat abated and the wind went round to the north-west but without any squall, in fact the weather moderated, the heavy bank of cloud had passed off to the eastward, and the stars came out clear and bright, the moon which had given considerable light was setting, no large ship was seen any where near us when the *Captain* had been last observed, although the lights of some were visible at a distance.

'When day broke the squadron was somewhat scattered and only 10 ships instead of 11 could be discerned, the *Captain* was the missing one. We bore up for the rendezvous, thinking she might have gone in that direction, but no large vessel being in sight from the masthead, I became alarmed for her safety, because if disabled she ought to be within sight, and if not disabled she ought to be in company with the squadron, and I signalled the following ships to proceed in the directions indicated to look out. *Agincourt* to the southwest, *Monarch* to the south, *Warrior* southeast, *Northumberland* east, *Bristol* northeast, *Bellerophon* north by east, *Minotaur* northeast. These vessels proceeded about ten to fourteen miles, but nothing could be seen of the missing ship.

'The greater part of the ships were recalled and formed in line abreast and steered, at three or four cables apart, to the south-east looking for any wreck. The *Monarch* first picked up a top gallant yard of the *Captain*, the *Lord Warden* another with sails bent, then some studding and booms, and on the *Psyche* joining me from Vigo at sunset she reported having passed two cutters painted white, bottom up, with a large amount of wreck, apparently the hurricane deck, among which was found the body of a seaman with 'rose' marked on his flannel.

'I have stated all that occurred under the eye of the flag captain and myself, and I much regret that I can come to no other conclusion than that the *Captain* foundered with all hands onboard, probably in one of the heavy squalls between

Where the *Captain* sank

ENGLAND

PORTSMOUTH

ATLANTIC

BREST

OCEAN

FRANCE

Bay of

Biscay

**CAPTAIN
sank here**

✗

Cape Finisterre

VIGO

SPAIN

How The Fleet Was Formed

Arrows show in which direction each ship was told to search for the *Captain*

WIND

N

COURSE WEST-NORTHWEST

LORD WARDEN

NORTHUMBERLAND

MINOTAUR

(CAPTAIN)

BRISTOL

AGINCOURT

WARRIOR

BELLEREPHON

MONARCH

Below:
HMS *Captain* was the first large ironclad to have a twin screw arrangement. Her substantial masting and rigging and her low freeboard are apparent in this 1870 picture.
Imperial War Museum (IWM)

1.30am and 2.15am of this morning at which time a heavy cross sea was running, but how the catastrophe occurred will probably never be known. I had the most perfect confidence in Captain Burgoyne, Commander Sheepshanks and the executive officers with whom I had come in contact. Captain Burgoyne himself was a thoroughly practical seaman, and it is impossible that the *Captain* could have been better commanded. The Service will mourn the loss of an officer of such ability and promise. I regret also that Captain Coles should have shared the same fate. He had been on several passages in his newly constructed ship, and took a deep interest in all that concerned her.

'I greatly deplore the sad event, which has cast a deep gloom on the whole squadron.'

I have etc
A. W. Milne. Admiral

Adm Milne was obviously worried about the ship's stability, otherwise why would he have personally 'constantly watched the ship' until 'her red bow light was no longer visible'? As will be explained, he was in fact watching the wrong ship, and was also wrong on the question of survivors. In fact there were 18 out of a total complement of over 500 because Gunner James May and 17 men managed to reach one of the ship's boats which had been washed overboard. After 12 hours and by stupendous efforts they reached the shore at Concubion Bay, south of Cape Finisterre and one of the very few places on that coast where a landing was possible. When they came to give evidence they were quite certain that the ship foundered at about 15 minutes after midnight. The ship Adm Milne had been watching from 1am to 1.30am must have been some other ship and all his remarks about the canvas the *Captain* was carrying and the amount she was heeling over was incorrect. Gunner May and the other survivors were sent back to Portsmouth in the fast *Volage* and May was sent straight up to the Admiralty in London to report.

The Court Martial was held on board HMS *Wellington* in Portsmouth and opened on 27 September 1870: the accused were nominally Mr May and the remainder of the survivors, but this was just a formality and they were all found not guilty. Actually the Court was convened to enquire into the whole circumstances of the loss of the ship and in particular her stability. The survivors told that on the watch being changed at midnight the ship gave a lurch to starboard, but soon righted herself. There was a full gale blowing and the ship was carrying her fore and main topsails, both double reefed, and her fore topmast stay-sail. The yards were braced sharp up and she had little way on her. A few minutes later the ship again lurched to starboard. Burgoyne was on deck and he shouted 'How much is she heeling?'. The reply was 18° and he immediately ordered 'Let go fore top-sail halyards' and followed it with 'Let go fore and main topsail sheets'. The men were unable to release the ropes in time so the heel increased and she slowly capsized and sank by the stern.

The Court findings were:

'Her Majesty's Ship *Captain* capsized in the morning of 7 September 1870 by pressure of wind assisted by the heave of the sea and that the sail carried at the time, regard being had to the force of the wind and state of the sea, was *insufficient* to have endangered a ship with a proper amount of stability'. (Authors italics) 'The Court, before separating, find it their duty to record the conviction they entertain that the *Captain* was built in deference to public opinion expressed in Parliament and through other channels, and in opposition to the views and opinions of the Controller, and his department, and that the evidence all tends to show that they generally disapproved of her construction. It further appears in evidence that before the *Captain* was received from the contractors, a gross departure from her original design had been committed, whereby her draught of water had increased about two feet and her freeboard was diminished to a corresponding extent, and that her stability proved to be dangerously small, combined with an area of sail under these circumstances excessive. The Court deeply regrets that if these facts were duly known and appreciated, they were not communicated to the officer in command of the ship, or that, if otherwise, the ship was allowed to be employed in the ordinary service of the Fleet before they had been ascertained by calculation and experience.'

That should have been the end of the affair, but it was fully discussed at the 1871 spring meeting of the Institute of Naval Architects. The Institute felt that it was up to it to investigate further, since it was the design of the ship that was at fault. The President of the Institute was the previous First Lord of the Admiralty, one Hampton, and in his opening speech he admitted that he had agreed to Capt Coles designing the *Captain*, against the advice of the naval constructors, but he added that the design was for a ship of over 300ft long and over 4,000 tons, but with only about 8ft freeboard. Hampton added: 'You know the result, the ship was proceeded with — the ship was launched — and to the astonishment of everyone, I think, and I confess I can never forget the dismay with which I heard it, instead of a freeboard of 8ft, the *Captain* was launched with a freeboard of only 6ft'.

From the discussion which followed it became evident that even naval architects did not fully understand stability in those days. The effect of squalls, as opposed to a steady wind pressure, had not been fully appreciated. It was stated that if the *Captain* had had 10% more freeboard she would have been safe or, alternatively, had she carried a smaller sail area, cut to perhaps just a jury rig, she would also have been safe.

Coles was a brilliant man and his idea of a rotating turret revolutionised naval gunnery, but he was a man before his time and was unable to appreciate the finer points of ship design, particularly in those days of the slow onset of steam. A ship with sails and steam engines proved a difficult combination in any case. Having designed *Captain* with more adequate freeboard, he should have refused to accept her when he found that the freeboard had been reduced by 25%. He cannot be wholly blamed for the disaster, since the Lords of the Admiralty should have had more sense than to entrust the design of a completely new type of ship to a naval captain, with little knowledge of ship design, against the advice of their professional advisers.

4

USS Memphis

The USS *Memphis* was an American heavy armoured cruiser, what perhaps in more recent years we might have called a slow battlecruiser. She was originally named the *Tennessee* and was launched on 3 December 1904, displacing 18,000 tons, with coal burning and two reciprocating engines giving her a maximum speed of 23kt. She carried four 10in guns in two turrets and these could outrange the guns of any battleship then in commission. In addition she had 16×6in guns and 22×3in guns: in total a formidable armament indeed.

In 1916 she was renamed *Memphis* in order to release the name *Tennessee* for a new battleship under construction. Many of the dockyard workers thought it spelt bad luck to change the name, and the superstition spread to the crew, but nobody took it really seriously. Her Commanding Officer was Capt Edward I. Beach, who had previously been in command of the *Washington* of the same class.

Shortly after the change of name the *Memphis* sailed from Hampton Roads for the harbour of San Domingo, the capital of the Caribbean Island of San Domingo (now the Dominican Republic). She was flying the flag of Rear-Adm Charles F. Pond, the Admiral commanding all the cruisers in the Pacific Fleet. San Domingo was a state in its own right and had a President, but her Government was highly unstable and the US authorities deemed it advisable to station a force of US Marines there to look after the interests of the American residents, and this came to mean looking after all foreign nationals on the island. The *Memphis* was sent there to support the Marines and generally act as guardship.

San Domingo harbour is virtually an exposed anchorage and it lies open to the south and the east. Neither Capt Beach, nor his Admiral, much liked the anchorage, but they had to make the best of it because the *Memphis* was likely to be stationed there for some time. As it was August and the hurricane season was almost upon them, Capt Beach proposed to keep four boilers alight at all times to enable him to get out of the harbour at short notice should a hurricane warning be received. However, the US Navy was in the middle of one of its periodic bouts of economy and there was a considerable accent on saving of fuel (coal). Adm Pond therefore told Beach to keep only two boilers alight in order to run the auxiliary machinery, but to have four additional boilers ready to be lit at a moment's notice.

This arrangement was to be put to the test on the evening of 22 August. The weather started to deteriorate and the barometer fell alarmingly. Capt Beach thought that a hurricane was approaching so he ordered the extra four boilers to be lit, and to make full arrangements for getting underway. The Admiral was entertaining the US Minister to the Dominican Republic, Mr W. W. Russel, to dinner and a film, but the threatened hurricane completely upset the arrangements: the film was cancelled and the boats were hoisted, leaving Mr Russel to spend the night onboard. However, the hurricane never arrived, a boat was lowered and Mr Russel went ashore. It was nonetheless a very good practice run and showed the Admiral and the Captain that steam could be raised in the short time of 40 minutes. This greatly reassured the Captain, and probably also the Admiral, as 40 minutes was considered well within the warning time that they should receive.

All was peaceful for another week, and there were no more signs of hurricanes. On Tuesday 29 August the day dawned fine with a light northeasterly breeze. The Admiral and Capt Beach had been invited ashore for an afternoon concert in the Cathedral, but Capt Beach begged to be excused as he had much work to do, and in any case he did not allow both officers and men to go ashore in working hours, and he thought he should set an example. The Admiral and two aides went and met the American Consul, who took them to the Cathedral.

As usual *Memphis* was at anchor in 55ft of water, with the USS *Castine*, a 1,200-ton gunboat, also at anchor some 600yd away. The Captain of the *Castine*, Cdr Kenneth Bennett, went onboard the *Memphis* for dental treatment at 12.50 and *Memphis* landed a recreation party at 13.00. The party proceeded in one boat to a point about half a mile upstream in the Ozama River, on the opposite side to Fort Ozama where the Marines were billeted. The party largely consisted of the ship's baseball team.

The first warning of an approaching storm was voiced by the Executive Officer, Lt-Cdr Williams. One of the ship's dinghies had capsized and he was supervising it being rehoisted when he noticed that the ship was rolling more than usual. She often rolled in the afternoons when the wind got up, but he noticed that there was no wind. He went below to report to his Captain, and found him in the company of Cdr Bennett who, having finished his dental appointment, had decided to call on Capt Beach out of politeness.

Williams was not very happy about the rising swell and he told the Captain that he had decided to send two boats inshore to pick up the recreation party. He described the rapidly rising swell and all three of them went on deck to have a look. They saw that both the *Memphis* and the much smaller *Castine* were rolling heavily, and they did not like what they saw. Capt Beach arranged to return Bennett to the *Castine* in a *Memphis* boat immediately. He also took a long look at the lee shore and could clearly see the surf breaking on the rocky shore. Turning to look to seaward he could see long waves rolling into the harbour from the east.

It was enough to trouble him, so he sent a message to the Chief Engineer to raise steam in the four boilers as fast as possible. He also told his Executive Officer to prepare for sea and to hoist all boats. One boat had already gone inshore for the recreation party and a second boat was on its way, but the swell was rising so quickly that Beach decided to recall it. Before the recall could be hoisted, the boat had got through the breakers near the shore and was entering the mouth of the river, so the recall was never made. Beach then sent a signal to the officer commanding the Marines, asking him to keep both boats and the recreation party for the time being.

He looked again out to seaward and, to his horror, saw an immense wave about 70ft high obscuring the horizon and approaching the harbour fast. He at once ordered the ship to rig for heavy weather, but there was hardly time enough even to start doing so. It was then 15.45 on the afternoon of 29 August.

The order to raise steam had been given at about 15.30, but the engine and

boiler rooms were experiencing great difficulties. Quite apart from the motion of the ship, which steadily got worse, spray started entering the engine rooms through large ventilators situated on the boat deck which had not been properly secured. It was the engineers' job to secure them, but by this time they could not spare anybody to go up top to do the job. The bridge was asked if they could do something and a party of men went on to the boat deck to try and prevent the water entering. They had some success with the closure of the ventilators and in covering them with canvas, but undoubtedly the water that had leaked into the engine room had had an adverse effect on raising steam. The bridge was asking continually what time to expect sufficient steam to move the engines and the engine room continued to say 16.35. When 16.35 arrived there was only 90lb of steam pressure in the engines; this was hardly sufficient, but the bridge could not wait any longer, particularly as the anchor cable was snubbing every few seconds and would part before very long. Capt Beach told the engine room to obey telegraphs.

Since 15.30 the swell had increased considerably and was now really enormous. *Memphis* was rolling very heavily and seas were washing right over her; spray was even coming down the funnels. Lt-Cdr Williams, the Executive Officer, was knocked out by a roll sending him flying into some lockers. He later recovered, but was still very shaky. Once or twice the officers on the bridge had felt a bump as the keel touched the seabed which, considering they had 55ft of water under them, meant waves of up to 40ft in height. The enormous wave which had blotted out the horizon was still approaching, but much slower than it had been, and was carrying before it a huge area of sand and mud. The nearer it got, so the swell increased.

Sometime about 16.00 the *Memphis* officers saw their motor launch, which had gone to fetch the recreation party, emerging from the mouth of the river. She was pitching alarmingly and it was obvious to the onlookers that she would never make it; even if she had done so, it would have been impossible to get the men in her onboard. As they watched, the inevitable happened and she capsized, throwing all her passengers into the sea. Capt Beach was understandably very upset, as he had specifically asked the Marines ashore, in his signal, to keep both boats and the recreation party. Possibly, however, the first boat had left before

31

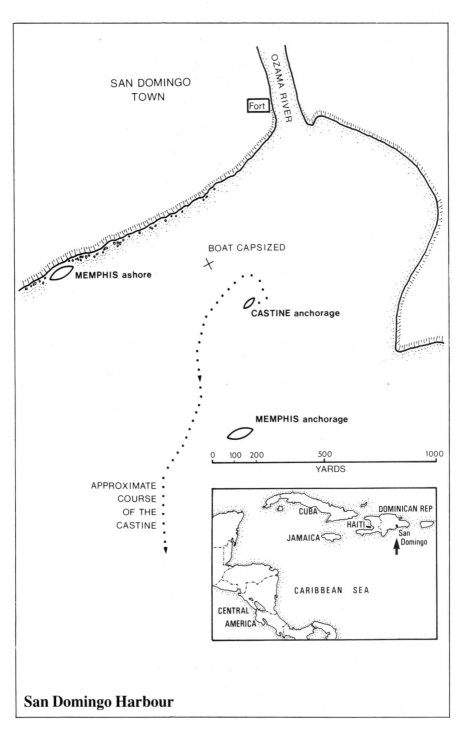

SAN DOMINGO
TOWN

Fort

OZAMA RIVER

BOAT CAPSIZED

MEMPHIS ashore

CASTINE anchorage

MEMPHIS anchorage

0   100 200   500   1000
YARDS

APPROXIMATE
COURSE
OF THE
CASTINE

CUBA

DOMINICAN REP

HAITI

JAMAICA

San
Domingo

CENTRAL
AMERICA

CARIBBEAN   SEA

San Domingo Harbour

the signal had been passed down to the embarkation point which was some way from the actual fort. The men were struggling in the water and there was nothing the *Memphis* could do, but the *Castine* had by this time weighed anchor and she very gallantly went into the surf to try and rescue the men. She too only had a small steam pressure as there had not been time to raise full pressure, but she went astern into the breakers, which were now assuming enormous proportions, towards the struggling men in the water. It was far too rough to lower a boat and all that she could do was to throw as many lifebelts and other objects which could float into the water for the men to hang on to. Cdr Bennett realised that his ship was in imminent danger of being thrown on to the rocks and he had to give up the rescue attempt. He rang down full ahead and started out to sea, passing close to the *Memphis* on his way. The *Castine* looked a sorry sight: her scuppers were pouring out water, she had a heavy list to port and her upperworks looked as if they had been hit by a shell. Nevertheless she got safely to sea and away from the rocky lea shore, and found the swell much less steep in deeper water.

Meanwhile the *Memphis* was rolling more than ever — about 60° to 70° either side — the main deck was continuously flooded and even the high boat deck, some 35ft above the water line, was being washed by the waves. In addition, to their astonishment, the crew saw green seas actually going down the funnels.

Capt Beach had made arrangements to drop the other anchor should he not get sufficient steam to move the ship. He actually ordered it to be dropped, but at that moment the engine room told him that the engines would be ready to move in another five minutes. He immediately cancelled his order, but in any case it would not have been possible as the seas were washing over the forecastle and it was impossible to put anybody on the forecastle to knock off the slip. Beach could wait no longer and he ordered starboard engine full astern and port engine full ahead in the hope of pointing the ship's head in the direction of the now rapidly approaching wave. In the event, the amount of steam was so little that the screws barely rotated and had no effect on the ship at all. Thus he was caught with the enormous wave just upon him and he was in the worst position — broadside on to it. At first a deep hollow or trough appeared ahead of the wave and on the ship's starboard side, with the face of the wave about a hundred yards behind it. The trough appeared to slow down and the wave to build up just before it struck. The vertical face of the wave started to curve over towards the horrified onlookers. One can imagine their feelings: the crest of the wave must have been some 30-40ft above them, it was a wave the like of which none of them had ever seen before, and for all they knew it might engulf the entire ship. The Captain cried 'hang on' and they gripped anything they could. Then with a roar like an express train the wave broke and the sea swept over, tons of water falling on them. Strangely, the water was quite hot. Slowly it drained away and they picked themselves up, battered, bruised, soaking wet and completely exhausted, but alive. The entire ship except the bridge, the four funnels and the two masts had been completely engulfed. Those on the bridge had at first thought that the ship had disappeared and they had been left alone on the top of the wave, but gradually the turrets, the boat deck and the main deck came into view and they realised that the ship was still afloat. They had distinctly felt the ship touch the seabed with a heavy bump when they were in the trough and they knew that the bottom of the ship must have been seriously damaged. Most of the crew were below decks and many of them were injured by the motion of the ship, although only a few of those who were badly burnt by escaping steam when the boilers exploded were seriously injured. Observers of the wave testified afterwards that it was in the form of three gigantic steps, each with a large plateau on top of it, and the whole rushing towards the shore at colossal speed. Each of the three steps had hit the *Memphis* with enormous force.

The wave was noted at the time as a 'tropical disturbance', and the subsequent Court Martial also recorded it as such. In fact it was a 'tsunami' (a Hawaiian word), a wave caused by underwater seismic action. In the book *Heavy Weather* by Rear-Adm Kotsch and Mr Henderson, a tsunami is stated to be, 'Ocean waves produced by a submarine earthquake, landslide or volcanic eruption. They are also called seismic sea waves, but they are popularly and incorrectly called tidal waves . . . Tsunamis steepen and increase in height on approaching shallow water and completely inundate low-lying areas'.

The bridge personnel saved their lives by taking refuge inside the cage-like structure of the foremast, which was quite common in US ships at that time, and they were reasonably safe from the fury of the waves, but the Captain's orderly was slow in getting inside and was washed overboard and drowned. As the third step of the wave passed, the *Memphis* had been grounded on the coral bottom several times, and on one occasion the whole of her port side was aground. In fact the 18,000-ton ship had been thrown on her beam ends, but had recovered to an upright position. A couple of seamen made gallant efforts to get on to the forecastle to let go the second anchor, but one of them was washed overboard. The other succeeded in knocking off the slip and very nearly lost his life too, but the cable ran out. It was too late nonetheless, as by then the ship was aground on the rocks at the edge of the harbour.

As the ship was rapidly carried ashore, fires from the exploding boilers spread and a number of people were burnt, but there was nothing the crew could do about it. The *Memphis* struck the first rocks at about 16.45 and as each succeeding wave pounded her she was pushed a little further ashore. The rocks were made of coral and they pierced her side time and time again. She was still rolling from side to side, although her keel was firmly aground, and the watchers on shore could see how her side and bottom were badly perforated with large gaping holes. At about 17.00 she was given one final push by the waves and she moved slightly further inshore. She was now firmly wedged on the rocks, but still rolling. The men below did not know what was happening, although they could hear the rocks scraping along her sides and, when she actually struck, the noise was terrific. They were thrown about and many suffered injuries and some were dying from their burns.

As soon as she was firmly aground, Capt Beach ordered all hands on deck and told them to get as high as possible in the ship. Ropes were rigged to assist them to get up from below, and the injured had to be hauled up. By now the ship had a heavy list to port and the upperworks were leaning towards the 20-30ft cliffs. This was fortunate as the distance between the ship and the cliffs was not as far as it might have been. Hundreds of Dominicans had gathered on the cliffs and the entire force of the Marines had been ordered there as well. In addition there were the remnants of the recreation party which had not been embarked in the first boat because it was full.

34

The crew were endeavouring to throw heaving lines to the men on the cliffs, but the wind was from offshore and it was still a long way. However, eventually a line was caught by some of the sailors of the recreation party. Its inboard end was secured to a 5in hawser and the men onshore were told to haul away. The shore end of the hawser had to be kept in hand all the time to allow for it suddenly tautening with the rolling of the ship, and for two hours the Marines and the recreation party veered and hauled on the hawser. A breeches buoy was rigged, having been quickly constructed onboard, and a snatch block held it to the hawser. Additional lines had also to be provided to haul it to and fro.

The Captain ordered the injured and disabled to be sent first, but this presented a problem because a number of the men were so badly burnt about the hands that they could not hold on to anything. Eventually they were sent in coal bags. More hawsers were then brought into use and in the end there were no less than five of them secured. Thus a continuous one-way shuttle was devised, with men going over to the cliffs at the rate of about five a minute. In all some 850 lives were saved by this method, but some 40 others lost their lives, mostly from the boats and from injuries received onboard.

Adm Pond had left the concert at about 16.30, quite unaware of what was happening except that it was too rough for him to go back onboard the *Memphis*. He was soon told and he and his party were taken in cars from the Cathedral to the cliff tops. It was never revealed at either of the two enquiries or the Court Martial that it had been he who had not allowed Capt Beach to keep steam in four boilers as he had wished, and one cannot but wonder if he remembered this at the *Memphis'* last moments while he watched from the safety of the cliff tops . . .

Capt Beach sent his Executive Officer, Williams, ashore among some of the first in order to organise the arrangements for their reception and accommodation. Williams was still very dizzy, but he did a magnificent job and quickly got the 800 men organised. As the rescue proceeded and it got dark, almost the entire population of the city of San Domingo assembled on the cliffs, arriving in cars and on foot. The cars were commandeered at once to turn their headlights on and illuminate the scene, since there were no street lights in the area. There had previously been some bad feeling between the Marines and the local population, but happily this was forgotten and the townsfolk played a leading part in the rescue and in comforting the injured, of which there were 180.

There were three power boats left to fend for themselves because it had been impossible to hoist them. All three were told to proceed out to sea and await the arrival of their parent ships. Two were from the *Memphis* and one from the *Castine*. They got outside the harbour and waited for hours, riding the reduced swell in the deeper water quite well. They had seen the *Castine* leave the harbour, but had lost sight of her. They could not see inside the harbour and had no idea what had happened to the *Memphis*. After dark, at some time before 20.00, they decided to make for the only shore light they could see, the San Domingo Lighthouse, some way to the north of them.

It was a wrong decision as they did not realise that the waves were much larger inshore and breaking heavily against the rocks. They soon got caught in the surf, but by then it was too late to extricate themselves. They had stuck together as far as possible, but one by one all three were broken up on the difficult shore and

Top:
The *Memphis* during the storm, and already forced aground.   *Paul Silverstone collection*

Above:
Memphis aground after the storm, with salvage already commenced.
Paul Silverstone collection

eight men lost their lives. Twenty-five men had also drowned when the *Memphis'* launch, bringing back some of the recreation party, capsized.

It did not take the *Memphis'* crew long to realise that the ship was a complete loss. She was badly stove in and her engines were a complete write-off. The only thing worth salvaging were the guns and they were later removed by the battleship *New Hampshire*, sent to the island for this purpose. *Memphis* was finally left alone on the rocks to await the arrival of the ship breakers — she had to wait for 21 years.

The inevitable Courts of Enquiry and the Court Martial of Capt Beach followed. The defence wished to call Adm Pond to give evidence on the question of the number of boilers to be kept alight in the open anchorage, and they invited him to attend. He refused, and Capt Beach also refused to subpoena him. Thus this vital evidence, which might have greatly helped Capt Beach, was never given.

The Court Martial brought out the fact that conditions detoriorated so rapidly after the engine room had given the initial estimate of the time when steam would be available (16.35) that it was impossible for the engineers to meet this deadline. The Court accepted that the ship was rolling so heavily and that water was coming down the funnels and dowsing the fires in the boiler rooms, thus actually preventing steam being raised. However, in spite of this, the Court found Capt Beach guilty on two charges of not keeping sufficient steam up to get underway at short notice, and of not properly securing for heavy weather. However, in addition, they added a unanimous recommendation for clemency in execution of the punishment prescribed. He was sentenced to lose 20 numbers in his rank of Captain on the lineal list of the Navy. This meant that instead of nearing the top of the list for Rear-Admiral, as he was, he would be put back below 19 other Captains and thus his promotion would be that much delayed. In fact he would reach the top of the list long after he had been retired because of age. This was cruel punishment for something which was palpably not his fault. The Secretary of the Navy agreed and subsequently altered the Court's sentence to the loss of only five places, but even then he had little chance of making Rear-Admiral.

However, the Navy did its best for him. He was at once appointed as the Commanding Officer of the Naval Torpedo Station, at that time one of the most important stations in the US Navy. He stayed there for 18 months and was then appointed to command the battleship *New York*, the flagship of the US squadron attached to the British Grand Fleet, probably one of the best appointments for a Captain in the whole of the US Navy.

The real truth of the matter was that none of the officers of the Court Martial had ever experienced a tsunami. It was completely outside their experience and they had no conception of the speed at which such a storm moved, or what tremendous waves it could raise in shallow water. This fact was soon realised by the Department of the Navy: indeed, the first mention of a seismic storm was made by them. Capt Beach was treated as leniently as possible because all the officers of the Court realised that but for the Grace of God, there went they.

It was a major disaster, but fortunately most of the crew had been rescued. Nobody really was to blame and it could have been called an Act of God — it is surprising that the Court Martial did not choose this way out. Everybody in their heart of hearts knew that Capt Beach could not be blamed. Indeed his subsequent appointments showed clearly that the Department of the Navy thought so too.

5

Victoria *and* Camperdown

In the days when warships frequently manoeuvred in close company, collisions between ships were a great deal more frequent than they are today. Nowadays ships of a force are much more widely spaced apart, partly so that they form a more difficult target for submarines and partly because of the nuclear threat.

The best known and most tragic Royal Naval collision in the last century was that between the battleships *Victoria* and *Camperdown*. The *Victoria* was launched in 1887. She was to have been called the *Renown*, but as she was ready for launching in Queen Victoria's Jubilee Year, her name was changed. She carried two enormous Armstrong 16¼in guns weighing 110 tons each and firing a 1,600lb projectile. They were so huge and heavy that only two guns could be carried and both were mounted in one turret forward, which of course meant that they could not fire astern. The Board of the Admiralty accepted this operational limitation because 'no British battleship would ever be called upon to fire astern'. The *Victoria* had only one sister ship, the *Sans Pareil*, which was in company with her when she sank. They both displaced 10,420 tons.

The *Camperdown* was a slightly older ship and displaced 10,600 tons. She was launched in 1883 as one of the 'Admiral' class, having an armament of four 13½in guns each weighing only 67 tons and mounted in one twin turret forward and another aft.

On a hot afternoon in the Mediterranean in June 1898 the British Mediterranean Fleet was about to anchor in formation off the coast of Tripoli. The fleet, consisting of 10 battleships or large armoured cruisers of about 10,000 tons each, and one despatch vessel, had been organised into two divisions and were formed in divisions in line ahead disposed abeam, with the *Victoria* leading the first division and the *Camperdown* leading the second division.

The fleet was under the command of Vice-Adm Sir George Tryon who flew his flag in the *Victoria*, and the second in command was Rear-Adm Markham in the *Camperdown*. Adm Tryon was an expert in fleet handling and had trained his captains to expect all sorts of complicated manoeuvres at any time. He was a great martinet, a large, taciturn man who sought counsel from nobody and seldom informed his staff of his intentions.

On this occasion, however, Tryon had discussed his anchoring plan with his Flag Captain, Staff Commander and Flag Lieutenant. He told them he intended to form up in two columns steering away from the coast with the columns 1,200yd apart, with ships in columns at normal station-keeping distance apart, which in those days was 400yd. At a given moment he intended to reverse the course of the fleet by turning the columns inwards, leaders turning together and each ship following in succession the next ahead. He then intended to close the columns to 400yd apart. Finally he intended to turn the whole fleet together 90° to port and then to anchor.

38

It was intended to be an impressive sight to the watchers ashore and indeed it would have been. Even in those days it was not often that it was possible to see 10 battleships anchoring together. The *Victoria* would have hoisted a two flag signal which denoted 'anchor instantly', the *Camperdown* would have repeated the hoist, and, as *Victoria's* signalman hauled it down, 10 blacksmiths with hammers would have knocked off 10 slips holding the cables and down would have splashed 10 anchors simultaneously. Ten lower booms would have swung out and 10 accommodation ladders would have been lowered. Adm Tryon had trained his fleet in such a manoeuvre and woe betide any Captain whose ship was only a few yards out of line, or whose blacksmith failed to knock off the slip with the first blow of the hammer.

The Staff Commander and the Flag Captain remarked to the Admiral that 1,200yd between columns was insufficient to allow the leading ships to turn together towards each other, and the Staff Commander suggested that 1,600yd would be better, but even that was insufficient. The Admiral agreed, but later told his Flag Lieutenant to make the necessary signal to close the columns to *1,200yd*.

The signal was hoisted and the Staff Commander, seeing 1,200yd was hoisted, told the Flag Lieutenant that he must have made a mistake as the Admiral had agreed to 1,600yd apart. The Flag Lieutenant therefore went to the Admiral, who was in his sea cabin, and queried whether it should be 1,200yd or 1,600yd and explained that 1,200yd was flying. The Admiral, somewhat tersely, told him to leave it at 1,200yd and to execute the signal as soon as possible.

Thus the fleet was formed. It should be noted that, when formed into columns like this, the normal distance between columns laid down in the manoeuvring instructions was in those days 'the distance apart of ships [400yd] multiplied by the number of ships in the longest column'. In this case the longest column had six ships in it and the distance apart of columns should have been 400×6=2,400yd, which would have left plenty of room to carry out the manoeuvre.

The distance between columns was worked out to allow for a favourite manoeuvre in those days — forming a single line by turning leading ships of columns together 90° to port or starboard, remaining ships following their leaders in succession. By this means one line could be formed at right angles to the original line of advance. If the distance between columns was too short the end ships of columns, in the direction of the turn, might have got muddled up with the leading ships of columns not in the direction of the turn with a consequent risk of collision. By making the distance between columns equal to the number of ships in the columns multiplied by their intervals apart, the end of the column in the direction of the turn should have fitted perfectly with the leading ship of the column away from the direction of the turn.

The fleet increased speed to 8.8kt and shortly afterwards, at 15.00, the Admiral directed his Flag Lieutenant to hoist two signals. One was addressed to the first division and directed it to turn in succession, preserving the order of the fleet, 16 points (180°) to port. The second was addressed to the second division and directed it to turn in succession, preserving the order of the fleet, 16 points (180°) to starboard. The two columns were thus to turn towards each other. The signals were made in two separate hoists and it would have been quite possible to execute one signal (by hauling it down) before the other. However, the Flag Lieutenant knew perfectly well what was in the Admiral's mind.

However, let us return to the collision. The turning circle diameters of *Victoria* and *Camperdown*, under tactical rudder, were each about 800yd. Thus, even the 1,600yd suggested by the Staff Commander was hardly sufficient. If the two ships had used full rudder, their turning circle diameters would have been reduced to about 600yd. It would have been possible, by about 20yd to turn without colliding if both ships had used full rudder. However, the instructions were that during manoeuvres tactical rudder (or helm as it was called in those days) was to be used.

It must have been obvious to all the captains in the fleet that the manoeuvre was a dangerous one, yet every ship with the exception of the *Camperdown* went close up (two blocks) with her answering pennant in complete acknowledgement (it was and still is the custom to keep the answering pennant at 'the dip' if a signal is not understood). *Camperdown*, being a leading ship, repeated the hoist, but Adm Markham, realising the danger of the manoeuvre, ordered the repeated hoist to be kept at the dip, signifying that he did not understand the signal. At the same time he ordered a semaphore signal to the flagship, saying that he did not understand the signal.

The semaphore signal was never sent as Adm Tryon, ever impatient, ordered *Camperdown's* pennants to be shown — a sign of derision which no Captain or Admiral would like — and sent a semaphore signal saying 'What are you waiting for?'. Adm Markham, seeing this and having faith in his Admiral, thought that he would solve the problem somehow. He therefore cancelled his semaphore signal and ordered the repeated signal to be hoisted close up.

At the subsequent Court Martial, held in Malta, Capt Burke, the Captain of the *Victoria*, and several of his officers were charged with the loss of their ship. Adm Markham was questioned closely why, when he knew the manoeuvre to be dangerous, if not impossible, he allowed the repeated signal to be hoisted close up? He stated that he had such faith in his C-in-C that he thought he must have some trick up his sleeve. He thought there were two possibilities: either the C-in-C would execute the signal to the second division first and, when they were safely turned, would turn his own division, or he would execute both signals together and turn *Victoria* with less rudder, and thus lead his division outside the second division.

Although it was not mentioned at the Court Martial, this excuse looks weak because the anchoring formation had been signalled to the Fleet earlier and Adm Markham knew that, in order to take it up, *Victoria* would have to be to port of him on completion of the turning manoeuvre signalled. The fleet was due to anchor at 16.00 in about 25 minutes time, and there would have been no time for the C-in-C to get his division to the other side of the second division. On completion of this reverse course manoeuvre the ships would have been in their correct relative positions for anchoring.

Thus the two signals ordering the two divisions to turn were executed together and *Victoria* started turning to port and *Camperdown* to starboard using tactical rudder. Even then, although it was obvious that a collision was bound to take place, both Captains were reluctant to go astern on their inner screws without permission from their respective Admirals. In fact Capt Burke had to ask three times for permission to go astern on the port screw.

The two ships met almost halfway between the columns, *Camperdown* striking *Victoria* on the starboard side and opening up an enormous hole through which

Left:
The 'Admiral' class
battleship
HMS *Camperdown. IWM*

Below:
HMS *Victoria's* design must be
considered a retrograde step
after previous Royal Navy
designs, mounting as she did
a limited main armament
which could only fire ahead
of the beam. *IWM*

the water rushed. Nowadays such a collision would not perhaps have resulted in a sinking, but in those days watertight sub-division was not as good as it is today. The *Camperdown's* bow had penetrated *Victoria's* hull by about 9ft at about 12ft below the waterline. It struck a transverse bulkhead almost directly and, as the two ships swung together, *Camperdown's* bow enlarged the breach to over 100sq ft.

Just before the impact, orders were given onboard the *Victoria* to 'close watertight doors and out collision mat'. As regards the watertight doors, the order was too late and only a few doors had been closed before the actual collision. Owing to the open doors, water was able to find its way into a coal bunker just forward of a stokehold. The ship began to list to starboard, and the list increased rapidly when water entered the battery in large quantities through armoured doors and broadside gun ports. It was a very hot day and every port or door that could admit air had been left open.

As soon as the collision occurred, 'Collision Stations' was piped and the crew lined up four deep on the port side facing inboard. Initially it was hoped to beach the vessel in shallow water and the gallant men in the engine room and stokehold were still keeping the engines running. However, by now, in addition to the list, she was down by the bows. Suddenly her bows went down and her stern reared up high in the sky with the screws still turning. She foundered almost immediately afterwards, only 13 minutes after the impact.

Intended Anchoring Formation

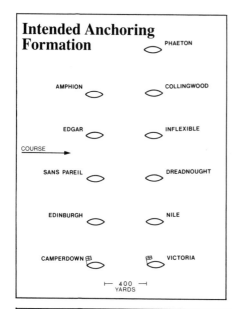

How The Collision Occurred

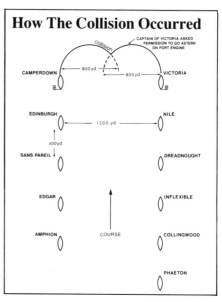

What The Distance Apart Should Have Been

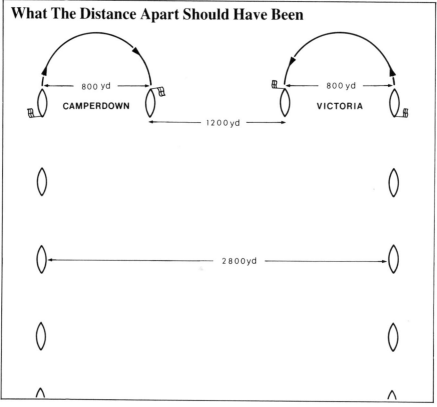

'Abandon ship' was ordered just before the end, and the crew who had remained in good order broke ranks and dashed for the side and into the sea. Owing to the list this was difficult and many men were left onboard and went down with the ship.

Boats from other ships of the fleet were soon on the scene and were able to save most of the men in the water. In all, 21 officers and 336 men were rescued and 350 officers and men were lost, including the C-in-C, Vice-Adm Tryon. Amongst those saved was the Executive Officer of the *Victoria*, Cdr Jellicoe, who afterwards became the C-in-C of the British Fleet at the Battle of Jutland.

The *Camperdown's* bows were badly damaged and she very nearly suffered the same fate as the *Victoria*. In those days it was the custom to cut drainage holes in the watertight bulkheads — which of course made the bulkheads not entirely watertight — and the water started pouring through them. (The practice of providing drainage holes was abolished shortly afterwards.) Quite a lot of water got into the *Camperdown* before the pumps could be started, but the ship's carpenter improvised a wooden barricade which helped to keep the water out. This, together with the collision mat which was promptly placed in position across the bows, did much to save the ship. Fortunately the sea was calm.

Adm Tryon was drowned. His last words were 'It's all my fault' and at the Court Martial he was found entirely to blame. No one can tell what was in his mind. It must have been obvious to anybody as experienced as he was that the distance between the columns was insufficient. One perhaps can only assume that he had some sort of mental blackout, as he was probably working under a strain.

What *is* quite inexplicable is how 11 Captains and one Rear-Admiral could all have acknowledged the signal ordering the turn as 'received and understood', and how Adm Tryon's own staff, who knew the manoeuvre to be dangerous, did not expostulate more with him when the signal was hoisted. The only explanation is that both his staff and his Captains had such infinite faith in him that they thought he had some last-minute manoeuvre up his sleeve to save the day. Also, it must not be forgotten that he was a difficult man to approach, and it was perhaps a brave staff officer who queried a manoeuvre he had ordered.

The loss of one of Britain's best battleships, the flagship of the mighty Mediterranean Fleet, coupled with the death of the Commander-in-Chief and so many officers and men, was a great blow to the country. Many stories circulated at the time, most of them mere rumour, but two which have survived to this day are worth repeating.

At a lunch party on the same day as the collision, held at the Naval Torpedo Depot at Weymouth in England, one of the officers' wineglasses broke of its own accord at the stem. Seafarers are notoriously superstitious of a glass ringing or breaking and one of the officers remarked lightly, 'that should mean a big naval disaster'.

The other story is even stranger. On the evening of the day of the disaster, long before the news had reached England, Lady Tryon, the Commander-in-Chief's wife, was giving a big reception at her house in London. Many of the guests remarked to her how nice it was for her to have her husband home again. She explained that he was still in the Mediterranean, but her guests insisted that they had seen him on the stairs, though none of them had spoken to him.

43

6

Vanguard *and* Iron Duke

This is the story of two battleships being in collision. It took place in September 1875 during manoeuvres, and it was primarily caused by fog.

The ships concerned belonged to the First Reserve Squadron under the command of Vice-Adm Sir Walter Tarleton, who had previously been Second Sea Lord. He was flying his flag in the *Warrior*, another battleship, and the squadron was carrying out a flag-showing cruise and manoeuvres off the west coast of Ireland.

The four ships concerned were ironclads, that is to say they were built of a wooden hull with a belt of iron armour plate round the hull in the most vulnerable places. *Vanguard* and *Iron Duke* were sister ships 280ft long, some 100ft shorter than the remaining ships of the squadron. As was the custom in those days both ships had a very pronounced ram, pointed at the outboard end and protruding from the bow below the waterline, suitably protected by iron plating. On top of the ram was a bowsprit which also protruded but above the waterline. The ships were both steam and sail propelled, their maximum speed under steam being up to 14kt.

The squadron sailed from Portland with a large number of reservists embarked and by the time of the collision had nearly completed its five-week cruise. Seven ships started out but two had been detached on the way, leaving the *Warrior* (flagship), *Hector, Vanguard, Iron Duke* and *Achilles*. They sailed from Dublin Bay on 1 September and were formed in single line ahead. After rounding the Kish Light, *Achilles* was ordered to part company and to proceed to the Mersey.

They sailed at 10.45 and at 12.30 the signal was made to form columns of divisions. The evolution was carried out by *Warrior* and *Hector* maintaining their course and speed, and *Vanguard* and *Iron Duke* altering course together 90° to port, and then at the correct distance turning 90° back again to starboard. The squadron was steaming at 7kt, but on turning back again to the original course they had to increase speed to 8kt to catch up the *Warrior's* division. Thus when they had got into station abeam of the other division the ships were formed in two divisions with *Warrior* leading one and *Vanguard* the other. The visibility was moderate, with perhaps a hint of fog in the air. Their course was almost due south and the divisions were four cables (800yd) apart. Two small ships were in sight but they presented no danger to the squadron. Unbeknown to the squadron, however, there was another sailing vessel which they could not see because she was behind a bank of fog.

The Captain of the *Vanguard*, Capt Richard Dawkins, went below for his lunch at 12.35 leaving Officer of the Watch (OOW) Lt Hathorn in charge. About the same time, Capt Hickley, the Captain of the *Iron Duke*, went below, leaving his OOW, Lt Evans, on the bridge. All seemed very peaceful when suddenly a dense fog enveloped them, bringing visibility down to less than a ship's length.

Top:
HMS *Vanguard* at anchor. *IWM*

Above:
HMS *Iron Duke*. *IWM*

Vanguard's OOW at once called Capt Dawkins and he went straight up to the bridge. *Vanguard* was then steaming at over 8kt as she was trying to get into station, but the regulations laid down that speed in a fog should not exceed 5kt. No signal ordering a reduction of speed had come from *Warrior*, but Dawkins thought that it was essential to reduce speed. Neither Dawkins nor this Chief Yeoman of Signals knew the correct signal to make, particularly as any signal would have to be made by the ship's siren. Whilst they were looking it up in the signal book, Dawkins ordered the siren to be sounded in prolonged blasts and also the ship's pendants to be made on it. He was consulting the signal book when his attention was diverted by a report of a sailing vessel right ahead. He was indeed in a quandary, because if he stopped, the chances were that the *Iron Duke* astern of him would ram him aft and if he carried straight on, he would undoubtedly hit the sailing vessel. He decided to stop.

He shouted to the OOW to 'stop her' and himself dashed forward to the forecastle. As he did so he heard the OOW order 'Hard-a-starboard', which in those days meant that the ship would turn to port. On arrival at the forecastle he saw a sailing vessel passing down his starboard side, reckoned that all danger had passed and he turned aft to shout at the OOW to go full ahead, because he was still worried about the *Iron Duke* coming up astern of him. As he did so he saw through the fog a ship coming straight towards him from the port side. The OOW had already reversed the wheel to hard-a-port, possibly to avoid his stern catching the sailing vessel, which he had seen passing very close down the starboard side. It was all to no avail; the ship was of course the *Iron Duke* and she struck the *Vanguard* with her ram and tore a great hole in her side about amidships.

It seems extraordinary in these days to think of a Captain leaving his bridge and himself going forward to see the approaching ship, but it must not be forgotten that in 1875 there were no raised bridges to which we have grown accustomed, but only a small platform a few feet above the flush deck of the ship to serve as a conning position. Capt Dawkins therefore did not have to clamber down ladders, but had only to step off the platform and rush forward a few feet to reach the forecastle.

Dawkins later argued that had *Iron Duke* been in her correct station, dead astern of *Vanguard*, and had she maintained her course instead of veering out to port, she would have avoided the *Vanguard* and passed her on the starboard side. This was correct, but the OOW in the *Iron Duke* had purposely veered out very slightly to port so that if *Vanguard* had stopped, he would have passed up her port side.

The *Iron Duke* struck in the worst possible place for *Vanguard*, just abaft the transverse bulkhead between the engine room and the boiler rooms, and both the rooms started to flood. The two ships remained locked together for about a minute before the *Iron Duke* went astern and got herself free. Meanwhile Dawkins had returned to the bridge and re-assumed command. He ordered the siren to be sounded continuously, which enabled *Iron Duke* to locate his stricken ship and to send boats. This was just as well because the *Iron Duke's* bowsprit had carried away most of the boats on the port side and those remaining on the starboard side were not enough to accommodate the whole ship's company of 384 men. The watertight doors had been closed but the Chief Engineer reported that the ship was sinking nevertheless. Dawkins told him to get the steam pumps going, but he was informed that the boiler rooms were already flooded, as was the engine room, and there was no steam. Dawkins then ordered the hand pumps to be used, but these made little difference.

Cdr Young of the *Achilles*, who was taking passage in the *Vanguard*, was ordered to get into a boat and mark the ship's side on the waterline to see if she was really sinking. He reported that indeed she was, at the rate of about 8in in 15 minutes. After the report Dawkins realised that there was nothing he could do to save his ship, so he concentrated on saving his crew. The starboard boats were in order and the *Iron Duke* sent all the boats she could. The crew entered them in an orderly fashion and all were saved, many without even getting their feet wet — the only casualty was Capt Dawkins' pet dog, of which he was very fond. Dawkins said later that the time taken from the moment of collision to the giving of the order to abandon ship was 40 minutes. He himself left the ship, and was the last to leave about 10 minutes later; the ship foundered 10 minutes after he left. Fortunately the weather was calm.

Let us now look at what happened onboard the *Iron Duke*. Left alone on the bridge, Lt Evans was doing his best to catch up the *Vanguard* as he had fallen astern of station, and the *Vanguard* herself seemed to be steaming faster than the 8kt which had been signalled. When last seen the *Vanguard* had been displaying flags indicating that she was proceeding at 8kt. He had already rung down for revolutions for 9kt and a few minutes later he asked the engine room to go 'as fast as possible'. This was indeed a dangerous request as the ship, with the boilers alight, was capable of at least 10-11kt, and Evans had no means of knowing exactly what speed the ship was going.

A few minutes later the ship ran into the fog. He lost sight of the flagship and the *Vanguard* and he knew he was in a somewhat dangerous position, so he ordered the quartermaster to steer a little bit to port of the course, thinking that if he should overtake the *Vanguard* he could avoid her by steering further to port. Capt Hickley took his time to come up to the bridge and when he arrived he did not like the idea of steering slightly wide of the course and he told Evans to get back into line, no easy matter as the *Vanguard* was out of sight. Evans did his best to comply and almost immediately *Vanguard's* siren could be heard, slightly on *Iron Duke's* starboard bow. Capt Hickley thought that this confirmed that *Vanguard* was slightly to starboard of him and he thought that she must be still proceeding at 8kt, particularly as there had been no signal to reduce speed.

The next thing that Capt Hickley saw was the shape of the *Vanguard* looming through the fog about half a cable (100yd) away and dead ahead of him. He went hard-a-starboard and stopped the port engine, then, seeing that a collision was imminent, he went full speed astern on both engines. It was too late and the *Iron Duke* struck the *Vanguard* on her port side. The *Iron Duke* was not badly damaged, her reinforced ram taking most of the blow, and she shortly afterwards backed away from the *Vanguard*.

A Court Martial was convened onboard the *Royal Adelaide* at Devonport on Friday 10 September 1875 and lasted for 15 days. The President of the Court was Rear-Adm the Rt Hon Lord John Day and he was assisted by another Rear-Admiral and seven Captains. Only three of the members of the Court had served in ironclads and the remainder had experience only of wooden ships. This fact soon became obvious from the many quite fatuous questions asked by the

The Collision of *Iron Duke* and *Vanguard*

Q WARRIOR

Q HECTOR

Q VANGUARD

1 *Initial Formation*
Single line ahead

Q IRON DUKE

VANGUARD Q

IRON DUKE Q

Q WARRIOR

Q HECTOR

2 *Required Formation*
Divisions in line ahead disposed abeam to port

3 *Method Used*
Vanguard and *Iron Duke* turned together 90° to port and when at correct distance turned together again 90° to starboard, thus finishing up well astern of station and necessitating an increase in speed to regain station

Q WARRIOR

Q HECTOR

4 *How the Collision Occurred*
Iron Duke slightly out of line to port. *Vanguard* sights sailing vessel and alters hard to port to avoid, thus crossing *Iron Duke's* bows, but *Iron Duke* was closer to *Vanguard* than either ship thought and she hit *Vanguard* amidships

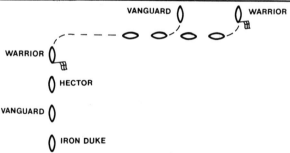

VANGUARD Q

Q WARRIOR

WARRIOR Q

Q HECTOR

VANGUARD Q

Q IRON DUKE

5 *What the Admiralty Said Should Have Been Done*
The squadron should have been ordered to turn in succession 90° to starboard. When all had thus turned, a signal should have been made for leading ships of the divisions to turn together to the original course, remaining ships following in succession. No ship would have lost bearing on the flagship and no alteration in speed would have been necessary

Court — indeed, the Court as a whole appeared heavily biased against *Vanguard's* officers, from the Captain down, and for no apparent reason. The accused were the whole of the officers and men of the *Vanguard*.

Capt Dawkins was asked. 'Is the Court to understand that when you put the helm hard-a-starboard and stopped engines (whilst avoiding the sailing ship), being the leading ship of a column, you did not make any signal to the ship astern?' Dawkins replied, 'There was little time to do anything, the stopping of the engines and moving the helm did not occupy more than a quarter of a minute before the helm was reversed and the engines put to full speed ahead'. Later he was asked why he reduced speed on entering the fog, below that authorised by the Admiral, without signalling the fact to the *Iron Duke*. Dawkins explained that at the time he was manoeuvring his column to take up his appointed station and for this he had increased speed, but on entering the fog he still considered that it was his duty to reduce speed, even though he was not yet in station. As regards not informing *Iron Duke*, he said that at the moment he could not think what the correct signal was, but he thought that by blowing his siren continuously and sounding his pendants, the *Iron Duke* would understand. Capt Hickley, however, said in evidence that he had not heard the *Vanguard's* siren at all, and even if he had he would not have taken a prolonged blast and the sounding of pendants as a signal to reduce speed. Apparently *Vanguard's* siren could not be heard onboard *Iron Duke* by anybody, but this is always a possibility in fog which can play strange tricks with sound.

Adm Tarleton supported Dawkins. He said that when last seen *Vanguard* was well astern of station and he expected Capt Dawkins to increase speed, but when the fog came down he also expected him to reduce the speed of his column.

Cdr Young, although only a passenger in the *Vanguard*, was regarded with suspicion by the Court. He was asked why he had not volunteered to assist in shutting the watertight doors. He very sensibly replied that he was not familiar with the ship and might have been more of a hindrance than a help. The Court then asked him why he had not suggested that all the spare sails should be jammed into the hole. Quite apart from the fact that the Captain might have been extremely annoyed at any suggestion from him, he replied that the ship was sinking so fast he thought that she would not remain afloat for more than another 10 minutes. In fact, although the Court did not know it at the time, there was not just one large hole in the ship's bottom but a number of smaller holes. The ram of the *Iron Duke* had not penetrated the innerskin of the double bottom, but had stopped just short of it. However, the shock of the collision had weakened a large number of rivets and it was through these that the water was penetrating.

Lt Evans told how he was the OOW in the *Iron Duke* and had ordered the quartermaster to steer just to port of the *Vanguard's* stern to avoid running into her if she should suddenly slow or stop. He asserted that it was a common practice and there is no doubt that it is done in fog even to this day. The Court treated him quite leniently, as it did anybody who was not onboard the *Vanguard*, but they did find that one of the reasons which caused the collision was the *Iron Duke* improperly leaving the line. They imposed no punishment on him, but the Admiralty ordered him to be dismissed his ship, which seems a little hard on an officer who was only taking a seamanlike precaution. Perhaps, however, my Lords thought that it was a little unfair that so many of the *Vanguard's* officers should take all the blame, particularly as the Court itself had said that *Iron Duke* steering out of the line was a contributory factor to the collision.

The Court was very critical of Mr Tiddy, the *Vanguard's* carpenter. He was asked why he did not repeatedly sound the compartments and report their state to the Captain. He pointed out that he had been ordered by the Captain to see that all ports and scuttles were closed and to rig the hand pumps. Apart from the fact that it was a direct order, he considered it was more important as he was receiving information about the flooding from his Commander (Tandy) and others. The Court was not finished with him yet and asked whether he attempted to stop the leak from either the inside or the outside. He replied that there was no power available and he had no other means of disposing of such a mass of water filling the engine room. He was also asked if he made any suggestions to his Captain as to how the leak could be stopped. He said he had not. The Court was obsessed with 'the leak' and seemed unable to understand that it was not one leak but a number of small leaks. They quite failed to grasp that it is not possible to stop a number of leaks by outside means. They also made much of the delay in getting the hand pumps working when it was discovered that no steam was available. They attempted to blame anybody they could think of from the Captain down to the carpenter. In fact, as was pointed out afterwards, the hand pumps would have been able to pump out a total of about half a ton a minute, whilst the water was entering the ship at the rate of about 600 tons per minute. The hand pumps would have made no difference even if they had been got to work earlier.

Finally, the Court gave its verdict, which read as follows:

'Having heard the evidence which has been adduced at this inquiry and trial, the Court is of the opinion that the loss of HMS *Vanguard* was occasioned by HMS *Iron Duke* coming into collision with her off the Kish Bank in the Irish Channel at about fifty minutes past noon on the First of September, from the effects of which she eventually foundered, and that such collision was caused:

1. By the high rate of speed at which the squadron (of which these vessels formed part) was proceeding whilst in fog.
2. By Captain Dawkins, when leader of his division, leaving the deck of his ship before the evolution which was being performed was completed, especially as there were indications of foggy weather at the time.
3. By the unnecessary reduction of speed of HMS *Vanguard* without a signal from the Vice-Admiral in command of the squadron and without making a signal to HMS *Iron Duke*.
4. By the increase of speed of HMS *Iron Duke* during a dense fog, the speed being already high.
5. By HMS *Iron Duke* improperly steering out of the line.
6. By the want of any fog signal on the part of *Iron Duke*.'

The Court was further of the opinion that the cause of the loss of HMS *Vanguard* by foundering was:

'A breach being made in her side by the prow of HMS *Iron Duke* in the neighbourhood of the most important transverse bulkhead, viz that between the engine and boiler rooms, causing a great rush of water into the engine room, shaft

alleys and stokehold, extinguishing the fires in a few minutes, the water eventually finding its way into the provision room flat and the provision rooms through imperfectly fastened watertight doors and owing to the leakage of Number 99 bulkhead.'

True to form, they went on to lay as much blame at Capt Dawkins' door as possible. They said that the foundering might have been prevented by him giving orders for immediate action to get all available pumps working, instead of employing his crew in hoisting out boats. They blamed Capt Dawkins, Cdr Tandy (the Executive Officer), Navigating Lieutenant Thomson and Mr Tiddy, the carpenter, for not showing more resource and energy in endeavouring to stop the leak from the outside with the means at their disposal, such as hammocks and sails, and they said that Capt Dawkins should have ordered Capt Hickley to tow the *Vanguard* into shallow water. They also blamed Lt Thomson for neglect of duty in not pointing out to his Captain that there was shallow water within a short distance.

They had not finished yet and they went on to blame the Commander, Tandy, for showing lack of energy as second in command; Mr Brown, the Chief Engineer, for want of promptitude in not applying the means at his command to relieve the ship of water; and Mr Tiddy, the carpenter, for not offering any suggestions to the Captain as to how to stop the leak and for not taking immediate steps to sound the compartments. Finally, once again, they blamed Capt Dawkins for exhibiting want of judgement, and for neglect of duty in handling his ship, and for want of resource, promptitude and decision in saving HMS *Vanguard* after the collision.

After such a blistering attack on all the principal officers of the ill-fated *Vanguard*, not one of them could expect to get off scot free, and so it was. Capt Dawkins was severely reprimanded and dismissed his ship. Cdr Tandy and Lt Thomson were severely reprimanded. Mr Brown and the wretched Mr Tiddy were reprimanded, and finally the Court graciously acquitted the remainder of the officers and men on the *Vanguard*.

There was a strong public outcry at the findings of the Court and many questions were asked as to why the officers of the *Iron Duke* had not even been arraigned before the Court. It seemed odd also that Lt Evans had been dismissed his ship without ever being given a chance to defend himself. After all, it was *Iron Duke* which actually sank the *Vanguard* and one might have expected Capt Hickley at least to have been one of the accused. The Admiralty was forced to

51

look into it and later issued a statement saying that it agreed with the sentences, but added the name of Lt Evans, the OOW in the *Iron Duke*, to the list of the convicted and ordered him to be dismissed his ship. The Admiralty said nothing about Capt Hickley of the *Iron Duke*, but did mention that he was justified in using high speed to regain his station. In fact, under the circumstances nobody could have blamed him if, when the fog came down, he had slowed right down or even stopped his ship. After all, there was no ship astern of him and it would have been the most seamanlike thing to do. Instead he continued at high speed for some little time after the fog enveloped him.

The Admiralty took the trouble to exonerate Vice-Adm Tarleton for proceeding with his squadron at high speed after the fog came down. It said that he was justified at continuing the speed until such time as he made a signal to reduce it. This seems an incredible remark. What it virtually said was that the Admiral was justified in continuing at high speed for as long as he liked, in spite of the standing regulation that speed in a fog should not exceed 5kt. In fact, if Adm Tarleton had made a signal to the squadron to reduce speed to 5kt the moment the fog came down, the collision might not have occurred at all. The trouble seemed to have been that there was no short signal, suitable for use on the siren, that anyone knew by heart. Even the Admiral's signal officer had to look it up in the book and by the time he had found it, the collision had occurred.

The Admiralty also criticised Tarleton for the method by which he formed into two columns from line ahead. They thought it would have been better for the leading ship of the four to have turned 90° to starboard and for the remaining ships to have followed her around. Then, when all four ships were in line ahead again, he could have ordered leading ships of divisions to alter course 90° to port, remainder in succession, ie back to the original course. Thus the two leading ships of divisions would have been formed abeam of each other with their two consorts astern of them. The squadron would thus have been in the required formation without the necessity of *Vanguard's* division having to judge when to turn back to the original course and without any ship having to alter speed. In fairness, Adm Tarleton, whose squadron was on a training cruise, might have thought that it would be a good training for Capt Dawkins to manoeuvre his division for a short time.

Three other points made by the Court are worth remarking on. The idea of towing *Vanguard* into shallow water was indeed quite a good one, but the shallow water was not all that shallow, being 10 fathoms deep as opposed to the 18 fathoms in which she was. Thus when she sank, *Vanguard* would still have been a loss but with perhaps her masts and yards above water. The Court members could never get it into their heads that the *Iron Duke's* ram never penetrated the wooden hull and thus there was no great rush of water. Plenty of water entered the ship but through small holes and rents caused by the shock of the collision, thus the Court's idea of stopping the leak with hammocks and sails was nonsense, as all the people convicted on that charge knew very well. Finally, it was quite absurd to blame so many people for lack of energy in getting the hand pumps going and in blaming Capt Dawkins for being negligent in not making every effort to save his ship. The fact of the matter was that very shortly after the collision it was obvious to all that nothing could be done to save the ship, and Dawkins and his officers were perfectly correct to concentrate on saving lives.

Three
Peacetime Collisions

Hood and *Renown*

A ridiculous collision between two major British warships took place on 23 January 1935. Two battlecruisers, *Hood* and *Renown*, each of some 35,000 tons and over 600ft long, were exercising together. No other ships were near and yet in full daylight on a fine day they succeeded in colliding.

The circumstances were as follows. The ships comprised the Battlecruiser Squadron and were under the command of Rear-Adm S. R. Bailey who flew his flag in the *Hood*. Whilst in harbour on the previous day the Squadron Navigating Officer in the *Hood* asked his opposite number in the *Renown* to come over and discuss the next day's exercises 'over a glass of gin'.

The exercises were to consist of a Range & Inclination exercise between the two ships. On completion *Renown* was to close *Hood* and together they were to carry out an anti-submarine exercise. A Range & Inclination exercise meant that the ships separated out to about 12 miles apart and then steered various courses, but keeping roughly abeam of each other. The rangefinders were exercised in taking ranges at frequent intervals and various officers made estimates of the other ship's course, and thus the angle she presented to the line of sight between the two ships. These two factors, in the days before radar, were all important to solve the gunnery fire control problem. A record was kept of the courses steered and subsequently the exercise was analysed and each officer could see how accurate he had been in the estimates he had made.

The two navigators worked out the courses required for opening out and closing on completion and the Squadron Navigator remarked that when *Renown* had closed to 1,400yd, *Hood* would be turned to a course of 180° ready for the next exercise. The result of their discussion was promulgated by signal from the Admiral which read:

'On Wednesday 23 January, the Battleship Squadron will pass through position two miles 148 degrees from Salvera Island Light. On passing this point, *Hood* is to steer 192 degrees and *Renown* 254 degrees at 12 knots. At 10.50 ships are to turn to 223 degrees when inclination exercises will be carried out. On completion, *Hood* and *Renown* are to steer 254 degrees and 198 degrees respectively to close. Course after rejoining will be 180 degrees, speed 12 knots.'

The inclination exercise was completed at 11.35 with *Renown* some 10-12 miles north-northwest of *Hood*. Both ships steered as ordered to close (see diagram). At 12.18 *Renown* had arrived in a position 320°, 900yd from *Hood*. *Renown* had received no further signal but was expecting *Hood* to turn to 180° at any moment.

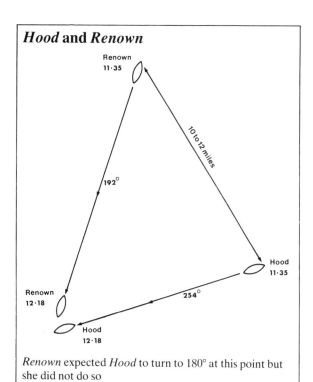

Hood and *Renown*

Renown
11·35

10 to 12 miles

192°

Hood
11·35

Renown
12·18

254°

Hood
12·18

Renown expected *Hood* to turn to 180° at this point but she did not do so

Below:
The battlecruiser *Renown*.
Real Photos (S1127)

Bottom:
HMS *Hood* on sea trials.
IWM

However, *Hood* did not make the expected turn and *Renown* found herself getting far too close, so she stopped engines and ordered hard-a-starboard. It was too late: her advance carried her rapidly towards *Hood* and although she went full astern they collided, her stern hitting *Hood* on the starboard quarter. Fortunately the damage was slight and there was no loss of life.

Two Courts Martial were held, one on Adm Bailey and the other on Capt Sawbridge. Adm Bailey's defence was that no signal was necessary to *Renown* to form astern. She was astern of *Hood* before she opened out for the inclination exercise and she should have come back into this position. Adm Bailey stated that he held strong views on training Captains to do without signals whenever possible. Yet he had made a long signal the day before telling each ship exactly what to do. The two do not quite tie up; the Court acquitted him.

Capt Sawbridge's defence was that it had previously been arranged between the two navigators that *Hood* would turn to 180° when *Renown* was 1,400yd away and had confidently expected her to do so and had thus placed himself to the northwest of her, so that when she turned to 180° he would be astern of her. When she continued her course he found himself in a difficult position and did his best to extricate himself. He was found guilty and dismissed his ship.

On the face of it the Court Martial finding would appear reasonable, but the Navy was astonished when a few days later the Admiralty issued a memorandum stating that Their Lordships dissented from the finding on Adm Bailey. They stated that he adopted an unusual procedure in ordering actual courses to be steered, and that, having done so, the responsibility rested on him to make a further signal to reform his squadron. As regards Capt Sawbridge, Their Lordships agreed with the finding of the Court, but reduced his sentence to that of 'severe reprimand' and they reinstated him in command of *Renown*. Their Lordships also apportioned some of the blame to Capt Tower, Captain of the *Hood*, who they said should have taken action earlier to avoid collision.

It is easy to be wise after the event, but one cannot but help being struck by the rigidity of the orders for opening out and closing. With the freedom of action allowed to the two ships during the actual exercise, their exact positions at the end of the exercise must have been in doubt and the rigid courses ordered may well not have been the correct ones to bring them back together. Surely it would have been better to have signalled the course the Admiral intended to steer and to have told *Renown* to open and close as necessary. This would have allowed freedom of manoeuvre to the *Renown* to steer so as to take station astern of *Hood*. It is nearly always wrong to order another ship to a definitive course: there may be a dozen reasons why she could not do so, wind and tide being the most obvious.

There was also the question as to what is meant by 'rejoining'. The Admiral's signal had said, 'Course after rejoining will be 180 degrees'. Could *Renown* be said to have rejoined when she was 900yd away on *Hood's* starboard bow? One would have thought that she could not be said to have 'rejoined' until she was in station astern of *Hood*. Capt Sawbridge would have been more sensible to have made for this position in the first place. *Hood* could then have altered to 180° when *Renown* was safely astern of her.

Capt Tower said in his evidence that when *Renown* got close he did not alter *Hood's* course and speed as he was the 'guide', but in fact as no manoeuvring signal had been made he was not, and this doubtless is why the Admiralty placed some kind of blame on him.

It seems incredible that two large ships commanded by experienced men could collide like this in broad daylight, but the fact remains that they did, and all three of the major participants in the drama received some blame for it. The two lessons learnt are very clear. Word of mouth conversations between two relatively junior officers should never be relied on unless they are clearly and specifically confirmed by signal or in writing. The Admiral's signal, for example, never mentioned that *Hood* would turn to 180° when *Renown* was 1,400yd away, but only said 'after rejoining'. The second lesson was that definite courses and speeds should never be laid down for ships to take: circumstances may not enable them to do so.

Melbourne and *Voyager*

The collision between the Royal Australian Navy ships *Melbourne* and *Voyager* was another example of two ships alone in the ocean colliding, but this time it was at night and the ships were steaming without lights.

Melbourne (19,930 tons), an aircraft carrier, and *Voyager* (3,550 tons), a destroyer, were carrying out night-flying exercises off Jervis Bay, New South Wales, on 10 February 1964. It was a clear moonless night with very light but variable winds, which, in a sense, were the cause of the disaster. During flying operations *Melbourne* had to chase what little wind there was and was making frequent alterations of course, many without signal, a habit by no means uncommon in aircraft carriers.

At 19.29 *Melbourne* made a signal to *Voyager*, 'Estimated course for impending aircraft operation is 180 degrees, speed 28 knots. Take plane guard station number one. My course 000 degrees, my speed 10 knots'. Plane guard station No 1 is between 1,000yd and 1,500yd on a relative bearing of 200° to the expected flight operations course. The expected course for flight operations was 180°, so *Voyager* positioned herself 200° relative to that course. As *Melbourne* was at the time in fact steering 000°, *Voyager* went to a position 20° on her starboard bow (see diagram at 'A'). Flight operations were postponed, due to lack of wind, and at 20.47 *Melbourne* signalled 'Turn together to 060°, ships turning to starboard' (see diagram at 'B'). Six minutes later *Melbourne* signalled 'Turn together at 020°, ships turning to port'.

This turn should have brought *Voyager* right ahead of *Melbourne* had she been in station (see diagram at 'C'). In fact she was not, and on completion of the turn to 020°, *Voyager* was noted in *Melbourne* as being slightly on her (*Melbourne's*) starboard bow (see diagram at 'D'). At 20.54 *Melbourne* signalled 'Estimated course for impending aircraft operations is 020°, 22 knots'. *Voyager* was then observed by Melbourne to turn to starboard and then immediately back again to port (see diagram at 'E'). The next moment she was observed to be steering about 270°, right across *Melbourne's* bows. *Melbourne* did her best to avoid her, but struck *Voyager* almost amidships and cut her clean in two (see diagram at 'F'). The *Voyager* sank and 82 officers and men were lost, including Capt Stevens, her Commanding Officer, and all the other officers who were on the bridge.

A Royal Commission was appointed to enquire into the accident, but because

Melbourne and *Voyager*

A Where *Voyager* was after signal at 19.29

B Where *Voyager* should have been after turn to 060° at 20.47

C Where *Voyager* should have been after turn to 020° at 20.53: eg right ahead of *Melbourne*

D Where *Voyager* apparently was after turn to 020° at 20.53: eg slightly to starboard bow of *Melbourne*

E *Voyager's* movements as seen by *Melbourne* after the signal made by *Melbourne* at 20.54: 'Estimated course for flying operations 020°'. This required *Voyager* to take up her correct plane guard station on the port quarter of *Melbourne*

F The collision

no bridge officer survived they found it difficult, if not impossible, to discover why *Voyager* acted as she did. We do know that Capt Stevens had his attention diverted to the chart table shortly before the collision and this might have been a contributory factor.

Arguments were put forward to the fact that the *Melbourne* had ordered a new course for impending flying operations did not require *Voyager* to change her station, and that if she was required to do so, a further signal 'take up assigned station' was required. However, very few plane guard Captains would have

Below:
Originally laid down as the light fleet carrier HMS *Majestic*, *Melbourne* was completed for the Royal Australian Navy in 1955. Having sunk the destroyer *Voyager* in 1964, she was also in a collision which sank the US destroyer *Frank E. Evans* in 1969.
Real Photos (N1102)

Bottom:
The unlucky destroyer *Voyager*, photographed off Sydney in December 1962.
Paul Silverstone collection

waited for such a signal, and it would appear that *Voyager* was only showing intelligent anticipation in moving to her new station.

If *Voyager* had been in her correct initial plane guard station she would have been bearing 020° true from *Melbourne*, ie right ahead; and on the new impending course being signalled, she should have moved to a position 200° relative to this course of 020°, ie 220° true from *Melbourne*. The shortest route to this new position would be down *Melbourne's* port side and therefore, had *Voyager* been in station, she should have turned to port.

However, as we know, she was not in station and bore something like 040° true from *Melbourne*. In other words she had to take up station on an exact reciprocal bearing. In this case, it would obviously have been prudent for her to turn to starboard and pass down *Melbourne's* starboard side and under her stern.

It looks therefore as if Capt Stevens first of all decided to do this and then changed his mind, perhaps because he realised that the quickest way from a bearing of 020° true from *Melbourne* to a bearing of 220° true from *Melbourne* was to turn to port. Of course his brief turn to starboard and back again had lost him a lot of bearing, and thus, when he did turn to port, he was a great deal nearer *Melbourne* than he anticipated.

The Royal Commission found that the evidence was insufficient to be able to state the exact cause of the collision but that it appeared to be an error of judgement on the part of Capt Stevens of the *Voyager*. The Commission remarked that the ships had not worked together before and they felt that the two Captains should have consulted together before the exercise.

It can always be argued that nothing replaces personal contacts between Captains of ships before any complicated or difficult exercises or manoeuvres. But acting as plane guard is not very difficult and any destroyer may be called upon to do it, particularly in wartime, and the instructions as to how they should act are quite clear. It should not be necessary for Captains to meet each other first. If it is, then there is something wrong with the manoeuvring instructions.

Diamond and *Swiftsure*

The collision between the cruiser *Swiftsure* and the destroyer *Diamond* occurred on 29 September 1953 during a major NATO exercise in the North Atlantic. A task group consisting of *Swiftsure* (flagship), the battleship *Vanguard* and six destroyers was patrolling to the west of Iceland. The ships were formed as shown in diagram A on page 61, the destroyers being on a bent line screen. It was dark and the ships were steaming without lights on a course of 020°, speed 10kt. The senior officer of the destroyers was in *Diamond* and she was leading the port side of the screen.

At 18.40 on the evening of 29 September, the Officer in Tactical Command (OTC) in *Swiftsure* signalled his intention to reverse the course at 20.00. He did not indicate his intention as to reorienting the destroyer screen, but it was assumed that he would do it by the method 'Rum', by which the ships on the screen changed sides.

At 19.50 the OTC made a signal to reorientate the screen to a course of 200° by method 'Rum' and appended the starboard pennant on the end of the signal group. This was in accordance with the instructions which stated that when the turn was exactly 180° the OTC must indicate which way the main body's reorientation was to be. The exact meaning of the starboard pennant used in this way was 'The direction of reorientation is to be to starboard'.

The 'Rum' method of reorientating the screen requires all ships on the screen to turn together outwards and then to take up their new positions so that they will be in the correct position for screening the main body when it turns, but ships on the screen in effect change sides. In other words, *Diamond* should have turned to port (outwards), increased speed to regain the leading position and finished up on the main body's starboard bow after the whole group had turned. It is a well known manoeuvre and one frequently used in those days, but unfortunately the Captain of the *Diamond* had been ashore for many years and was unfamiliar with the signal books.

When the signal was executed he was in the Operations Room and quite correctly ordered 'Port 10' and the ship started to turn to port. However, his officers in the Operations Room, who should have known better, assured him that the addition of the starboard pennant inferior to the signal group meant that all ships were to turn to starboard. The Captain therefore reversed his wheel and ordered 'Starboard 10'. *Diamond* thus started turning to starboard and with only 10° of wheel her turning circle was large. The Captain appreciated this and saw from his plot that he was going to turn very close to *Swiftsure's* track (the main body was continuing on a course of 020°). He therefore ordered more starboard wheel to try and turn inside her track and to pass *Swiftsure*, with *Vanguard* astern of her, port to port.

On looking at the plot again, he saw that he was only 1,000yd from *Swiftsure's* track, so he proceeded to the bridge and, realising that there was now definite danger of collision, he ordered navigation lights to be switched on and also ordered 'hard-a-starboard' and stopped the starboard engine. He also ordered one short blast to be made on the siren, indicating that he was turning to starboard. He could just see *Swiftsure's* shape in the dark and thought she was end on to him, but when she switched on her navigation lights — which she did almost simultaneously with *Diamond* — he could only see her starboard green light. He thought therefore that she must have altered course to port (see diagram at B). In fact, *Swiftsure* did not alter course at all and *Diamond* had crossed her bow, a fact never appreciated in the *Diamond's* Operations Room, due probably to delay in plotting (see diagram at C).

Had the Captain not increased his starboard wheel he would probably have passed down *Swiftsure's* starboard side and all would have been well. As it was, by the time *Diamond's* officers had realised that their ship was in fact on the starboard bow of the *Swiftsure*, it was too late and, in spite of going full astern, the *Diamond* rammed *Swiftsure* on her starboard side about abreast the bridge. The collision caused a fire in *Swiftsure* and extensive damage to both ships. Forty officers and ratings were injured but there were no fatal casualties.

At the subsequent Court Martial, the Captain of *Diamond* argued that the manoeuvring instructions were not entirely clear as to the meaning of the starboard pennant inferior. He pointed out that 'the direction of re-orientation is to be to starboard' might be misinterpreted to mean ships were to turn to starboard. In fact, if the full instructions are read, it is perfectly clear that ships on either side of the screen turn outwards and this argument was not accepted by the

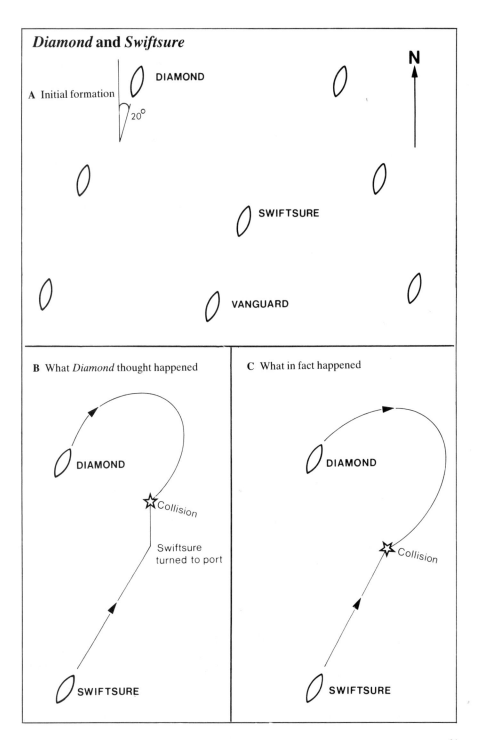

Diamond and _Swiftsure_

A Initial formation

20°

DIAMOND

N

SWIFTSURE

VANGUARD

B What _Diamond_ thought happened

DIAMOND

Collision

Swiftsure
turned to port

SWIFTSURE

C What in fact happened

DIAMOND

Collision

SWIFTSURE

Court and the Captain was found guilty of hazarding his ship. However, it is of interest to note that the manoeuvring instructions were subsequently amended to read 'The direction of the reorientation of the screen axis must be indicated by the port flag or starboard pennant'. The only reason for the port flag or the starboard pennant is to show the screening ships which way the main body is going to turn so that they can adjust their positions to port or starboard as necessary after they have turned.

What then were the causes for the collision? The initial error undoubtedly lay in *Diamond* changing her turn from port to starboard and this was due to wrong advice tendered to the Captain by his officers. It is obvious that neither these officers, nor the Captain, had read thoroughly the appropriate instructions. A warning was given over an hour beforehand that course was going to be reversed and one would have thought that this should have given ample time for the instructions to be read on all methods of carrying out this manoeuvre.

Even after having turned the wrong way, a collision could have been avoided had the plotting in *Diamond* been accurate and up to date. Radar was in use and accurate positions of the two ships should have been shown, but it must not be forgotten that in those days the bearings and ranges of radar echoes were 'told' to the plot by voice over a telling line and quite considerable delays between the range and bearing having been obtained and it actually being plotted were common. It was therefore more than likely that the plot was behind the actual situation. A more experienced Captain would have realised this, but in fact it led to the officers in *Diamond* thinking that the *Swiftsure* was further away than she actually was. Nowadays radar echoes appear automatically on the plot almost as soon as they are obtained, so this type of error is unlikely to occur again.

The Royal Navy has almost always suffered from having too few ships, so it is inevitable that Commanding Officers spend more time in shore jobs than at sea and get out of date with the signal books, the complications of manoeuvring and ship handling. There are excellent refresher courses available and manoeuvres can be practised on a tactical table in a most realistic fashion, but nothing can replace actual sea training.

Below:
A wartime view of the 'Minotaur' class cruiser HMS *Swiftsure. Real Photos (S1654)*

8

Untamed *and* Affray

This is the story of two submarines which were lost with all hands for no apparent reason. The first was the *Untamed* which was lost in 1943, during the war, but enemy action did not enter into it. The second was the *Affray* in 1951 and the reason for her loss has never definitely been established.

Untamed

In May 1943 HMS *Untamed* was detailed to act as a target submarine for a number of anti-submarine ships practising underwater detections and the hunting of submarines off the west coast of Scotland. It was very much a routine exercise, especially for the submarine, and *Untamed's* job was known as the 'Clockwork Mouse'. All she had to do was to act as an enemy submarine, within strict limits to make life easy for the untrained hunters, while the surface ships practised detecting her with sonar, or ASDIC as it was known in those days. She dived to 60ft well below the keels of the destroyers with whom she was exercising, and put herself in positions where she knew she would be detected. It was a boring exercise for the crew and they had little to do.

However, after an hour or two, her patent log broke down. The log is used to measure the distance run by the submarine and her speed. It was not required for the exercise and the young officer in command thought that it would be a good exercise for his crew to try and repair the unit. To do this, it would have to be withdrawn inside the boat and the hole, in which it fitted in order to protrude into the sea, blocked off so that no water entered. This was easily done by a hand-operated valve.

The necessary order was given to close the valve, but unbeknown to anybody on board the gearing between the operating lever and the valve itself was incorrectly connected, so that when the indicator showed that the valve was shut, it was in fact open. On withdrawing the log, a solid stream of water 4in in diameter came through the hole and started to fill the fore end of the boat. Because of the pressure of the water it was impossible to close the hole, and in minutes the fore end was nearly half-full. The only thing to do was to evacuate the compartment and to shut the watertight door which would isolate the flooded compartment from the rest of the submarine. Further, with the door shut, the water in the compartment would stop rising when the pressure of the air on top of it became equal to the pressure of the sea. When this occurred, it would be a comparatively simple matter for one or two men to re-enter the compartment and block off the hole. The compartment could then be pumped out.

With the weight of the water in the fore end, the submarine started a deep dive. The Captain in the control room was doing all he could to counteract it by blowing ballast tanks, and in fact he did succeed in levelling the boat off before she hit the

Above:
Unrivalled, sister-ship of *Untamed*, seen in 1942.　*Real Photos (S1686)*

bottom at 160ft. Of course the deeper the boat went, the greater became the pressure of the water and the higher it rose in the flooded compartment. The Sub-Lieutenant and a rating had entered the compartment and they had arranged a code of signals by banging on the bulkhead, but no signals came.

The Captain was in a quandary. He did not like the idea of abandoning the submarine with two of his men in the flooded compartment and he waited, hoping that they would get out or that he might yet succeed in getting the boat to the surface. It was his first command and he lacked experience, but he had plenty of other experienced submariners on whom he could call. He tried for four hours to lighten the submarine, but all to no avail. Efforts were made to pump out the fore end with a 2in pipe, but as the water was entering through a 4in hole it was a hopeless task. What the crew probably did not realise was that they were beginning to feel the effects of carbon dioxide poisoning, of which the first symptoms were loss of reasoning power.

The Captain at last gave the order to abandon ship and moved the whole crew into the engine room, which is abaft the control room, and shut the watertight door between the two rooms. This virtually halved the amount of space available for the men and increased the action of the carbon dioxide, as in the small space available the atmosphere came under even greater pressure. The twill trunk was rigged and the order was given to flood the compartment, but on opening the flood valve no water came in. After the boat was salvaged it was found that the handle of the valve had been mounted incorrectly, so that when the indicator showed open, the valve was in fact shut. Other valves were opened and flooding commenced, but at a very slow rate. The water rose painfully slowly and as it rose it increased the pressure and thus the carbon dioxide poisoning. Breathing became a terrible effort and some men started to breathe oxygen from the DSEA equipment, but breathing oxygen under pressure is fatal and they probably succumbed. In fact it looked as if very few of the crew survived long enough even to attempt an escape.

The water had still been coming in very slowly and the reason for this was found after the boat had been salvaged. One of the valves they opened was in fact connected to a small bore drain pipe which led through the after bulkhead of the engine room into the bilges of the after end. Because of this the pressure in the engine room could not be equalised, until the pressure in the after end was also equalised, and the tiny pipe was only allowing a very little water through.

On the surface the exercise had been stopped and the ships started searching with their sonars for the submarine, and firing charges underwater from time to time to indicate that they were there and that the crew could escape if desired. After some hours of fruitless searching they abandoned it as it was obvious that nobody could have survived for so long. Occasional bubbles of air had been coming to the surface, and initially they knew that some of the crew must have been alive, but after about four hours even the bubbles had ceased.

Untamed was salvaged six months later and was towed into harbour. The gruesome task of investigating the interior of the submarine began. The bodies of most of the crew were found grouped in the engine room waiting to go into the twill trunk, and the Chief Stoker's body was found at the top of the ladder inside the trunk. The control room was found to be quite intact with the air in it at atmospheric pressure, but contaminated with carbon dioxide to about 4-5%. The pressure in the engine room, from where the attempt was being made, had risen to nearly six atmospheres and the concentration of carbon dioxide was about 25-30%. As the air was being compressed very slowly, the carbon dioxide content must have also built up slowly, but it is probable that after a time the men hardly noticed it and went off into a deep coma, followed by a peaceful death.

It was the first time that it had been possible to test the air inside a submarine which had been lost when submerged, and the heavy content of carbon dioxide surprised many people, but it must not be forgotten that there were a large number of men in a very confined space which was gradually being put under pressure, and it was already known that compressing the atmosphere tended to increase the carbon dioxide content. For all that, it shed some light on the *Thetis* disaster of some years before, and proved that most of the crew must have been dead before noon on that fatal day in June.

Affray

Affray was a large and modern submarine of the 'Acheron' class and displaced 1,120 tons (1,445 tons submerged). In addition to her crew of about 60, she embarked at Portsmouth 23 junior officers and a small detachment of Royal Marines which she was to land on a beach in Cornwall.

Her orders were to proceed down Channel at her best speed, either dived or on the surface at the discretion of the Captain, until she reached the Western Approaches, probably between Start Point and Lands End. She was then to play the part of a submarine on war patrol and to carry out dummy attacks on shipping in the area, proceeding either down or up the Channel, for the benefit of the young officers under training. The exercise was to last three days and after that she was to close the Cornish coast and land the Marines at a secluded bay. The Captain had complete freedom of action and could go anywhere in the mouth of the Channel between the English and French coasts and was not required to make frequent diving and surfacing signals, but could make one diving signal when he commenced the exercise and one surfacing signal when he completed it.

Affray sailed for the exercise at 16.15 on 16 April 1951, only 15 months after the *Truculent* submarine disaster. She was grossly overcrowded, with nearly 80 persons onboard in a submarine built for 60, and not for just one day but for three or four days. One wonders why two completely unrelated exercises were combined in one submarine and why her orders were obviously not framed to take into account the possibility of any mishap. Complete freedom of action meant that nobody on shore had any idea as to where she was at any time; she had onboard an entire class of specially selected young officers whose loss would strike a severe blow to the submarine service; and no-one would know if she suffered a mishap because no regular diving and surfacing signals were required.

She was reported soon after sunset on the 16th off the Isle of Wight, at 21.00 she made a signal saying that she was diving for the night and would surface by 08.00 the next morning, before starting the exercise of attacking shipping in the Channel. No surfacing signal was ever received and at about 09.00 on the morning of the 17th the executive order to commence Operation 'Subsunk' was given.

'Subsunk' is the code word for a massive national and international submarine search for a submarine believed to be missing. It affects thousands of people and organisations. In this case, over 40 ships were sent out to search, Fleet Air Arm and RAF aircraft and helicopters were deployed, and salvage ships along the whole south coast were alerted, including the Navy's deep diving ship HMS *Reclaim*. An American squadron of destroyers visiting Plymouth sailed to join in and the French and Dutch were alerted. If this seemed a very large force, it must not be forgotten that for all anyone knew, *Affray* might be anywhere from Land's End to off the coast of Dorset, or on the other side of the Channel between Ushant and Cherbourg. In all it amounted to an area of several thousand square miles. The whole operation was controlled from the headquarters of C-in-C Portsmouth, Adm Sir Arthur John Power.

In the Operations Room at Portsmouth the staff reckoned that they had at the most 18 to 24 hours to find *Affray* in time to save life, assuming that something had happened to her towards the end of the night. When no reports of any clues, no bodies, no sign of wreckage, or no submarine indicator buoys were received, the despondent team in the Ops Room decided to turn the operation into one of salvage instead of one of rescue. No less than 14 naval salvage vessels were on alert along the Channel ports. The heavy German lifting craft *Energris* and *Adedauer* were made ready to be towed across the North Sea; all British naval divers' leave was cancelled and every conceivable contingency was catered for. It all took time and by now it had become obvious that there could be nobody left onboard alive, but there was still hope that they had escaped and had been picked up by some craft without radio. There was also the possibility that *Affray* might have dived into one of the numerous wrecks which are to be found in the Channel and be caught in it unable to surface. A team of salvage experts was gathered at Portsmouth to work out a plan for getting a wire around her stern and pulling her out, but opinion varied as to whether it would take four months or four hours.

In the end, the experts had to face the fact that *Affray* was definitely lost and all onboard her must be dead, so on 19 April Operation 'Subsunk' was called off and the long-term search for the submarine was started.

It proved to be a most laborious job, and lasted over two months. A probability area was first established and the search concentrated on that. The area stretched from her diving position just west of the Isle of Wight to her furthest on position at 09.00, assuming her best dived speed. In the north-south direction it was confined from off the English coast to mid-Channel. A flotilla of frigates was detailed to carry out sonar searches in the area, but allowing for delays in investigating non-submarine echoes it would take them some considerable time.

They had with them two survey ships to carry out more detailed investigations of anything the frigates detected, and backing them up was the deep diving ship HMS *Reclaim*. The idea was that any find thought worthwhile investigating even more thoroughly would be reported to C-in-C Portsmouth and he would decide, after sifting all the available evidence, whether it was worth pursuing. If it was, the *Reclaim* would be ordered to proceed to the spot, moor over the precise location and send down divers.

Reclaim had to be moored with four moorings to ensure that she did not move more than a few feet when the divers were down, to avoid dragging them along the bottom. Further, as the tides were often very strong, the *Reclaim* could only work for about two hours each slack water and the divers only about three-quarters of an hour. This meant that there were only four periods of about two hours each when the operation could be carried out and only about a total of three hours in 24 during which the divers could actually submerge. It was a time-consuming and infuriating business, particularly as contact after contact proved to be old wrecks. The divers took incredible risks and there were a number of cases of them having to be brought to the surface more dead than alive.

After this method of searching had been in use for about six weeks, the Admiralty Research Laboratory suggested that its underwater television camera might be able to help. Underwater TV in those days was far less sophisticated than it is now, and was generally mistrusted by the diving fraternity. However, the offer was gratefully accepted and proved at once to be a great time saver. The camera was placed onboard the *Reclaim*. It had its own operating team, commanded by Cdr Crabb, who subsequently lost his life when clandestinely diving on a Soviet cruiser in Portsmouth harbour.

It was found that the camera could be used for several hours at each slack water, a great improvement on the divers' three-quarters of an hour. It was also possible to identify the non-sub contacts with comparative ease as the camera was quite good enough to differentiate between an old rusty wreck of a merchant ship and the new wreck of a submarine. In addition the swarms of fish, showing white in the powerful flashlight attached to the camera, were a sure indication of an old wreck, since fish do not feed near a new wreck. All this greatly speeded things up.

By the end of May the original probability area had been completely covered, so it was decided to move to the next most probable area, further south and nearer to the French coast. A sonar contact was obtained with some underwater object and looked hopeful. It was labelled Contact 'Jig' and *Reclaim* was called in to investigate it. A diver was sent down in an observation chamber and he reported a white rail, the first time anything not covered in rust had been seen. The diver was recalled and a TV camera was sent down instead. It at once revealed a picture of rails round a submarine's gun tower and furthermore the letters FFRAY could be discerned. The search was over.

Affray lay in 278ft of water, somewhat south of Guernsey. She was pointing in the right direction, towards the northwest, and was lying on a level, gravel bottom with a slight list to port. Her radar antenna and her after periscope were both raised, indicating that she was probably at periscope depth when the accident occurred. All her hatches were shut and her hull was undamaged. There were no signs that any attempt had been made to release her indicator buoys. Both hydroplanes were to the hard-a-rise position, indicating that a last frantic effort

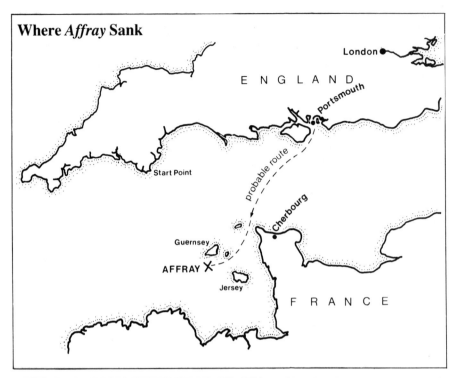

Where _Affray_ Sank

Above:
A wartime picture of HMS _Affray_.   *Real Photos (S1998)*

had been made to hold her up or possibly to level her off before she hit the bottom.

Reclaim made a second attempt to find out more about what had happened. She found out that _Affray's_ 35ft 'snort' was snapped off a few feet above deck level and was leaning over her port side, the side to which she was listing, and was only attached to the boat by a thin strip of metal. This indeed was a significant find. The 'snort' is a tube down which fresh air is drawn when at periscope depth in order to keep the diesel engines running when submerged. Had she been at periscope depth, which seemed likely, the 'snort' might quite well have been raised. It did not appear to be damaged towards the top end, as it would have been had it collided with some ship; therefore the assumption must be that it had snapped off due to the strain on it as the submarine ploughed through the water, but this is a fairly constant pressure and unlikely to sever a large steel 'snort'. The only other conclusion the experts could come to was that the 'snort' had suffered some form of metal fatigue and eventually the metal had succumbed to the pressure of the sea against it and broken off, perhaps because of a sudden speed increase.

With this theory in mind, the authorities ordered that the 'snort' must be recovered at all costs. The job was given to the *Reclaim*. After much deliberation it was decided to grapple for the head of the 'snort', put a strop around it and gently lift it up, hoping that the thin bit of metal holding it to the submarine would break away. Every effort was made to avoid damaging the actual fracture as this was the vital part which the metallurgists would want to examine. It took the *Reclaim* and her divers two days to secure the strop, but on an unusually fine day on Sunday 1 July the job was done and the order was given to haul in. The entire 'snort' came up without difficulty and the piece of thin metal sheered as expected. The 'snort' was laid along *Reclaim's* deck and she made all haste back to Portsmouth.

Meanwhile the submarine experts had been thinking as to whether the breaking off of the 'snort' would have been enough to sink the *Affray*. They realised that water would enter the submarine at the fracture point, but not in overwhelming quantities, and in any case there was an induction valve at this point, especially for this sort of emergency, and it should have been possible to close this remotely. Whether or not attempts had been made to close this valve would entail recovering the entire submarine and opening her up.

The tests on the recovered 'snort' showed that there had indeed been a metal weakness at the point of fracture and at once all submarines of the same class were told not to use their 'snorts' until further orders. Many trials were carried out on *Affray's* sister ships, but no defective 'snorts' were found and the theory that her loss was directly attributable to the breaking off of the 'snort' was losing ground to a theory that an explosion had occurred onboard. One argument was that had the 'snort' broken off, the flooding would have been in the after end of the boat, but it appeared that she had taken the bottom in a nose-down position and she was undamaged aft. However, it seemed likely that the fractured 'snort' must have had something to do with the accident. Many theories were put forward, but nothing definite ever emerged and would not do so until she was salvaged.

Eventually the Admiralty decided not to attempt to salvage her. It would have been a difficult and expensive job, so *Affray* was left to lie in her watery grave, where she still lies today.

The Admiralty issued the following statement: 'It is possible that there had been an explosion of battery gases in the early hours of the morning of 17 April which had split the battery ventilation shaft, thus allowing water to flood into the batteries. In any event, it appeared that the crew must have been killed or drowned almost instantaneously'.

It was a sorry business, but we can take heart that it was the last submarine disaster in the Royal Navy and that it took place over 35 years ago.

9

Squalus

The *Squalus* was a brand-new conventional (diesel-electric) submarine. She was nearly 300ft long and had only been out of the builder's hands for 11 days when she sailed from Portsmouth, New Hampshire, on 23 May 1939. She was going to sea to carry out her first 'crash dive', as frequently practised by conventional submarines. It is the dive effected when an enemy suddenly appears and it is necessary to dive as rapidly as possible to avoid being seen or detected. Nuclear submarines do not 'crash dive' because of their size and the fact that they are so seldom on the surface in enemy waters, but conventional submarines may often have to carry it out, particularly when surprised on the surface by an enemy aircraft.

For the practice dive, *Squalus* would be running on her diesels on the surface and at a given moment the Captain would give the order 'crash dive'. In American submarines this would be followed by a prolonged blast on the diving klaxon. The Captain and the bridge crew would collect all loose gear on the bridge and make all haste to go down the vertical ladder to the control room; the last man down, usually the Captain, would shut the hatch firmly behind him. The vents at the top of the main ballast tanks would be opened with all speed, allowing the air inside them to rush out and the water to enter. Main ballast tanks are normally open to the sea, the pressure from the air inside them preventing the water from entering; by opening the vents on top of the tanks, the pressure of the water pushes the air up and out and the water rushes in to replace it.

All went according to plan at first; the Captain, Lt Naquin, gave the order to crash dive and climbed down the ladder into the control room, where the First Lieutenant was in charge of the actual dive. Naquin was anxious to see how successful his crew were in this, their first 'crash dive', for much might depend on them in a real emergency, but he soon saw that they knew their jobs. The boat slipped steeply under the waves and the First Lieutenant levelled her up by use of the hydroplanes. The idea was to dive to periscope depth, probably about 40ft, but just on reaching this depth there was a frantic cry over the intercom, 'Water flooding into the engine room'.

The state of all openings into the sea is indicated in a submarine by an illuminated indicator panel, where red and green lights were shown. All eyes in the control room turned to this panel. Every light was showing green, indicating that all openings were shut, yet it was obvious that the sea was entering somewhere aft as the stern began to drop and the boat, instead of being nose down, was rapidly sinking by the stern. The engine room was quickly evacuated and men from it came staggering into the control room. The First Lieutenant gave the obvious orders, 'blow the main ballast tanks' and 'close watertight doors'. This had the effect of halting *Squalus* in her rapid downward path, but only for a brief moment. She then continued sinking by the stern even faster and she hit the bottom with a large jolt which knocked most people off their feet. As they scrambled up, she slowly levelled off and came to rest firmly on the seabed lying upright with about a 12° nose-up angle.

Naquin held a rapid conference with his officers. They came to the conclusion that the cause of the sinking must have been that the 'high induction valve' had remained open, but that for some unexplained reason the indicator had shown closed. This valve is a large one situated inside the conning tower casing, slightly above the level of the conning tower hatch. It should be closed at all times, unless specifically ordered to be opened. It is used to enable air to be drawn into the boat to keep her diesels running in rough weather when rough sea may occasionally wash over the conning tower hatch. It is operated from the control room and on carrying out a 'crash dive' one member of the crew should have been responsible for shutting it. Evidently he had failed to do so, perhaps because he had seen that the indicator had shown that it was already shut.

Naquin and his officers decided that it should be possible to shut the valve from the outside and then pump out the engine room. It would necessitate getting a diver out to work on it. However, the conference was rudely interrupted by a cry from forward, 'fire forward', and at that moment all the lights went out. The fire was an electrical one and the Chief Electrician's Mate had broken the switches from the batteries to prevent the fire spreading. The crew's position, already desperate, changed in a brief second to highly perilous.

By groping around with torches they established that it would be impossible to restore the lights and power which meant that not only would they have to work in the dark, but they would be unable to operate the sonar or indeed any electrical apparatus. There was no heating (the water temperature outside was 34°F) and it would now be impossible to get a diver out. Naquin took a count of the men remaining and found that there were 33 alive, all in the control room or the forward compartments, and that the submarine was undamaged forward. They were at 242ft, just about the maximum for the use of the Momson Lung, a form of self-breathing apparatus worn individually by men endeavouring to escape.

However, Naquin knew that the newly designed McCann Rescue Bell was actually onboard the USS *Falcon*, at New London, not very far distant. He reckoned that before long the *Squalus* would be rated as overdue, as no surfacing signal would have been received by those on shore at the time expected. He thought that the *Falcon* could be got to sea and could be with them in perhaps 12 hours. He therefore decided that they would wait for an external rescue. The cold was intense and he had ever in mind the necessity of the men not generating too much carbon dioxide by heavy breathing. He ordered all the crew to turn in to their bunks, to keep absolute silence and to conserve their strength. He ordered the release of the indicator buoy which also carried a telephone. Finally he ordered the release of one red underwater grenade. This grenade would ignite on reaching the surface and give off a cloud of red smoke for some 15 to 20 minutes. Naquin would appear to have been a most sensible young man — all the orders he gave were absolutely correct and he was fully aware of the dangers of carbon dioxide poisoning.

Ashore in Portsmouth the Base Commander, Rear-Adm Cole, an ex-submarine officer, was worried by the non-receipt of *Squalus'* surfacing signal when it was due. He rang the submarine base at New London and asked them to get the *Falcon* ready for sea with the diving bell onboard as soon as possible. In addition, by great good fortune, the submarine *Sculpin* was due to sail from Portsmouth at 11.30 that morning, so Adm Cole himself went down to her berth and asked her to go through *Squalus's* position on her way and see if they could find out anything. He also informed the Bureau of Ships.

By what was almost a miracle, the *Sculpin* found the red flare launched by the *Squalus* and the indicator buoy. She grappled the buoy and in no time her Commanding Officer, Lt-Cdr Wilkin, was in conversation with Naquin, who was an old friend of his. Naquin just had time to tell him what the situation was onboard when the wire connecting the telephone to the submarine parted in the rough seas and *Squalus* was lost again. *Sculpin* anchored immediately to act as a marker for the submarine, and reported to the base at New London by radio. The full alarm was raised and things began to move. Adm Cole proceeded to the scene of the disaster by an old dockyard tug, the only vessel available. In spite of her slow speed, she was the first ship to arrive after the *Sculpin*. She immediately started dragging for the submarine, but as the afternoon faded she had still not found her.

Onboard the *Squalus* the hopes of the crew were greatly raised by the telephone conversation, only to be dashed when the wire parted, but the noise of the tug's propeller could be clearly heard and this, at least, told them that help would soon be at hand.

Falcon, as bad luck would have it, was carrying out a short self-maintenance period and her boilers were cold, but she broke all the rules and was ready for sea in a few hours. Her Captain, Lt Sharp, lost no time in putting to sea with the massive bell onboard, but he soon ran into a nasty head sea which slowed him down a lot. However, he pressed on, with the bell straining at her securing ropes, and at 04.15 sighted the lights of the *Sculpin* and the tug. The *Sculpin* informed him that the tug's drag wire had caught in something which they thought was the *Squalus*. The *Falcon* was asked to get divers down as soon as possible to verify it. By this time the weather was really bad and *Falcon* had to try and moor exactly on top of the *Squalus* to avoid having to move with the divers down, and thus dragging them through the water. The mooring took four precious hours. The *Falcon* had to put out several anchors in order to hold her steady in the strong wind, right on top of the *Squalus*. By now the time was 10.30 in the morning and *Squalus* had been stranded submerged for just over 24 hours.

The man chosen to make the first dive was Bosun's Mate (second class) Sibitzky, a large man renowed for his great strength. He climbed on to the diving platform and was swung over the side. The weather, fortunately, chose this moment to improve and three minutes later the waiting officers in the *Falcon* heard his voice over the telephone telling them that he had landed right on the deck of the *Squalus* within 6ft of the forward hatch. He could not have been better placed for there was a lug on the hatch to which to secure the downhaul wire of the bell. He first of all inspected the hatch and found that the wire of the indicator buoy had run foul of the hatch and was lying across it, just where the bell's hatch would have to mate with it. Unless the wire was cleared away, the bell would be unable to get a seal. Meanwhile, onboard the *Falcon*, they had lowered the downhaul wire of the bell to Sibitzky. He got hold of it and was able to shackle the end of the wire on to the lug of the hatch, and he told those on the surface to haul

Above:
The submarine rescue ship *Falcon* with the tender *Wandank* anchored over the sunken *Squalus*. *US Navy*

Left:
The McCann rescue bell alongside the rescue ship *Falcon* at the scene of the *Squalus* disaster. *US Navy*

Below left:
In 1940 the ill-fated *Squalus* was put back into service under the name *Sailfish*, after a refit costing $1.4 million.
Paul Silverstone collection

73

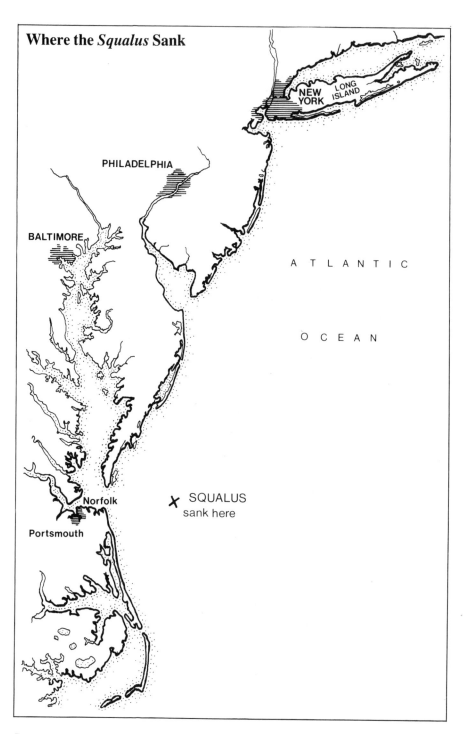

Where the *Squalus* Sank

NEW YORK

LONG ISLAND

PHILADELPHIA

BALTIMORE

A T L A N T I C

O C E A N

Norfolk

Portsmouth

X SQUALUS
sank here

away on it until it was taut. He then started his long return to the surface and the welcome company of his friends. The dive was a magnificent effort. He had to work at about the depth limit in those days for a diver, in almost pitch darkness, in a bitter cold sea and all by himself, knowing that the lives of the 33 men onboard the *Squalus* depended upon him and him alone.

On the surface, other ships had arrived by this time, including one with Cdr McCann and some of his divers onboard. Cdr McCann had invented the diving bell and this was the first time that it had ever been used in action. He was most anxious that it should prove successful. He now took charge and put his two best men inside the bell.

The bell was swung out and lowered into the water and the two men started the electrical winch which slowly pulled the bell down towards the submarine. The men could see little, but eventually they felt a slight bump and, on peering out, they saw that they were right on top of the *Squalus*. Following the drill which they had practised they blew the water out of the lower compartment of the bell, using compressed air supplied by the *Falcon* down the hose pipe, into a ballast tank provided for the purpose, thus maintaining the same weight of the bell so that she did not suddenly rise. When this was completed the air inside the lower compartment was at the same pressure as the sea outside, but of course they had to get this air down to the same pressure as the air inside the submarine. They therefore had to vent the air out through another hose to the surface. From then on it was a relatively simple matter to open the submarine's hatch which had a wheel on top of it for the purpose. The hatch swung open and one of the rescuers shone a torch down into the control room and casually announced 'Hullo fellas, we're here'.

It had been previously agreed that before attempting any evacuation, the *Falcon* would supply fresh air to the submarine to enable the crew to recover from their ordeal, observing that they had by now been submerged for 28 hours without any external air. The bell was already connected to the *Falcon* by an air hose and the *Falcon's* compressors blew fresh air down into the bell and thus into the *Squalus*. The bell could only hold nine men, two of which were the crew, thus only seven men could be rescued at a time, and while the bell was away the submarine would have to be closed again, hence the necessity for plenty of fresh air. Whilst the fresh air was being blown into the submarine, opportunity was taken to hand the crew hot drinks, food and carbon dioxide absorbers to mop up any of the gas remaining. The first seven passengers entered the bell and, by reversing the processes of flooding and blowing, the bell was made positively buoyant and rose to the surface, paying out the downhaul wire as it went and also using it as a brake to prevent them coming up too fast and possibly hitting the bottom of the *Falcon*.

On surfacing, the bell was rapidly hauled alongside the *Falcon* and the seven men emerged. Thus the first rescue made by the bell was completed successfully. However, there were still 26 men below, and at only seven men at a time the rescue would not be completed for 10 hours, as each sortie of the bell from the surface down to the submarine and back to the surface took two hours. Adm Cole thought that 10 hours would be too long, even in spite of the ventilation from the *Falcon*. Further, he was worried that the weather might not hold. He therefore decided that they must get the men out in three trips instead of four. This would mean two trips with nine passengers and one with eight. There was considerable doubt as to whether the bell would have sufficient buoyancy, but it was a risk that had to be taken. The first two trips went perfectly; the bell's buoyancy seemed sufficient and spirits rose high. There were only eight men remaining, but the atmosphere inside the *Squalus* was deteriorating rapidly, chlorine gas was rising from the battery and the air was very foul.

At last the time came for the remaining men to make their attempt. They filed into the bell one by one, with Naquin the last man to leave, and the bell cast off from the submarine and started its ascent. Then after eight minutes the downhaul wire jammed on the winch and went bar taut. They stopped dead and could not rise any more. They telephoned to the *Falcon* and were told to let ballast water out and to return to the submarine and they would send a diver down to clear the wire. The trapped men then eased the bell down on to the casing of the *Squalus* and waited for the diver. He eventually arrived and had a desperate struggle to try and clear the wire, but failed. As a last effort, although nearly unconscious, he took out his wire cutters and severed the wire. The bell was freed but now had no brake for its ascent, which would have to be very carefully controlled.

Cdr McCann himself took over the telephone and assured the men inside that they would be perfectly alright, provided they obeyed his instructions completely. He told them to blow the water out of the lower chamber into the ballast tanks very slowly until the bell started to ascend, reporting to him the depth showing on their depth gauge every few minutes. If it came up too fast, McCann told them to admit water; if too slow, to blow with the compressed air again. Very slowly he talked them up, speaking always in slow, measured tones and remaining perfectly calm. His air of assurance greatly heartened the men below and inch by inch the bell rose. After four hours it broke surface close to the *Falcon* and was quickly grappled and brought alongside and the men got out. They had been nearly 40 hours in the submarine and the bell and were very exhausted.

The McCann Bell thoroughly proved its worth and effected a magnificent rescue, but it must be said that the conditions were favourable. The weather, although rough at first, calmed down; the bell was already onboard the *Falcon*, which itself was quite close to the scene of the disaster; the submarine was lying upright, so mating with it presented no difficulties; and there were no tides. All this, however, does not detract from the heroism shown by the divers and the astonishing stamina of the crew. Their long endurance against carbon dioxide poisoning was partly due to the good sense of Lt Naquin who made sure they did not over-exert themselves in the initial stages. Some men were of course lost. Her crew would have numbered about 45 persons and only 33 were saved. The remainder were undoubtedly trapped in the after part of the submarine when the engine room flooded, particularly as the watertight door between the engine room and the control room had to be shut to prevent further flooding, whether or not it would entail trapping some of the men.

The Americans still have the McCann Bell for shallow rescues, but for deep water rescues they have now developed a much more sophisticated device known as the Deep Submergence Rescue Vessel which can move through the water under its own power and can also mate with a submarine lying on its side at an angle. Fortunately it has never been put to use in a real-life rescue, although mock rescues have been carried out with great success.

10

Thetis

HM Submarine *Thetis* commissioned at Cammell Laird's yard at Birkenhead near Liverpool on 4 March 1939 under the command of Lt-Cdr 'Sam' Bolus, a very well-known and experienced submariner in the Royal Navy. She sailed for initial trials on 30 April that year, but her forward hydroplanes jammed and she had to return to Birkenhead before she even dived.

Whilst waiting for the repairs to be completed she carried out torpedo equipment trials. Amongst other things this involved testing the bow caps of the torpedo tubes, both to see that they closed properly and to see that the 'spit cocks' functioned correctly. Spit cocks are small cocks in the rear doors of the tubes which can be opened by hand to test whether the tube is dry or wet. If the tube has been filled with water and the bow cap has been closed, there will be a small trickle of water out of the cock, but if the bow cap is open, the pressure of the sea will cause a definite spurt of water out of the cocks.

After the trials, an employee of a sub-contractor of Cammell Laird applied Bitumastic to the inside of the tubes but, as it eventually turned out, he failed to ensure that the spit cocks were clear of the paint-like material. This is an essential precaution since the Bitumastic might clog the spit cocks and prevent the water from passing through them.

On Thursday 1 June 1939 the *Thetis* again sailed from Birkenhead to carry out diving trials. *Thetis* was a 'T' class submarine, diesel-electric driven with a maximum speed on the surface of 16kt and when submerged of 10kt on her electric motors. She displaced 1,090 tons and was 169ft long. She cost £350,000.

On this occasion she carried 103 persons, 50 of her own crew and about 50 additional workmen from Cammell Laird and sub contractors. Amongst the supernumeraries were Capt H. P. K. Oram, who commanded the flotilla which *Thetis* was to join, and Engineer Captain S. Jackson from the staff of Flag Officer Submarines, an old and valued friend of the author and his wife. There was sufficient Davis Submarine Escape Apparatus (DSEA) onboard for the crew and the passengers. The DSEA set was a form of self-contained breathing apparatus which should provide sufficient oxygen for a man to effect an underwater escape, but it could only be used in relatively shallow water.

On all initial submarine trials a tug accompanies the submarine and on this occasion it was the tug *Grebecock*. She carried onboard Lt R. H. Coltart as the submarine expert on the spot. He was in fact the First Lieutenant of the *Taku*, another submarine of the 'T' class. The tug was also to disembark any of the workmen who were not required for the trials, but they all expressed a wish to dive in the submarine, so in the end nobody was disembarked.

Lt-Cdr Bolus sent a signal, timed 13.40, to Flag Officer Submarines at Fort Blockhouse in Portsmouth saying he was diving for three hours. It was received in Blockhouse at 14.03. This was the normal diving signal, but in fact Bolus expected to surface long before that time. On reaching the surface he would send a surfacing signal. If no such signal was received in three hours, the shore authorities would act because he would be overdue.

Meanwhile Bolus gave the order to dive and went below into the control room. Onboard the *Grebecock*, Coltart watched the *Thetis* for more than 50 minutes endeavouring to dive, but he was not particularly worried as a boat straight out of dockyard hands is often at a different weight to that calculated, and it is by no means unusual for the first dive to take some time. She had arranged to come up after the initial dive to check her trim and then was to dive again to a greater depth; finally she would go down to 60ft and fire smoke candles to show that she was alright. However, she did none of these things, but she did manage to dive. Coltart, watching, thought that she disappeared rather fast, but was not unduly worried; nevertheless, he did send a signal to Flag Officer Submarines enquiring the length of time that *Thetis* had said she was diving for. It did not reach Blockhouse until 18.00 as it was sent by commercial radio by the tug.

The Flag Officer himself was sick and he had left his Chief of Staff, Capt I. A. P. Macintyre, in charge. *Thetis* was due to surface by 16.40, three hours after the diving signal, and at 16.45 Capt Macintyre began to worry. However, he remembered that the diving signal had taken 25 minutes to get through and presumably the surfacing signal would take about the same length of time. As a precaution, however, Capt Macintyre ordered Blockhouse to try and establish communication with the *Thetis* and he enquired of the Admiralty and the staff of C-in-C Plymouth whether they had any news. The first dive of a new submarine straight out of the builders' hands is always an anxious time and Macintyre was quite right to be a bit worried.

Let us now return to the *Thetis*. When the main ballast tanks were flooded and the submarine refused to dive, the First Lieutenant, Lt Chapman, ordered the auxiliary tanks also to be flooded, and Bolus put the hydroplanes hard-a-dive and ordered the engines to be put to half ahead. The Admiralty official who had calculated the trim was onboard and Chapman asked him what he thought was wrong. He replied that his calculations were worked out with Nos 5 and 6 tubes flooded to represent the weight of torpedoes in the tubes and he thought that, through some miscalculation, they had not been flooded.

The Torpedo Officer, Lt F. Woods, was of the same opinion and he decided to make sure that they were indeed flooded. He opened the 'spit cocks' of both tubes, but no water came out and he reported to Chapman that Nos 5 and 6 were empty, but was instructed to make a further check. There is a pointer on each tube which indicates the state of the bow cap and he checked that all six indicators were showing the bow caps closed. The indicators are pointers and he noted that all six pointers were in the same direction. He knew from his previous checks with the spit cocks that tubes Nos 1 to 4 were empty and, seeing all the indicators in the same position, he naturally concluded that all the bow caps were shut. However, to make doubly sure he once again tested all the spit cocks. No water came in tubes 1 to 5, but in 6 there was a slight trickle. He then ordered the rear doors to be opened in sequence starting with No 1. Nos 1 to 4 were indeed dry. He then decided to leave 6 and came to No 5. He tried the spit cock again and no water came out so he ordered a Leading Seaman to open the rear door. As soon as the last clip on the door was freed it swung open with a crash and a tremendous flood of water under pressure poured in.

Woods knew that the water was under too high a pressure to be merely the contents of the tube escaping and that it must be open to the sea. He was so confident with his checks that he thought the tube must have fractured, so he made no effort to close the door. He called the control room on the telephone and reported 'We are flooding through No 5 tube. Blow main ballast'. By this time there was no possibility of shutting the rear door against the water pouring in, so he ordered the evacuation of the compartment into the next compartment further aft, the spare torpedo stowage space, intending to shut the watertight door behind him to prevent further flooding. The evacuation was rapid and the men shut the door but could not clip up because one of the clips had become jammed in the door. Woods then ordered that compartment to be evacuated also. This was done and the watertight door between it and the rapidly flooding compartment forward of it was shut and secured. However, it meant that the two forward compartments were flooded and full of a considerable weight of water.

Bolus went full astern on the electric motors and put the hydroplanes to hard-a-rise, but it had no effect and the submarine was at an angle of about 40° down by the bow. The bows hit the mud and stuck. The depth was less than 160ft and *Thetis* was 169ft long, thus only a small portion of the stern was just above water. Bolus, Woods and Capt Oram conferred together and it was only then that the error in the bow cap pointers was discovered. By then, Bolus had stopped blowing to conserve compressed air and had also stopped engines to avoid wasting the battery. *Thetis'* stern came slowly down until she was lying level on the bottom.

Efforts were made to reach the forward compartment with the idea of trying to shut the bow cap of No 5 tube. It meant crossing two compartments under water to do so and this entailed using the DSEA equipment. Three attempts were made. The First Lieutenant, Chapman, went first but he was soon overcome with dizziness and almost fainted because he was breathing oxygen under pressure. This fact was not appreciated, so Woods and the torpedo gunner went next. The torpedo gunner fainted and they gave up the attempt. For the third attempt Woods and the second coxswain volunteered, but the Petty Officer was soon overcome. It was then decided to abandon any more attempts.

It was now about 18.30 and Coltart's signal, asking how long *Thetis* had said she was diving for, had arrived in Blockhouse. It showed Capt Macintyre that those onboard the tug must have thought that something was wrong, but he still did not believe that it was necessary to issue the emergency signal which would have put the full rescue organisation into effect.

Meanwhile, onboard the *Thetis*, a conference of all officers was called in the Wardroom, and it was decided that the only thing to do was to pump out the water forward using the compressed air, but they found that there was no compressed air left as they had used it all when the main ballast was blown after the initial flooding. They realised that they would have to rely upon compressed air being blown into the boat from outside, and this meant from a ship of which as yet there was no sign. Even then special adaptors would have to be made to fit the ship's air hoses. The Engineer Officer wrote out full instructions of what would have to be done, so that when a ship arrived, someone, armed with the instructions, could attempt to escape through the escape chamber.

Whilst waiting they decided to lighten the stern by pumping out the after trim tanks and shifting water from aft to forward. They hoped that they might raise the stern sufficiently to bring the after escape hatch above the surface of the water, but even if it did not work, it would at least reduce the pressure on the escape chamber which would make escape that much easier, and it would keep the men occupied during the night. In this they made a mistake. Nowadays it is accepted practice that when there is risk of carbon dioxide poisoning, the crew should rest as much as possible, thus minimising the amount they breathe out. Had they done this, it might have prolonged their lives by a few hours — but even then rescue would not have been at hand. However, their efforts during the night did raise the stern until it was just protruding above the water, but not protruding enough to bring the after escape hatch above the water.

Action was beginning to be taken in the outside world. The destroyer *Brazen* was on passage in the Irish Sea and she received a signal to proceed with all despatch to Liverpool Bay and search for the *Thetis*, while Abbotsinch Naval Air Station was ordered to organise an air search with Anson aircraft. Both *Brazen* and the Ansons arrived at about the same time of 21.00, just on sunset. *Brazen* managed to make contact with the tug *Grebecock* which was lying at anchor nearby. The latter told *Brazen* the rough position of the *Thetis* when last seen and her intended course when dived. In fact the submarine never took up this course and *Brazen* wasted much time in carrying out a sonar search on this line.

In Portland, on the south coast of England, were eight destroyers of the Sixth Destroyer Flotilla. They were brand-new ships of the 'Tribal' class and were reckoned to be the Navy's finest destroyers. They were ordered to proceed to Liverpool Bay with all despatch and to carry out a sonar search on arrival, but even at their maximum speed of over 30kt, they would not arrive until the following forenoon. The salvage ship *Vigilant* was ordered out of the Mersey and the Navy's diving ship, the *Tedworth*, proceeded from Inverary.

Onboard the *Thetis* the atmosphere got progressively worse and by 04.00 even

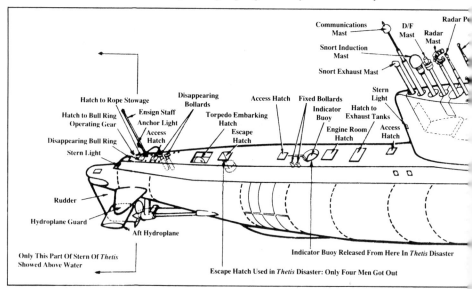

to breathe was an effort. Work was stopped and everybody lay down as best they could, to conserve their rapidly diminishing energy and oxygen. They had not heard the *Brazen*, but Bolus decided that if he waited much longer nobody would be able to escape at all, and the carefully prepared instructions to the rescuers would be wasted. He decided that an attempt should be made at 07.30 and called for volunteers. Capt Oram volunteered as he felt that a senior submarine officer should be on the surface to conduct rescue operations. Lt Woods was selected from other volunteers to accompany him because of his intimate knowledge of how the flooding had taken place.

Promptly at 07.30 they both stepped into the escape chamber, and at that moment they heard *Brazen's* signal charges exploding, signifying that she had arrived and was overhead. Both made a perfectly normal escape, in spite of the fact that the boat was at an angle of about 40° or more to the horizontal. They were quickly picked up by *Brazen's* whaler. They explained that it was the intention to continue the escape in pairs from the after escape hatch, each pair to consist of one sailor and one civilian, but it was not until 10.00 that there was the tell-tale swirl of water alongside the submarine and two more exhausted men were hauled onboard the whaler — Leading Stoker Arnold and Mr Shaw of Cammell Laird.

They had a terrible story to tell. Conditions onboard the *Thetis* had worsened rapidly and the atmosphere had become fouler and fouler. Many of the men were already dead and few of those alive had the strength to haul themselves up the steep slope into the escape chamber. Bolus was being held by two men against the door of the engine room to prevent him slipping, and was still giving orders. Therefore the First Lieutenant, Chapman, realising that the situation was desperate, had ordered four men to go into the escape chamber at a time in order to speed things up. Four men had entered, but had found difficulty in opening the escape hatch: then one man had panicked and tore out the mouthpiece of his

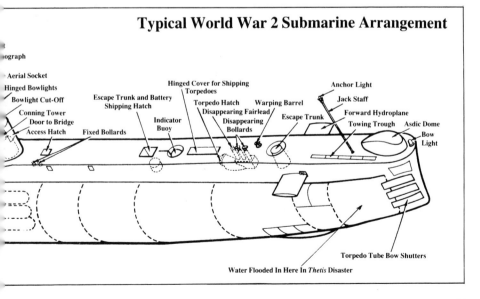

Typical World War 2 Submarine Arrangement

ograph

Aerial Socket

Hinged Bowlights

Bowlight Cut-Off

Conning Tower

Door to Bridge

Access Hatch   Fixed Bollards

Escape Trunk and Battery Shipping Hatch

Indicator Buoy

Hinged Cover for Shipping Torpedoes

Torpedo Hatch   Warping Barrel

Disappearing Fairlead

Disappearing Bollards

Escape Trunk

Anchor Light

Jack Staff

Forward Hydroplane

Towing Trough   Asdic Dome

Bow Light

Torpedo Tube Bow Shutters

Water Flooded In Here In *Thetis* Disaster

DSEA set, and in so doing dislodged the sets of the other three. The men outside the chamber, in their weak state, had taken twice as long as normal to drain it down and get the men out. On opening the door, three men were seen to be dead and the fourth was dying. The whole incident had had a very bad effect on the morale of the remainder of the crew, most of whom by this time had resigned themselves to death. However, Leading Stoker Arnold, who was a powerful man and a good swimmer, had volunteered to make an attempt and he found a ready volunteer in Mr Shaw, who was an engine fitter at Cammell Laird. They too had trouble in pushing up the hatch, but Arnold's great strength forced it open and he had dragged Shaw up behind him. They had arrived on the surface completely exhausted, but were quickly picked up and brought onboard the *Brazen*. No more escapes were made, possibly because by now the men were too weak to attempt it.

Shortly afterwards the ships of the 6th Flotilla arrived and anchored in a semi-circle around the stern of the *Thetis*. Their funnels were burnt and blistered by the colossal heat of producing full power for over 12 hours. Their Captain (D), Capt R. S. G. Nicholson, went onboard *Brazen* to take charge, accompanied by his medical officer. Capt Nicholson was not a submariner and had no experience of salvage work. Although he now had Capt Oram to advise him, neither Oram nor Woods had not yet fully recovered from their frightening experience. Nicholson therefore asked his officers if any of them had any submarine experience, and the author, who was his signal officer, said that he had previously served as signal officer of a submarine flotilla in the Mediterranean and had been to sea in submarines on many occasions, but he was no expert. Nicholson decided to use him for the time being until Oram had fully recovered.

The stern of the *Thetis*, raised by the crew's actions, was still above the water, but the rising tide had reduced the amount showing. The author was ordered to try and communicate with the crew by tapping with a hammer, in Morse, on that portion of the stern. The Morse code is a combination of short and long sounds making the dots and dashes. When tapping, however, the shorts have to be indicated by light taps and longs by heavier taps and it is not always possible to distinguish between the two. Continued efforts for about two hours brought apparently answering taps, but no coherent message could be obtained from them

Below:
Attempts being made to rescue the crew of the *Thetis* in Liverpool Bay.
Liverpool Daily Post & Echo

and regretfully it was decided that the taps heard must have been produced by some loose piece of metal swinging around inside the submarine and hitting the side in the light swell that was running. It is interesting to note that when the divers went down some nine hours later, they also reported hearing taps from inside the submarine, but on this occasion the *Thetis* was on the bottom and perfectly steady. No explanation has ever been found, unless by some miracle somebody onboard was still alive.

On return to his ship, the *Somali*, the author reported that there was a manhole cover plainly visible just above the water and it was apparently bolted on to the hull. It was thought that if it could be removed, it might be possible to haul out any members of the crew still alive. At 13.30 the wreck master from the *Vigilant*, accompanied by the author, went in a boat to the stern and started to unscrew the bolts, but as he loosened them, air started to hiss out and it was thought that the loss of air might destroy the buoyancy in the stern which was, perhaps, holding the submarine up. The bolts were hurriedly replaced.

The *Thetis* was in a very precarious position, so Capt Nicholson called a conference onboard the *Vigilant*, which both Oram and Woods attended, to discuss whether the *Vigilant* and another tug which had arrived could tow the stern into a more upright position and thus expose the escape hatch. Whilst discussions were in progress, and before a definite decision had been taken, the Master of the *Vigilant*, which had a wire round the stern of the *Thetis*, started to try and push the bows of the *Vigilant* against the stern to push her more upright. As he went slow ahead, his bows slipped round the stern and the securing wire parted with a loud report. Free of the wire, the stern sunk and *Thetis* disappeared completely beneath the waves. Her indicator buoy stayed on the surface, but its wires later parted and all contact with the *Thetis* was lost.

There was little that those on the surface could do, and by now (about 16.00) there was little hope of anybody onboard being alive. No fresh air had entered the boat for over 24 hours, and the atmosphere onboard her must have been very foul indeed. However, naval divers had been sent for and other divers were believed to be on their way. Late in the evening a destroyer came dashing out of the Mersey with four civilian divers onboard.

These divers were probably the most experienced divers in the world at that time and they had been diving on the remains of the German battle fleet scuppered in Scapa Flow in 1919. Their leader, Tom Mackenzie, was contacted by the Admiralty and without hesitation he pulled them up from the depths of Scapa Flow, got them ashore, commandeered a car to Longhope airport on Flotta and took them to Inverness. There they changed planes and flew to Speke airport near Liverpool. After a hair-raising drive to Birkenhead, they joined a destroyer waiting for them and finally arrived in Liverpool Bay at 19.00. By 21.00 they had borrowed diving equipment, were on the bottom of the sea and had found the *Thetis*. Theirs was a most magnificent piece of work.

The divers had been told by the Admiralty that the *Thetis* could remain submerged with no external air for 36 hours with the crew still alive. Armed with this information they were determined to save the crew. Unfortunately the information was incorrect: whoever had supplied it was using the figures for an 'I' class submarine with a normal complement. Onboard the *Thetis* there were so many supernumeraries that the figure would have been considerably less: 18 to 20 hours would have been a better estimate. In other words the crew were probably all dead by the time the divers arrived. However, not knowing this, the divers continued, and attempts to secure pontoons to the hull were made, assisted by more divers who had arrived in the Naval Diving Ship *Tedworth*. All attempts failed and the *Thetis* remained stubbornly on the bottom. At 16.10 on Saturday 3 June, over 50 hours after her initial dive, the Admiralty announced that all hope for those onboard must be officially abandoned.

Ninety-nine men lost their lives and the public found it hard to believe that, when the stern of the submarine had been seen and had been secured to the salvage vessel, with the escape hatch only a few feet below the surface of the sea, she could have been lost. There were strong criticisms of the rescuers in the press.

The author well remembers the terrible sense of guilt felt by all, when eventually the papers arrived, full of criticism. With hindsight, though, what else could have been done? The unfortunate loss of the stern when the *Vigilant* tried to push the *Thetis* into a more vertical position was perhaps the criticism which hurt the most, but in fairness to the *Vigilant's* Master, he knew that time was very short and he did not believe in long conferences from which no apparent result emerged. In any case, as we now know, even if the stern had been kept above water the crew were all undoubtedly dead by that time. It would also have been some time before the arrival of a powerful enough salvage vessel and the necessary pontoons capable of lifting the submarine higher out of the water.

The Americans, flushed with their success with the *Squalus* only a short time before, declared that had the Royal Navy used a diving bell there would have been no tragedy. Apart from the fact that the Navy had no suitable diving bell, it would have been very difficult to get it into position over the escape hatch with the submarine lying at such a steep angle and in the strong tides that run in Liverpool Bay. In addition, it was Admiralty policy that no reliance should be placed on external rescue methods, and that escape must be made by DSEA equipment, provided there were surface ships in the vicinity to pick up survivors.

An official enquiry was held by Mr Justice Bucknell, the same judge who later took part in the *Queen Mary* and *Curacoa* enquiry. Much of the enquiry centred around the bow cap of No 5 torpedo tube and how it came to be open. Some time was also spent on whether Woods carried out sufficient tests on the tube before opening the rear door. As regards the bow cap, Mr Bucknell said that, in his opinion, the bow cap was only opened a few minutes before the accident. However, most submariners would disagree with that. In the first place, if it had been opened just before the accident, the crew onboard the submarine would have noticed the sudden additional weight in the bows and in fact it would probably have enabled her to dive. In the second place, it seems probable that when the dockyard workers were told to see that Nos 5 and 6 tubes were full of water before the *Thetis* went to sea, they filled them by opening the bow caps. This would have been much easier than flooding them from the tank provided for that purpose under the tubes, or by using the submarine's main pumping line. Both of these methods would have meant calling in other dockyard departments, which would have caused delays. As regards Woods not checking the tubes sufficiently, it did emerge that it was by no means unusual for the spit cocks to get blocked up and that a special 'riming' tool was provided close to the tubes for clearing them. It had not been used.

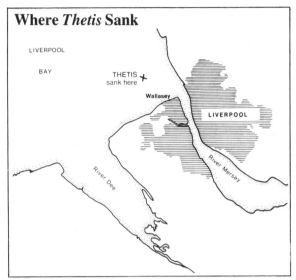

Where *Thetis* Sank

LIVERPOOL
BAY

THETIS
sank here ✕

Wallasey

LIVERPOOL

River Mersey

River Dee

Left:
Grappling the stem of the submarine *Thetis*. Efforts were made to communicate with the crew by tapping with a hammer.
Liverpool Daily Post & Echo

Below:
Thetis beached in Liverpool Bay, preparatory to salvage.
Liverpool Daily Post & Echo

The Admiralty set up its own enquiry under Sir Martin Dunbar Nasmith, a submarine hero of World War 1. This enquiry thought there was no question that the spit cocks in Nos 5 and 6 tubes had been blocked by Bitumastic. It also considered that the failure of the attempt to get into the flooded tube compartment was because escape training was carried out in tanks only 15ft deep. The enquiry recommended that the tanks should be at least double that depth.

The Nasmith enquiry also recommended that escape chambers should no longer be fitted, as such small chambers had a bad effect on the men, leading to panic. The members recommended instead that the Navy should revert to the old twill trunk method of escape. The advent of the war shortly afterwards meant that many of the proposals were not put into effect, at least for some years. However, the *Thetis* disaster did show the danger of carbon dioxide (CO_2) poisoning in submarines with no fresh air entering, and led to scientists redoubling their efforts to find a solution.

Little was known about it at the time, but it has now been fully investigated. Briefly, men breathe in a mixture of oxygen and nitrogen, but breathe out carbon dioxide. Normally the CO_2 is dissipated and absorbed by the atmosphere, but in a confined space there is not enough pure air to absorb it. CO_2 is a poisonous gas and will eventually result in death, but before this occurs, personnel will get drowsy, lethargy will set in and their movements will become unco-ordinated. Nowadays the CO_2 is absorbed by special absorbers (often known as scrubbers) filled with soda lime. In nuclear submarines a more complicated method of absorbing CO_2 is used, because they have to remain completely submerged for weeks on end. In a small submarine, such as the *Thetis*, the CO_2, even with absorbers, will start to accumulate, and when it reaches 3-4% of the atmosphere, men start to get drowsy and rational thinking is impaired. When it reaches 10% extreme dizziness is felt and consciousness is lost. When it reaches 20% the atmosphere is lethal.

Onboard the *Thetis* the lethargy level must have been reached by about 04.00 on the morning after the disaster. Soon after Oram and Woods had escaped, the crew must have been starting to lose consciousness and by about noon on that day they must have been dead.

Although not realised by those on the surface, it was really essential to get the submarine up or some fresh air into her by about 11.00 at the latest. But this involved pontoons and heavy lifting equipment, which had been ordered but which took time to arrange: in fact they did not arrive until the following day and even then it was not possible to lift the submarine. Mr Justice Bucknell remarked on it. 'The organisation', he said, 'was somewhat cumbersome for the case; it absorbed an amount of energy which was quite out of proportion to the value of the *Thetis*.' This is a remark that might have been better expressed because it was really the 99 lives that were at stake.

It is interesting to compare this disaster with that of the American submarine *Squalus*, which had occurred only a few months earlier. The two submarines were much the same size, both were brand-new and both sank due to a large portion of the submarine becoming flooded. The British rescue policy was to escape from reasonably shallow depths using self-breathing apparatus, whereas the Americans, although they had similar apparatus, tended to rely more on external rescue.

The *Thetis* only got four men out from a total of over 100 men onboard, perhaps due to some presumed malfunction of the escape tower, perhaps because the crew were already beginning to succumb to carbon dioxide poisoning. The Americans rescued 33 men by the bell, losing some 12 members of the crew who had drowned inside the submarine before help was at hand.

The *Thetis* had to cope with tides; the *Squalus* did not have this problem. In addition the *Thetis* was at a steep bows down angle which made the use of the escape tower very difficult. The 99 persons onboard the *Thetis* succumbed to carbon dioxide poisoning in an estimated 20 hours in a space about the same size as that of the *Squalus*. The 33 men of the *Squalus* survived some 30 hours and could probably have survived even longer, but of course they had only one third of the men breathing out carbon dioxide. Finally, the divers in the *Thetis* disaster arrived too late to be of any use. The *Squalus* divers arrived in good time, as did the bell.

Nowadays submarines are infinitely safer and are unlikely to suffer the fate of the *Thetis*. Nuclear submarines, for example, can carry out an entire six-week patrol without any fresh air entering the hull at all. In addition, there is a highly efficient NATO-wide 'Subsunk' organisation which will quickly get aid to a submarine unable to surface. There is also the American DSRV, a specially fitted rescue submarine which the Americans have kindly made available to NATO for rescue of submarines in trouble in deep water.

The *Thetis* was eventually salvaged by the Liverpool & Glasgow Salvage Association. The first attempt, using pontoons, failed and eventually a merchant ship the same length as the *Thetis* had to be used. The 3,500-ton ship, the *Zelo*, was specially fitted with heavy beams and bollards for the job.

Thetis was refitted and went back into service as HMS *Thunderbolt* in December 1940. For three years she carried out many wartime patrols and sank an Italian submarine, but in the end she was sunk by depth charges, from an Italian escort vessel, the *Cicagna*, when she tried to attack an Italian convoy in the Mediterranean.

11

Thresher

The *Thresher* was one of the early US nuclear attack submarines. The first nuclear submarine, apart from test vehicles, was the uss *Nautilus*, laid down in 1952. The first batch of SSNs, as they were called, was the 'Skate' class of which the name ship was laid down in 1957. These were followed by the 'Skipjack' class, built between 1958 and 1961, and then came the 'Thresher' class of nine nuclear submarines, built between 1959 and 1961. *Thresher* was the first of the latter class and was launched on 9 July 1960. She was way ahead technically of the other nuclear submarines and the US Navy was very proud of her.

Thresher displaced 3,210 tons (4,100 tons submerged). She was 278.5ft long and had one nuclear reactor and two steam turbines driving one screw which gave her a speed of 20kt on the surface and 30kt submerged.

She commissioned on 3 August 1961 under Cdr Axene. After commissioning, she carried out a series of trials and short cruises for nearly a year, during which she visited the Bahamas and Puerto Rico. The trials of course included many dives, some of them deep. In July 1962 she entered Portsmouth Naval Shipyard, New Hampshire, for a 10-month refit, and during the refit Cdr Axene was relieved by Lt-Cdr John Harvey. Harvey had great experience of nuclear submarines and his previous job had been as the Executive Officer of the uss *Seadragon*, one of the 'Skate' class. *Thresher* was, however, his first command.

As is customary in any navy, after such a long refit, *Thresher* had to undergo once again a series of trials before becoming operational. She sailed from Portsmouth on the morning of 9 April 1963. Onboard was a total of 129 persons; 12 officers and 96 men of the crew, a submarine staff officer, three other officers and 13 civilian employees from Portsmouth Naval Yard, an expert from the Naval Ordnance Laboratory and three representatives from the builders, General Dynamics' Electric Boat Division. One officer was left behind because his wife was sick and three enlisted men also missed the ship, one because he was in Washington for an interview for officer rank, one was away on a course and one was sick.

The *Thresher* first of all carried out some surface trials and then rendezvoused with the rescue ship *Skylark* — submarines on trials after a long refit are always accompanied by a surface ship in case they get into any trouble. The *Skylark* was to attend all the diving trials and in particular the *Thresher's* deep dive to her 'test depth'. She was fitted with an underwater telephone and was to remain in communication with the *Thresher* at all times when dived on trials.

The first day passed off without incident and at about 15.00 *Thresher* told the *Skylark* that she was finished for the day and ordered her to rendezvous with *Thresher* at 06.30 the following morning (10 April), 200 miles east of Cape Cod where the water was quite deep enough for the test dive. In fact it was very deep, more than 8,000ft.

During the night, *Thresher* carried out tests including a full power trial

Left:
A 1961 bow view of
USS *Thresher*. *US Navy*

Below:
The interior of a US nuclear
submarine. *US Navy*

submerged. She arrived at the rendezvous punctually at 06.30, but did not surface, only coming to periscope depth to sight the *Skylark*. She then communicated with her on the underwater telephone.

At 07.47 *Thresher* told the *Skylark* that she was preparing to dive to the test depth. Before her refit, *Thresher* had dived to her test depth on a number of occasions and to the crew it was just a routine dive. Test depths are never disclosed and, when using the underwater telephone, the submarine's depth is given with reference to the test depth, as it is possible that potentially hostile ships or submarines may also be listening. No scrambler is fitted to the underwater telephone.

Test depth is the maximum depth at which a submarine can work and fight. It is not as deep as she can go but is never exceeded except in an emergency. Below test depth, fittings onboard, such as pipes or other devices bolted to the bulkheads begin to give way and come adrift. This is a sure warning that the submarine should go no deeper. If she has to go below test depth, it is highly advisable not to go too far below it. After the initial breaking off of fittings, the deeper she goes, so the increasing weight of the water exerts a tremendous pressure on the hull and bits of the hull start being pulled out of shape, leaks occur and eventually the submarine would be crushed like a squeezed orange — a position known as the collapse depth.

At 07.52 *Thresher* reported that she was at 400ft and was checking for leaks. At 08.09 she told the *Skylark* that she was at half the test depth and at 08.35 she reported that she was at minus 300ft, meaning she was 300ft above the test depth. Nothing more was heard from her until 08.53 when she stated that she was 'proceeding to test depth'. At 09.02 *Thresher* asked for a repetition of a course reading and was given it. At 09.12 the two vessels made a routine communications check with communications appearing good. About a minute later Lt (junior grade) Watson, who was manning the telephone, heard *Thresher* report 'Have positive up angle [portion of message missing] am attempting to blow up'. 'Blowing up' in submarine parlance meant blowing compressed air into the ballast tanks to bring the submarine to the surface. There was some controversy about what was actually said by the *Thresher*. The Captain of the *Skylark*, Lt-Cdr Hecker, thought that she had said 'Experiencing minor problem . . . Have positive angle . . . Attempting to blow'. An enlisted man, who also heard the message, thought that what was said was 'Experiencing difficulty, attempting to blow, will keep you informed'. Immediately after the message many people onboard the *Skylark* heard over the underwater telephone loud speaker the sound of air under pressure. The official log of the message read 'Have position up angle . . . attempting to blow'. No time was placed against it in the log, and the word 'position' is obviously a mistake for 'positive'. At 09.14 the *Skylark* told the *Thresher* that she had no contact on the telephone and asked her to give her course and speed and a bearing of the *Skylark* from her. She did not reply, but at 09.17, a garbled message from *Thresher* was heard, but was unintelligible, except that Lt Watson thought that the message ended with 'test dive'. He also reported that he had heard 'the sound of a ship breaking up'. He was familiar with such sounds as during the war he had heard a ship break up on the sonar.

Skylark continued to try and make contact and started a search of the area, also dropping some signal grenades to indicate that communication had been lost and that she was still there. She originated a signal to the Commander of the 2nd Submarine Flotilla as follows:

'Unable to communicate with *Thresher* since 09.17. Have been calling on UQC [underwater telephone] and by CW [Morse] every minute. Explosive signals every 10 minutes with no success. Last transmission received was garbled, indicated *Thresher* was approaching test depth. My present position 41° 43′ N, 64° 57′ W. Am conducting expanding search.'

The message was sent with an Operational Immediate priority, but it took a very long time to get through as atmospherics were bad and the *Skylark* only had old radio equipment. Capt Sneed Schmidt, Commander of the 2nd Flotilla, received the message at 13.02 when he returned from lunch. He was not unduly perturbed as he frequently got similar messages which nearly all turned out to be false alarms. However, he did telephone the Headquarters of the Atlantic Fleet in Norfolk, Virginia, and spoke to Adm Elton W. Grenfell, commander of all submarines in the Atlantic and Capt Schmidt's boss. Things then started to move. The C-in-C Atlantic Fleet ordered the nuclear submarine *Seawolf*, the conventional submarine *Sea Owl*, the rescue ship *Sunbird* and an aircraft to *Thresher's* last reported position. The Commander of Submarine Development Group 2, Capt Andrews, flew out to the frigate *Norfolk*, off Cape Cod, and she also proceeded to the search area. Capt Andrews had been the *Thresher's* immediate boss whilst she was still undergoing trials and it was agreed that he should take charge of the search for the time being.

The Chief of Naval Operations, Adm George W. Anderson, was told of the situation about 15.40. He had been at a meeting of the Joint Chiefs of Staff and did not return to his office until that time. The Secretary of the Navy was told soon afterwards and he called the White House and asked them to tell the President, John F. Kennedy, himself an ex-naval officer. The Canadian Navy was asked to assist in any way possible, observing that *Thresher's* position was only about 100 miles off the tip of Nova Scotia. The Canadians at once ordered a British submarine, which was visiting Canada, to prepare to get under way. Half the crew were ashore on liberty leave and had to be recalled. Messages were flashed on screens in Halifax's cinemas and the press got wind of it. A television station in Halifax heard the rumour and came out with a news flash saying: 'US submarine reported in danger of sinking or in trouble on the high seas'. The search was on and the news was out.

Meanwhile the various ships, submarines and aircraft were starting to arrive in the search area. The weather started to worsen, but at about sunset on 10 April, only a few hours after *Thresher* had disappeared, the rescue ship *Recovery* spotted a calm patch of water in the rapidly increasing seas, and shortly afterwards began picking up some heavy yellow plastic and bits of cork. Both were quite often found in submarines. There were also patches of oil, and although *Thresher* did not use fuel oil, she did have lubricating oil onboard. The oil and debris confirmed the surface watchers' worst fears.

The Department of Defense decided to make a formal announcement of the loss of the *Thresher* at about 20.00 that night, but before doing so they made every effort to inform all relatives personally of the fact that she was overdue and presumed missing. Promptly at 20.00 the loss was announced in the name of Adm Anderson, the CNO, who at 21.30 went on television. He stated that an oil slick had been found and that, if the *Thresher* had sunk, it would have been in 8,400ft of water and that 'rescue would be absolutely out of the question'. He also announced that Vice-Adm Bernard L. Austin would head the formal enquiry into her loss.

Out at sea the weather grew steadily worse. The search was centred about 220 miles east of Cape Cod. Capt Andrews was in charge onboard the *Norfolk* and he had with him two destroyers and two recovery ships, the *Skylark* and the *Recovery*. The prime sensor in use was sonar, both active and passive, but the ships concentrated more on listening for any noise the *Thresher* might make rather than transmitting and hoping to obtain echoes. It was hoped that perhaps she had had an electrical failure and that when she had repaired it, she might be able to transmit on her sonar. Nothing was heard and the rescuers grew more and more pessimistic. Excitement however rose when the submarine *Seawolf* reported that she had heard sonar noises. Unfortunately the Navy's experts were quickly able to report that the sonar signals heard were not those of the *Thresher*, but probably those of other ships in the search, or were water noises.

The search dragged on day after day and all hope of finding the crew alive had long since disappeared. Various visitors went out to the scene. Rear-Adm Ramage, a very experienced submarine officer, arrived in the destroyer *Blandy* to take charge of the search operation from Capt Andrews. Two more destroyers joined the force with an oiler and the oceanographic ship *Atlantic II*. The Secretary of State for the Navy and Adm Grenfell flew over the area and talked to the *Norfolk* by radio, but there was little to do but search the seabed by all possible means. These included sonar, underwater cameras, magnetic anomaly detectors (to see where the earth's magnetic field had been disturbed by the presence of the large metal hull), and even drag ropes were used.

At 10.30 on the morning of 21 April Adm Anderson met the press again and Adm Grenfell personally called on Mrs Harvey. At the press conference Adm Anderson said:

This is a very sad occasion. I have come to the conclusion that the USS *Thresher*, which we had for sometime presumed missing, has indeed been lost. We are unable to communicate with her in any way, there is the evidence of the oil slick and the debris, so I have concluded, with great regret, and sadness, that this ship with 129 fine souls aboard is lost.'

In answer to a journalist's question, 'Did the last message from the *Thresher* indicate that everything was proceeding normally?', Adm Anderson replied 'Yes'. In fact this was not so; Lt-Cdr Hecker, the CO of the *Skylark*, had not mentioned to anybody at that time about the message which said she was experiencing minor problems, and he was later hauled over the coals for not doing so. In answer to another question, Adm Anderson assured the press that there were no Soviet or Communist ships in the area at the time of the *Thresher's* dive. He also assured them that Adm Rickover, the Navy's great nuclear specialist, had told him that there was no danger of a nuclear leak.

Determined not to give up until the *Thresher* was found, the Navy redoubled its efforts. More ships were sent to join the search and more use was made of the *Atlantic II*, a very modern research vessel belonging to Woods Hole Oceanographic Institute, together with eight other research ships. Underwater cameras were deployed and many photographs of objects on the seabed were taken. Hopes of finding the *Thresher* soared up and down for at least another month.

The Navy produced an idea of sinking an old submarine, roughly the same size as the *Thresher*, so that the sonar operators and the cameramen could see what a submarine on the seabed looked like, but just as the submarine was ready, underwater cameras started finding certain objects which were definitely believed to belong to the *Thresher*. In particular a number of small packets, with rings inside them were dredged up. The packages had stock numbers typed on them. They were identified as having been issued to the *Thresher* and the find gave the searchers fresh hopes. Very shortly afterwards the underwater cameras started getting photographs of pieces of metal which the men on the surface were sure must be from the *Thresher*, only to have their hopes dashed when they were examined by the Naval Photographic Centre which said they were definitely *not* part of the *Thresher*.

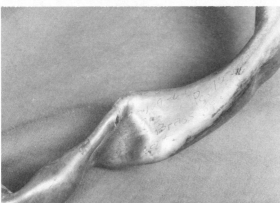

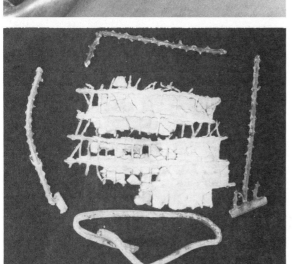

Above:
The *Trieste* operating in Boston dockyard. It was due to this bathyscaphe that the remains of the *Thresher* were finally found. *US Navy*

Left:
This battered brass pipe from the *Thresher* was recovered from the seabed by the *Trieste*. *US Navy*

Below left:
Part of a battery belonging to the *Thresher*, recovered by the *Trieste*. *US Navy*

Then, in mid-June, the Oceanographic Research Ship *Conrad* obtained some highly significant photographs of debris on the seabed and, so certain were the experts, it was decided to summon the deep diving ship *Trieste* which had been standing by for use when *Thresher* was definitely found.

The *Trieste* was what is known as a bathyscaph and was capable of going down to very great depths. It consisted of a large tank with a observation gondola slung beneath it. Inside it were two smaller tanks filled with petrol, which, being lighter than water, allowed the craft to float. At either end of the *Trieste* were two air tanks and to start her on its way they were flooded with sea water. As she submerged the pressure of the sea outside her would be equalled by the pressure of the petrol inside so that the craft would not buckle in. In the bottom of the petrol tanks were two containers, connected by tubes to the top of the craft. By careful adjustment of the water inside the two tanks at either end, the craft was brought to a state of just positive buoyancy. To make her sink, more weight, in the shape of steel pellets, had to be added by pouring the pellets down the tubes into the tanks provided. The object of this, apparently rather old-fashioned method, was to enable the craft to surface again. Having accomplished her mission, the steel pellets were released by opening two doors controlled by electro-magnets. Should the electrics fail for any reason the pellets would be released automatically. The gondola would hold two men normally, but it was possible to squeeze a third man in if required.

The US had purchased the *Trieste* from her inventor, Professor Picard, in 1958 and she was used for deep oceanographic work. She was based at San Diego and the first thing that had to be done was to get her over to the east coast. This was done by shipping her in a dock landing ship, the *Point Defence*, through the Panama Canal to Boston where she arrived on 26 April. She was made fully operational and she carried out a test dive off Boston of some 700ft. She remained in Boston, waiting for the *Thresher* to be found, for over six weeks.

After many false alarms her chance had finally come. Although the *Thresher* had not definitely been found, the evidence was so strong that it was decided that the *Trieste* could carry out some exploratory dives. They would be very limited as she could only move on battery-driven electric motors for about 1.5 miles in four hours. However, she was fitted with underwater cameras outside her hull and she had a sonar with a range of about 400yd. On 19 June she was towed out to the search area by a salvage ship called the *Preserver*. The voyage took four days.

Trieste then had a period of nearly 2½ months, diving at frequent intervals, looking and searching for any clues which would pinpoint the *Thresher* once and for all. She was dogged by bad weather and bad luck. During the period at least three Soviet merchant ships approached the area and had to be warned off. It was obvious that they were looking and listening for anything they could find. The crew of the *Trieste* were originally Cdr Keach and a civilian scientist called Mackenzie, but many others went out in her from time to time. During the period she twice went back to Boston for repairs and rest.

Eventually she was withdrawn to Boston on 2 September, her task completed. No news had been issued all this time as to what she had found, but on 5 September a press conference was called and the journalists found displayed before them many of the pathetic remains of the once-proud *Thresher*. They included a bent and twisted pipe, identified as part of a filtration system of the submarine's galley; a hatch cover; battery plates; portions of the sonar equipment; and many other items. There was absolutely no question that these, coupled with the many photographs, had definitely identified the *Thresher*. No human remains were found.

The Court of Enquiry had lost no time in meeting. It first assembled only three days after the accident, on 13 April, at the New London submarine base. The President was Vice-Adm Watson, who was then the President of the Naval War College, and he had with him on the Court no less than five submarine officers. After the initial session the Court moved to the naval yard at Portsmouth and all the remaining sessions were held there. The very first witness to be called was Cdr Axene, the first Commanding Officer of the *Thresher*. He said that, as far as he knew, *Thresher* had no major defects but there were some minor ones, many of them before she even commissioned. He went on to talk about her first dive to her test depth. 'The dive', he said, 'took place in the same area as *Thresher's* last dive. However', he went on, 'I had to halt the dive before we reached the required depth, because of trouble with certain instruments onboard. They indicated that something was wrong and they were contradicting each other. I cancelled the dive because of this.' He gave as his opinion that the accident to the *Thresher* must have been associated with some flooding problem.

Numerous witnesses were called. One of the most important was Lt-Cdr Hecker, the Captain of the *Skylark*. It came out that for some three days he had told nobody about the final messages from the *Thresher*. In fact the first the Court heard of the final message from her was from Lt Watson, on the afternoon of the first day of the enquiry. In particular Hecker had made no mention of Watson having heard sounds 'like a ship breaking up'. Hecker was cited by the President for failing in his duty in not fully reporting this sooner and was named as a 'party' before the Court, which meant that he might appoint a counsel to act on his behalf and had the right to cross-examine witnesses. The citation almost went as far as saying that he himself was on trial. He did in fact appoint a counsel, who pleaded that he had no case to answer, and after much argument the Court withdrew the obvious slur on his name with the words 'The Court agrees that it no longer appears that Lt-Cdr Hecker is involved in a material degree in the matter under investigation. His designation as a "party" is accordingly withdrawn.' In fact, of course, whether he had mentioned all the last words and sounds from the *Thresher* or not, it did not make the slightest difference to the Court's findings.

The Court carefully questioned Lt-Cdr McCoole, the *Thresher* officer who had stayed in Portsmouth because of his wife's illness. He was asked about the *Thresher's* air systems and he said they had been a continuing problem. He also said that 20% of the hydraulic valves had been installed backwards, that the periscope mechanism had been found to be faulty, and that the diving planes and rudder had also been found to be faulty and parts of them were replaced the day before she sailed on her last voyage. He went on to talk about *Thresher's* 'fast cruise'. The fast cruise is a dockyard trial carried out by submarines when nearing the end of a refit. It consists of running as much of the equipment as possible with the submarine still attached firmly to the jetty. *Thresher's* first effort had been stopped by the Captain because of difficulty with the submarine's air system. However, the fast cruise was eventually carried out successfully.

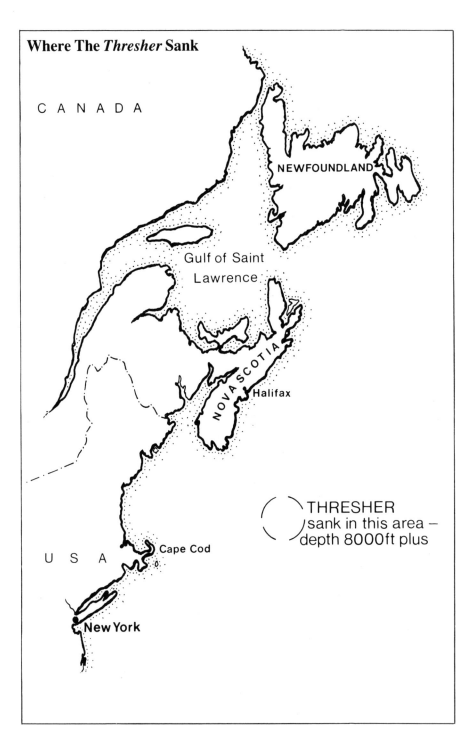

Where The *Thresher* Sank

CANADA

NEWFOUNDLAND

Gulf of Saint
Lawrence

NOVA SCOTIA

Halifax

THRESHER
sank in this area –
depth 8000ft plus

USA

Cape Cod

New York

Many enquiry sessions were held in private because classified matters were likely to be discussed, but towards the end of the inquiry it became obvious that the Court was veering towards the theory that some pipe inside the boat had burst and had sprayed with water under pressure, some vital parts of the submarine's electrical equipment. It was decided that the members of the Court should witness such a spray and themselves be sprayed to see the effect. The following day all the members, dressed in waterproof clothing, looked on as a mock-up of a submarine control panel was subjected to jets of water at roughly the same pressure as it would have been if a pipe had burst at depth. The first jet lasted only 3½ seconds, and so powerful was it that it dented the control panel, and there was a thin wisp of smoke. The next jet of water was kept on for seven seconds and apparently caused a great deal more damage. The members of the Court also got wet. The effects of the jets were discussed in a closed session, but they evidently impressed the Court.

The inquiry was adjourned on 6 June, just under two months from when it first started. It had examined 120 witnesses and 1,700 pages of testimony had been gathered. The result of the Court's deliberations was announced to the public by a press release from the Department of Defense. A great deal of the release was taken up with an account of *Thresher's* last voyage, but the nub of the report was contained in these words:

'A flooding casualty in the engine room is believed to be the most probable cause of the sinking of the nuclear submarine *Thresher*, lost on 10 April 1963, 220 miles east of Cape Cod with 129 persons onboard.

'The Navy believes it most likely that a piping system failure had occurred in one of the *Thresher's* salt water systems, probably in the engine room. The enormous pressure of sea water surrounding the submarine subjected her interior to a violent spray of water and progressive flooding. In all probability water affected electrical circuits and caused loss of power. *Thresher* slowed and began to sink. Within minutes she had exceeded her collapse depth and was totally flooded. She came to rest on the ocean floor 8,400ft beneath the surface.'

Thus ended the saga of the *Thresher*. It was a tremendous blow to the US Navy and to the man in the street, comparable only to the loss of the space ship *Challenger*. For a number of years the public had been told that nuclear submarines were extremely safe and could dive to colossal depths with no difficulty. For their very latest submarine to be lost with all her crew shocked the American public, particularly as the first nuclear ballistic missile submarine, the *Lafayette*, had commissioned only 14 days after the *Thresher* tragedy occurred. People asked, if it can happen to *Thresher*, will the monster ballistic nuclear submarines be any safer?

However, it must not be forgotten that America was still in the early days of nuclear submarines and prospective submariners can take heart in the thought that no other nuclear submarine has been lost in the Western world to date, although the Soviets may have lost two or even three. There is no doubt that the modern submarine, whether nuclear or conventional, is extremely safe, and nuclear submarines will still remain the greatest deterrent to any future nuclear war.

12

Titanic

The White Star Liner *Titanic* was launched on 3 May 1911 and sank, after collision with an iceberg, on 15 April 1912, less than a year after her launch. She was built by Harland & Wolff and was registered as 41,000 tons.

In 1907 Cunard, White Star's great rival, had started operating the large fast liners *Lusitania* and *Mauretania* of 31,550 and 32,937 tons respectively. They were turbine ships and designed for speeds of 25.5kt, but both exceeded these speeds on trials and in service. White Star Line's answer to these two great ships was to order three even larger ships of between 40,000 and 41,000 tons, but with the lower cruising speed of 22kt. The new vessels were the *Olympic*, the *Titanic* and the *Gigantic*; the latter's name was later changed to *Brittanic*. *Brittanic* never entered service with White Star and was commandeered as a hospital ship, being subsequently sunk in the Mediterranean by mines or torpedoes.

The *Olympic* came into service in June 1911, but collidied with the Royal Navy cruiser HMS *Hawke* in early 1912 and put out of commission for six weeks. She played quite a large part in the *Titanic* disaster, because her Master, Capt E. J. Smith, universally known as 'E.J.', transferred to the *Titanic* shortly before she sailed on her fateful first voyage, as did Chief Officer H. F. Wilde and First Officer W. M. Murdock. *Olympic*, having just completed her repairs, was also one of the ships to come to the *Titanic's* aid.

The *Titanic* left Belfast for trials at 06.00 on Tuesday 2 April 1912, and returned the same evening to disembark the Harland & Wolff officials and workmen. However, their Managing Director, Thomas Andrews, who had also been the chief designer of the *Titanic*, remained onboard for the voyage to New York, together with a number of other Harland & Wolff employees. All subsequently lost their lives in the collision. *Titanic* then sailed for Southampton to prepare for her maiden voyage. At Southampton she was badly affected by a national coal strike and had to borrow coal from other White Star liners in port. Even then she had to sail with not all her coal bunkers filled.

Wednesday 10 April, her sailing date, dawned reasonably fine. Boat trains arrived from Waterloo and the passengers were all embarked before noon (her sailing time). The total number of persons embarked were: 337 first class, 271 second class, 712 third class, 915 crew; a total of 2,235. They were extremely comfortably accommodated — at least in the first and second classes — and the ship sported a gymnasium in the first and second classes, swimming pools, a squash court and Turkish baths. There were rumoured to be at least 10 millionaires (probably dollar ones) onboard, and the first class included also a large number of well-known people onboard, ranging from actors and actresses to businessmen, including Colonel Astor and his wife. Also among the passengers were Mr Bruce Ismay, the Managing Director of the White Star Line, and Mr Andrews, already mentioned.

Above:
Titanic leaving for trials in Belfast Lough, shortly before her disastrous maiden voyage of
April 1912. *BBC Hulton Picture Library*

Some of the passengers had been transferred from the *Olympic* and some from
the *Oceanic*, the latter's voyage had been cancelled owing to the coal strike, and
of course the three officers from the *Olympic*. Even so the passenger
accommodation was only half full, because she had accommodation for 2,603 and
only 1,320 passengers embarked. In addition to the passengers the *Titanic* carried
3,245 bags of mail, 6,000 tons of coal and 900 tons of baggage and freight.
Amongst the freight were numerous dresses of exclusive design for the New York
spring displays, a number of very expensive diamond necklaces and a
consignment of continental wines. Valuable though the cargo was, there is no
trace of there being a really large consignment of valuables such as would justify
the raising of the great ship, as now proposed.

Titanic's departure from Southampton was not entirely without incident. The
tugs pulled her off the quay and into the dredged channel, and she was gathering
way under her own power when she passed the American Line ship *New York*.
The interaction between the two great ships dragged the *New York* off the quay
and parted her stern wires, but *Titanic* at once stopped engines and a collision was
avoided.

She called first at Cherbourg and then at Queenstown in Ireland where a
number of passengers, mostly immigrants, were embarked. She sailed from
Queenstown at 14.00 on Thursday 11 April and took the great circle route for
New York. The route was used by all liners, and it stretches from the Fastnet
Rock to a position 42° N, 47° W, thence on a rhumb line to Nantucket Island,
thence to New York. The route is outside the normal southern limit of the ice, but
inside an area on the chart was marked 'Icebergs have been seen within this line in
April, May and June'.

On Thursday evening, being the second night out, everybody in the first class
dressed for dinner, the men in dinner jackets or tails and the ladies in dinner
gowns. The food, as always with White Star, was magnificent; passengers were
getting to know each other; and an excellent orchestra, under the direction of Mr
W. Hartley, was playing. After dinner there was dancing. The officers were telling

their dinner companions that the ship was the safest ever built: she was so large and so high out of the water that no rough sea could ever wash over her.

Capt 'E.J.' came down to dinner for the first time. He wore a large white beard and looked every inch a sailor. Very experienced, he had crossed the Atlantic many times, but unbeknown to most of his passengers he had only a few weeks before been involved in a collision, as Captain of the *Olympic*; though no blame had been attributed to him.

The weekend came all too soon. Saturday night was a gala night and all three classes of passengers celebrated it in their own way. Sunday 14 April dawned bright and cheerful and the sea was exceptionally calm, but towards evening it felt decidedly colder. It is a well-known phenomenon that icebergs in the vicinity chill the water, which in turn chills the air. However the fact was known to only a few of the passengers, most of whom continued their happy drinking before dinner.

The significance of the colder weather was not however lost on Capt E.J. At 20.55 he appeared on the bridge because he knew by various radio reports that the ship was approaching an area where icebergs had been sighted. Second Officer Lightoller was on watch and he chatted to his Captain for five minutes. 'We spoke of the weather, the calmness of the sea and the clearness of the night', he said afterwards at the US Senate Enquiry.

At 21.30 E.J. left the bridge, saying 'If you are in the slightest degree doubtful, let me know'. Lightoller warned the crow's nest to keep a specially good look out for icebergs and the great ship settled down for the night, still steaming at 22kt, E.J. being anxious to meet his deadline in New York, particularly with his Managing Director onboard. At the Senate Enquiry much was made of this, but no evidence was ever produced to show that any undue pressure had been put on the Captain to arrive on time.

At 22.00 the watch changed. First Officer Murdock (late of the *Olympic*) was the Officer of the Watch and he had with him two junior officers, Fourth Officer Boxall and Sixth Officer Moody. The crow's nest was manned by two men, Flint and Lee, well wrapped up against the cold.

For an hour or so all was peace, but suddenly it was shattered by one stroke of a gong. It was the danger signal from the crow's nest and signified 'object right ahead'. It was followed by a telephone call to the bridge from the crow's nest saying 'iceberg right ahead'. Murdock immediately ordered 'Hard-a-starboard' (in those days steering orders referred to the helm or tiller, so 'Hard-a-starboard' turned the ship to port). He also immediately ordered 'full speed astern'. Murdock could now see the iceberg and it appeared to him that the ship was heading straight for it. The ship took her time to turn, probably because the engines were going astern, but eventually she started swinging to port and for a moment it appeared that she might just miss a collision. Murdock then reversed the helm and ordered 'Hard-a-port', thinking that he had cleared the edge of the iceberg and wishing to swing his stern away from it. It was too late and she struck the iceberg with her starboard bow.

The effect was not dramatic and it felt onboard as though she had shuddered, as if she had hit a jetty too hard whilst berthing. Unfortunately though the iceberg extended well below the water line and the damage to the ship was almost entirely below the water. It was enough to wake E.J., who was lying fully dressed on his bunk. He rushed up to the bridge and on arrival ordered the watertight doors to

The *Titanic's* Collision

A Iceberg sighted by look-out

B *Titanic's* Officer of the Watch orders hard 'a starboard; *Titanic* starts to turn to port

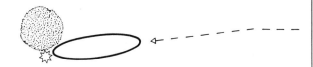

C *Titanic* collides with iceberg

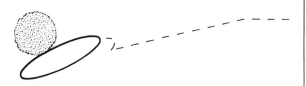

D Iceberg slides along starboard-side of *Titanic*

be shut, but Murdock told him that he had already closed them. He then asked what had happened. E.J. was not distressed at first because ships had knocked against icebergs before and had survived. However, when the reports of the damage started to come in, he realised that the ship was making water fast. He sent for Mr Andrews and together they went below to inspect the damage.

The forepeak was certainly filling, but it would not hold very much water. The much larger No 1 cargo hold was also flooding, so was No 2 cargo hold. It was obvious that the iceberg had not only holed the forepeak but the two cargo holds as well. Andrews then told him that the ship had been designed to allow four compartments to be flooded but no more. They then inspected No 3 cargo hold and to their horror found that it too was filling with water. Becoming more and more alarmed, they then went further aft to No 6 boiler room only to find that it was being abandoned by the firemen who reported that the whole of the starboard side of the ship seemed to have caved in and that the iceberg must have scraped along the side, opening up a tremendous gash.

Andrews then gave E.J. his verdict. The ship, he said, would trim by the head as soon as No 6 boiler room was fully flooded. Water would then lop over and fill the next boiler room abaft it, No 5. When this was full, it would lop over into No 4 and so on until the ship sank. He gave the whole process only 1½ hours.

On his return to the bridge, E.J. ordered all boats under davits to be got ready. He then told the wireless room to start sending out distress messages as soon as they had got the ship's position. A few minutes later he returned with the position written on a slip of paper and the operators started sending out the messages. The *Titanic* had a powerful transmitter and the call was heard by a number of ships. Among them were the *Baltic* and *Olympic* (now repaired) of the White Star Line, the Norddeutscher Lloyd *Frankfurt*, the Canadian Pacific *Mount Temple*, the Cunard *Caronia* and the Cape Race shore station in Newfoundland. The small *Carpathia* had only one radio operator who had just gone off watch, but he caught the signal as he was taking off his headphones. Of all the ships which had heard the distress message the *Carpathia* was the nearest to the *Titanic's* position, just 58 miles away. Her Captain, Rostrom, unable to believe that the *Titanic* was really sinking, nevertheless set off for her position.

The situation onboard the *Titanic* has been described by many people, from actual survivors to fanciful authors. It was also described by Walter Lord in his dramatic book *A Night to Remember*, which was later made into a film. Shorn of drama the following aims to give a true picture of what actually occurred, but of course survivors' stories differ: some remember it as the most awful and agonising moment of their lives, others (the lucky ones) got into the boats when they were told and were picked up very shortly afterwards; they remember it as an exciting incident. All their accounts differ so the real truth is hard to discover.

At first, many of the passengers did not realise the gravity of the situation. The more experienced might have noticed that the ship was very slightly down by the bows, although they became slightly more disturbed when they heard the stewards shouting 'All passengers on deck with lifebelts on'. The work of preparing the lifeboats was proceeding on both sides of the ship, but did not proceed very quickly at first as the lifeboat crews were slow in arriving on deck, and some of the crews of the lifeboats did not know their stations.

At 00.20 the order was given to swing out the boats, but there was considerable confusion due to the noise of the steam escaping through the safety valves and the general reluctance of passengers to enter the boats. First Officer Murdock, on the starboard side, ordered No 7 lifeboat to be lowered to the water line, but had the greatest difficulty in filling the boat with passengers, as most of them felt much safer onboard. Second Officer Lightoller, one of the few officers to be saved, was having the same difficulty. In fact the first boat he lowered had only 24 women and children and two crew in it. The boat was capable of holding 65 persons.

At about the same time, rockets were fired from the ship with the object of attracting the attention of a ship whose lights could be seen some four miles away, of which more anon. The lowering of the boats went on, albeit not very fast and not very professionally. The boats had to be lowered until the boats were level with the boat deck where they were filled with passengers. When the officer in charge thought that they had sufficient passengers onboard, the boats were then lowered into the water. At the subsequent enquiries it was established that few of the officers had any real idea as to how many persons the boats could hold whilst they were still suspended from the davits. There was a general feeling that they might buckle if too many persons got onboard them before they were in the water. Some boats were restricted to only about 25 people, but others were safely lowered with as many as 50 persons in them. Nowadays all boats have to be marked with the number of persons they can hold whilst still on the davits.

At 01.40 the last boat on the starboard side had left, and the later boats were better filled as more men were allowed into them when no women and children appeared on deck to fill them. On the port side the last boat left at 02.05, only 15 minutes before the vessel foundered.

Bruce Ismay was helping passengers on the boat deck, but as the last boat on his side left ('C' Collapsible), he found a space in it and jumped in at the last moment. He was heavily criticised later for his action. Andrews went down with the ship he had designed. He was apparently last seen in the first class smoking room standing alone and looking completely stunned. He must have felt he had nothing to live for.

There was a certain amount of rushing to board the boats by men, including some of the cooks and stewards. The officers had been told by their Captain that the order 'women and children first' was to be strictly enforced and they were stationed around the ship to see that it was. There were at least two cases of officers using their revolvers to stop concerted rushes for the boats, but they aimed wide and nobody was hurt. First Officer Murdock was seen by some of the passengers to use his revolver and Fifth Officer Lowe testified at the subsequent Senate Enquiry that he was in boat No 14, which had some 50 people onboard; in his opinion this was enough, if not too many, with the boat still to be lowered into the water. He saw a crowd of Italian immigrants by the ship's side about to rush the boat and he fired one shot from the boat, which effectively stopped the rush.

Later the Italian Ambassador to the USA complained of his statement that they were Italians and he was forced to change it to read 'a crowd of immigrants belonging to Latin races'. It was an honest mistake as he knew that many of the passengers in the steerage were in fact Italians.

The earlier boats were not completely filled for fear of overloading them at the davits and because not enough women and children came forward. Later on they were better filled but even so a number left half full because there were simply not enough people on the boat deck to fill them. It must have been obvious that many of the steerage class passengers had not found their way to the boat deck. This was borne out a little bit later, after all the boats had left, when a crowd of people including women and children swarmed up on to the boat deck from the steerage part of the ship. This was probably due to confusion as to which deck they had been told to muster. They apparently thought it was 'A' deck, but were later told that they should proceed to the boat deck. It was strongly denied by the surviving officers and men that there had been any form of forcibly preventing the steerage class passengers from leaving their part of the ship.

The total boat accommodation was 1,178 persons in 16 boats at the davits and four collapsible boats (which had to be manhandled over the side). The British Board of Trade was satisfied with this as there were in addition 3,560 lifebelts and 48 lifebuoys. The *Titanic* had 2,235 persons onboard. In fact the boat accommodation was completely inadequate. It is true that if the boats had all been filled some 200 extra might have been saved, but this would have been a small proportion of the 1,522 who were lost.

Survivors all confirmed that the band onboard was absolutely heroic. There were eight of them including their bandmaster, Mr Hartley, and they played popular tunes of the day whilst the ship was sinking under them. It had a wonderful effect on the passengers who tended to think that if the band was playing, things could not be too bad. Various accounts of the disaster credit the band with playing either 'Nearer my God to Thee' or 'Autumn' as their final tune, played when the water was rising over their feet. In fact it seems probable that, whilst the bandsmen might have known the popular tunes by heart, they would have been unlikely to have known any hymn tunes without the music, and it is very doubtful if they had hymn music with them. Anyway it was a gallant effort, and it is sad to record that all eight bandsmen were lost.

All boats except two collapsible types, were clear of the ship by about 02.15, but there were over 1,500 people still onboard. The water was rising fast and the bows dipped lower and lower. People were being swept away by the rising water, including First Officer Murdock who was never seen again. Second Officer Lightoller was seen to dive off the roof of the officers' quarters into the sea. He managed to reach a collapsible boat, which was already overcrowded, and later transferred to a larger *Titanic* boat. He did an immense job amongst the boats, taking complete charge as an officer should. He survived and was one of the chief witnesses at the subsequent enquiry.

The boats had been told by E.J. to stick together and to make for the lights of a ship which both E.J. and many others saw about four miles away. They were also told to secure the boats one to the other by their painters so that they did not drift apart. At 02.15, just after the last boat had got away, the great ship started to raise her stern as the bows went down, until she was nearly vertically upright, then suddenly the stern settled back a bit. There were numerous explosions onboard and many people thought that she had broken in two. This was discounted at the enquiries, but it is significant that when she was found in September 1985, her stern was missing. A minute or two later the stern started sinking again and at 02.20 it disappeared under the water. The *Titanic* sank in just over 200 fathoms of water. As the ship sank there was a rush of those still onboard towards the stern, but as it finally disappeared they were all washed off.

Above:
An artist's impression of the
Titanic's last moments.
BBC Hulton Picture Library

Left:
The official notice posted at
Lloyds, informing of the loss
of the *Titanic* 'after collision
with ice'. *Lloyds*

Above:
HMS *Carpathia. Real Photos (S2349)*

The sea was bitterly cold and many of them must have perished due to the cold, although some at least were still alive and shouting for help: but most of the boats which had just got away and were not far off failed to pick them up even though they were half-full. However, seven boats did manage to pick up a very few survivors. The boats were heavily criticised at the Senate Enquiry for their lack of common humanity. The surviving officers who had been in the boats explained that they wished to do so and ordered their oarsmen to give way and pull towards them, but the passengers in the boats objected so strongly that they had to give up the idea and they made for the rescue ships which by then had arrived.

The scene must have been terrible: the pathetic cries of those in the sea turning gradually to silence as one after another succumbed to the cold, this lingered in the survivors' minds for years after. At the Senate Enquiry a number of witnesses refused to answer questions about that part of the disaster, saying that it was too terrible to talk about. Many did in fact break down and cry.

The first of the rescue ships to arrive was the *Carpathia*, which arrived at 04.00, 1hr 40min after the *Titanic* sank. At first the survivors in the sea could not be seen because it was still dark, but as daylight dawned many scattered lifeboats came into view. Capt Arthur Rostrom wasted no time in launching his own boats to look for survivors in the water, but it was too late. A number of bodies were found but they were all dead. Other ships began to arrive, prominent among them being the *Olympic*, having sailed from Southampton shortly after the *Titanic*. They too lowered boats to search, and recovered many bodies.

All the *Titanic's* boats made for the *Carpathia* where the half frozen occupants were made welcome and given hot drinks. When it was obvious that nothing more could be done, *Carpathia* sailed for New York with 711 survivors onboard. She arrived at 21.30 on Thursday 18 April in a thunderstorm.

New York, with typical American hospitality, had prepared 5,000 beds for the survivors. Hospitals, doctors and ambulances were alerted, and crowds of people,

106

many of them relatives, thronged the quay. *Carpathia* had not replied to many requests from newspapers and others for the names of survivors, so many of the relatives had no idea whether their loved ones had been saved or not.

One of the first onboard was Signor Marconi, the head of the Marconi Wireless Co. He went straight to the wireless office where he found one of the two *Titanic's* wireless operators helping out the *Carpathia's* sole operator. The man was called Bride and he gained some notoriety for being the first person to give an authentic account of the sinking to a reporter from the *New York Times*.

'There were men in the water all round me', he said: 'The sea was dotted with them, all depending on their lifebelts. I felt I simply had to get away from the ship, so I swam with all my might. She was a beautiful sight then, smoke and sparks rushing out of the funnel and there must have been an explosion, but we heard no noise, we only saw the big stream of sparks. The band was playing and I guess they must all have gone down.

'When I was about 150ft from the ship she went on to her nose. With the after quarter sticking straight up into the air, she began to settle slowly. When at last the waves washed over her rudder there wasn't the least bit of suction that I could feel. She just kept going as slowly as she had been.'

Soon after the *Carpathia* reached New York, the White Star Line issued figures of the known persons lost, and they have been amended since. Here, for what they are worth, are the final figures.

Class	Women and Children Saved	Men Saved
First	98%	31%
Second	87%	16%
Third	47%	14%
Crew	87%	22%

Out of the 2,235 persons onboard, 1,522 perished. It must be recorded that most of these were from the third (steerage) class, not necessarily because favouritism was shown to the first and second class, but because the steerage passengers were much further from the boat deck and possibly because they were held back by members of the crew to avoid overcrowding the boat deck, and when they were released it was too late for them.

Two points remain to be cleared up: the behaviour of the *Californian* and that of Mr Bruce Ismay, the Managing Director of White Star.

It will be remembered that the lights of a ship were seen from the *Titanic* shortly before she sank and that E.J. directed the boats to steer for them. The lights were seen by the boats and numerous witnesses testified at the enquiry that the lights were those of a steamship, because they could see the red (port) light and the green (starboard) light. However, many other witnesses were not so sure and testified that they could only see one white light. Others said that they could not see any side lights, but only two masthead steaming lights. Yet others said that there were no lights at all, only stars low down on the horizon. In other words the witnesses' testimony was not 100% certain.

In the author's own experience it is quite possible to mistake a low star for a masthead light, particularly on such a clear night as this. It would however be difficult to mistake a star for a red or a green light.

It then appeared that the Leyland liner *Californian* had been in the vicinity of the *Titanic* on the night of Sunday 14 and Monday 15 April. Most surviving observers agreed that the lights sighted were off *Titanic's* port bow and at that time the ship was probably heading north, in other words the lights were somewhere to the north and west of the *Titanic*.

Rumours ashore led to newspaper reports that the *Californian* was well within reach of the *Titanic* but did nothing to help her. Her Master, Capt Stanley Lord, confirmed that he was in the area, but 17 to 19 miles from the position reported in *Titanic's* SOS. He had in fact stopped engines because he was surrounded by ice floes and deemed it too dangerous to proceed until daylight. His one radio operator, received a somewhat garbled SOS from the *Titanic*, relayed by the German Line *Frankfurt*. During the middle watch (00.01 to 04.00) the *Californian* saw some lights, apparently from a ship, and Capt Lord ordered the OOW to call the ship up by Morse lamp. This was done repeatedly during the night but she made no reply. However, during the watch a number of rockets were sighted very low down on the horizon. The Captain was informed but he stayed in his cabin and took no action.

It should be pointed out that the night was exceptionally clear and the visibility extreme, thus it might well have been that the rockets had been fired from over the horizon and only seen when they were at the top of their trajectory and thus above the horizon.

The lights of the supposed ship was in a direct line with the rockets which led the men on watch to think that they had been fired by her and the Captain was told this. One might have thought that Capt Lord would have endeavoured to approach the supposed ship, but he did not, perhaps because he deemed it dangerous to move in the ice at all, or because he thought that the rockets were shooting stars, a mistake easy to make on a clear night. However, afterwards the officers onboard the *Californian* reported that eight rockets had been fired, which was the exact number fired by the *Titanic*.

An engineer, called Gill, who was unable to sleep, went on deck about 00.40 and saw what he thought to be a shooting star, but eight minutes later he saw a second 'shooting star' and came to the conclusion that they were rockets. However, there is some discrepancy in the time because the *Titanic* did not start firing rockets until 01.45 (*Titanic* time). Probably the *Californian* was still keeping New York time and *Titanic* might have been going to put her clocks back just before arrival.

Three enquiries were made into the disaster, an unofficial one in New York, the second the official Senate Enquiry in Washington, headed by Senator Smith, and the third a British enquiry headed by Lord Mersey, a Wreck Commissioner. Both Senator Smith and Lord Mersey condemned Capt Lord, but Senator Smith put it most strongly. They both came to the conclusion that the lights seen by the *Titanic* must have been the *Californian* and that either her position or the *Titanic's* must have been in error. From this they concluded that the *Californian* must have been a great deal closer to the *Titanic* than '17 to 19 miles'. They both apparently failed to check at what time the *Californian* started to move towards the *Titanic* and at what time she arrived at the scene of the disaster. This, surely, would have told them how far away she was in the first place.

As regards Bruce Ismay, the American press criticised him severely for leaving the ship relatively soon after the collision and also for finding himself a place in a boat (albeit a collapsible) when not all the women and children had been evacuated. The Senate Enquiry cleared him of all these insinuations, but the hostile questioning by Senator Smith left everybody with the impression that he should have stayed aboard the *Titanic* until he was washed off or went down with the ship. This seems very unfair. In any case he was only a passenger (he had in fact resigned from the White Star board a month before but had not yet left), and whilst the Captain might be expected to be the last person to leave a sinking ship, no-one has ever suggested that a member of the management board of the shipping line should also be expected to do likewise.

The British and the American enquiries more or less came to the same conclusion. The US Senate Enquiry, headed by Senator Smith, was more critical than the British Enquiry. On its conclusion, Senator Smith made a speech to the Senate outlining his findings. He was an eloquent speaker — some thought too eloquent — and his speech was full of flowery comments, but in general he made the following points:

(a) The *Titanic's* boats had insufficient accommodation for all the persons onboard. The crews were unfamiliar with them and the lack of discipline in embarking the passengers meant that more lives were lost than should have been.

(b) The tests made during trials on the boilers, equipment and lifesaving facilities were not sufficient.

(c) Officers and men were strangers to each other and unfamiliar with the ship.

(d) The ship had received plenty of ice warnings.

(e) Capt Smith was guilty of over-confidence and neglect, mainly because he did not reduce speed in the known presence of icebergs, neither did he double the look-outs. He also failed to issue a general warning to all passengers.

(f) Finally, he bitterly criticised Capt Lord of the *Californian*, virtually calling him a liar over the position of his ship when he stopped in the ice. He said he must have been much closer to the *Titanic* than he had admitted.

The British enquiry was held at the Scottish Hall, Westminster and at Caxton Hall from 2 May to 30 July 1912. As mentioned, Lord Mersey was the Chairman and he had five assessors sitting with him. He said that he had received confirmation that at least four ice warnings had been received. One important one was from the steamer *Mesaba* and was actually addressed to the *Titanic* in addition to all eastbound ships. It read: 'Ice report in Lat 42° North, to 41° 45′ North, Long 49° West to 50° 30′ West. Saw much heavy pack ice and large number icebergs.' The ice was definitely in the *Titanic's* path, but unfortunately the report was not delivered to the bridge because the operator was very busy trying to clear messages from passengers. He also probably did not appreciate the importance of the message. The operator concerned was drowned.

Lord Mersey dealt at length with the fact that Capt Smith took no avoiding action by altering course well to the south, thus avoiding the ice field altogether. Somewhat surprisingly Lord Mersey did not blame E.J. for not altering course, neither did he blame him for not reducing speed, because, he said, 'It had been the practice of liners using this track for many years, when in the vicinity of ice at night in clear weather, to maintain their speed and trust to a sharp look-out to enable them to avoid the danger'. This practice, he said, had been justified by experience, no collisions having resulted from it.

Lord Mersey, dealing with the question of insufficient boats, found that the Board of Trade was working on an Act of 1894 which contained a table of boats required by ships of various tonnages, but did not include any ships over 10,000 tons. He thought that the number of boats should depend upon the number of passengers and not the tonnage. This has now been accepted and by international law ships must carry sufficient boats to accommodate all persons onboard.

The enquiry members exonerated the White Star Line from the charge that third class passengers had been unfairly treated by being held below until it was too late. However, like Senator Smith, they came down hard on Capt Lord of the *Californian*. In Lord Mersey's summing up, he said that the mysterious lights seen by the *Californian* were in fact the lights of the *Titanic*, and that the rockets his officers had seen were also fired by the *Titanic*. He thought that the *Californian* must have been from five to eight miles from the *Titanic*.

The British enquiry made a number of important recommendations, most of which have been accepted and have become international law. They included:

(a) Lifeboat accommodation to be in line with the number of persons onboard.
(b) One or more of the boats should be mechanically propelled.
(c) The number of persons that can be safely carried in the each boat whilst it is being lowered to be clearly marked.
(d) Boat and other emergency drills to be held as soon as possible after sailing and thereafter at weekly intervals.
(e) Company regulations should clearly state that when ice is reported on or near a vessel's track, she should proceed at a moderate speed or alter course to go well clear of the danger area.

Finally, what happened to the principal characters in this terrible drama?

Joseph C. Boxall was the *Titanic's* Fourth Officer and the officer responsible for determining *Titanic's* position when she was sinking. He stayed with the White Star Line and eventually became the First Officer of the Cunard White Star line's *Aquitania*. Protagonists of Capt Lord challenged the position Boxall gave, but he adamantly maintained its accuracy. He died in 1967, aged 83, and, at his request, his ashes were scattered at sea over *Titanic's* last resting place — 41° 45' N, 50° 16' W — the position he had defended throughout his life.

The *Carpathia* served in World War 1 but was sunk by a mine or a torpedo 170 miles off Bishop Rock.

Frederic Flint was one of the two crow's nest lookouts in the *Titanic*. After 24 years at sea, he joined Harland & Wolff, then on his final retirement he sold newspapers on the street corner of his home town, Southampton. In January 1945, two weeks after his wife died, he hanged himself with a clothes line in his garden at the age of 76.

International Mercantile Marine (IMM), the parent company of the White Star Line, never really recovered and in spite of receiving some £2 million of insurance money it steadily declined into obscurity.

J. Bruce Ismay, the Managing Director of the White Star Line and a Director of IMM, faced the US enquiry and was also called upon to testify at the British enquiry. He underwent a gruelling examination which in the end proved nothing, but the questions showed clearly that the British board thought that he should not have abandoned the ship as early as he had — a similar result to that in the US enquiry. He was attacked by the British press in much the same way that he was attacked in America. Ismay wanted to defend himself but the directors of the White Star Line thought that it would be bad for business and dissuaded him. He gave up business life in 1913 and retired to County Galway in Ireland, but not before he had contributed £10,000 to the creation of the Mercantile Widows Fund. He became a diabetic and it led to him having to have his right leg amputated. He returned to England and died at the age of 74.

Charles H. Lightoller, the *Titanic's* Second Officer and the senior survivor, saw service in the Royal Navy in World War 1 then returned to the White Star Line. He remained with the company until he retired at the normal retiring age. The White Star never gave him a command, perhaps because he had always defended Ismay.

Capt Stanley Lord of the *Californian* for many years suffered under a cloud of being a Captain who had failed to go to the assistance of a vessel in distress, even though this was never convincingly proved: the Leyland Line asked him to resign. During World War 1 he had command of a Nitrate Products Steam Ship Co's ship. He later continued to try and clear his name and to get the Board of Trade to re-open his case, but it repeatedly refused. A well known marine author, Peter Padfield, published a book in the early 1960s (*The 'Titanic' and the 'Californian'*) in which an excellent case was made out to prove that the *Californian* was not closer to the *Titanic*, but really was 17 to 19 miles away. The book certainly opened the eyes of the public to the gross wrong to this long suffering man, but still failed to get the case re-opened. Lord died in 1962 at the age of 84.

Harold C. Lowe, *Titanic's* Fifth Officer, figured largely in the American enquiry, served in the Royal Navy in World War 1 and reached the rank of Commander. He then retired to his native Wales where he entered local government, but he died at the early age of 61 in 1964.

The *Olympic*, sister ship of the *Titanic*, was given a major refit at Harland & Wolff after the disaster, largely to make her safer in the light of the lessons learnt from the *Titanic*. After the refit she was able to withstand flooding in six compartments without sinking, a great improvement on the 'unsinkable' *Titanic* which had been built to withstand flooding in only four compartments. During World War 1 she became a troopship and succeeded in ramming and sinking a German U-boat which tried to attack her. After the war she was converted to fuel oil and in May 1934 she collided with the Nantucket Light Vessel in the approaches to New York in dense fog. The seven men onboard the Lightship were all lost and the US Government sued White Star for her loss. She was broken up in 1935.

Capt Arthur Rostrom, the Captain of the *Carpathia* which embarked most of the survivors, took command of the *Mauretania* and from 1928 to 1931 he commanded the *Berengaria* as Commodore of the Cunard Fleet. He then retired and died in 1940.

Senator William Alden Smith, Chairman of the Senate enquiry, knew nothing of maritime matters, a fact that became only too obvious during the enquiry. He continued to serve in the Senate until 1919. He lost his only son from pneumonia shortly afterwards and he himself died from a heart attack in 1934 at the age of 73.

Finally, the *Titanic* herself. Although the position of the wreck was known, it was only approximate and for over half a century explorers and divers have been trying to find the actual position of the wreck with a view to salvage. Now at last it has been found, by the USS *Knorr*, a USN oceanographic research ship, on 1 September 1985. The *Knorr* was assisted by a robot submarine called the *Argo*, fitted with black and white and colour television cameras. The submarine was developed to operate in such deep water by the Woods Hole Oceanographic Institute of Massachusetts.

Onboard the *Knorr* was a team of Franco-American scientists, led by the Chief Scientist of Woods Hole, Dr Robert Ballard. The *Titanic* is lying on her side in 13,230ft of water some 300 miles into the Atlantic off the coast of Newfoundland. The exact location is being kept secret to avoid would-be treasure hunters finding the ship and looting it.

Dr Ballard is reported as saying that some parts of the ship were in remarkably good condition, having apparently been preserved by the icy water. The stern of the ship is, however, missing. Colour photographs have shown cases of wine apparently quite intact and other domestic utensils in pristine order. Even the jackstaff is still intact and standing proudly in the bows. The under part of the bow is however badly damaged; not, according to Dr Ballard, due to the impact with the iceberg, but due to the fact that the hull was compressed by the collision and this caused many rivets to 'pop out quietly but lethally'. Apparently so many rivets came out that the water rushed in, and this gave rise to the theory that there was a huge gash in the bows caused by the actual impact with the iceberg. Dr Ballard said that he and his divers found no trace of this. His theory is agreed by many of the survivors of the disaster who all agreed that the impact was hardly noticeable. The forward of the four funnels is missing, but otherwise the ship is reasonably preserved.

There are various rumours of attempts to salvage her, which may or may not be made. They are largely spurred on by the belief that she was carrying a considerable amount of bullion, jewellery and other valuables, but arguments have been put forward that she should be left where she is as a memorial to those who died in her. There is also some doubt as to whether she carried any bullion at all. She was insured for about £43 million by a consortium led by the Commercial Union, but whether this included her cargo is not clear. Dr Ballard asserts that she has sunk as much as 50ft into the seabed and that salvage is out of the question.

Thus ends the story of the most famous marine disaster in peacetime the world has ever known. It was a disaster which could have been avoided if greater caution and more vigilance had been shown, and the large loss of life could have been minimised if adequate lifeboat accommodation had been available. With hindsight all the mistakes have now been rectified by international law; unfortunately for 1,522 souls it is too late.

Andrea Doria *and* Stockholm

The *Andrea Doria*, built by Ansaldo of Sestri, near Genoa, was the flagship of the Italian Line and was the pride and joy of all Italians. Captained by Peiro Calamai, she was a beautiful ship, luxuriously furnished with gorgeous murals and paintings in her public rooms. She was some 690ft long and her tonnage was 29,083grt. Steam turbines and two screws gave her a cruising speed of 22kt and she was the first passenger ship to be built in Italy after World War 2. Her home port was Genoa. At the time of the collision (July 1956) she carried a total of over 1,700 persons, of which 190 were first class passengers, 267 cabin class, 672 tourist class, and the crew numbered over 570.

The author visited her in 1956 shortly before her last voyage and was highly impressed with her fine lines and her superb furnishings. She was a supreme example of the best of Italian artistry.

The *Stockholm* was built in Sweden by Gotaverken of Gothenberg. She was not so large, being only 12,644 tons, and her propulsion was by two diesels giving her a cruising speed of 19kt. She was the fourth liner named *Stockholm*. The first one was launched in 1904 and was just a little larger than the new *Stockholm*. The second ship was destroyed during the war before completion at her Italian berth. The third ship, also building in Italy, was never completed because of the war. The new *Stockholm* was launched in 1943 and was owned by the Swedish-America Line. Her master was Gunnar Nordensen.

The *Andria Doria* left Genoa on 17 July 1956 and called at Naples, Cannes and Gibraltar. She was due in New York on 26 July. Capt Calamai's plan was to make for the Nantucket Light Vessel outside the approaches to New York, and to pass south of her. The *Stockholm* sailed from New York on 25 July and also intended to pass close to the south of the Nantucket Light Vessel. Although neither Captain then knew it, both ships were to pass close to the south of the Light Vessel at about the same time. The stage was set for one of the worst disasters ever known at sea.

When about 150 miles from the Nantucket Light Vessel the *Doria* ran into fog, not unknown at that time of the year, and it slowly thickened. All normal precautions were taken — such as closing watertight doors, sounding the siren, posting look-outs, etc — and her navigational radar was turned on and seemed to be working perfectly. A token reduction of speed of about 5% was made. This reduced her speed from 22kt to 21kt. The collision rules specify that ships must proceed at a 'moderate speed' in fog and defines 'moderate' as such a speed that the ship can be stopped within the visibility distance. Certainly 21kt by no stretch of the imagination could be termed a 'moderate' speed, but too many passenger liners proceed far too fast because their Masters are very hidebound by their timetable. Calamai was no exception, as he felt that he had to arrive on schedule or there would be complaints made to his owners. In any case, he thought that with his radar there was no danger.

At 20.00, when it was getting dark, visibility was down to half a mile and there were three echoes showing on the *Doria's* radar, one astern and two ahead, and all them going in the same direction as the *Doria*. Calamai kept a close watch on the two echoes ahead, but at 21kt *Doria* soon overtook them.

Just before 21.30 another small echo appeared on the radar screen, apparently steaming at the same speed as the *Doria*, but it did not take long to work out that in fact it was stationary and was probably the Nantucket Light Vessel. With his ship heading straight for it, Calamai altered course 6° to port in order to leave the lightship well clear on his starboard hand. At 22.20 the Officer of the Watch reported that the Light Vessel was abeam to starboard at a distance of only one mile. The fog was too thick to see it but its fog signal could be clearly heard on *Doria's* bridge. It appeared that the ship had been set to the north by a current of about ¾kt.

At about 22.45 the OOW, Second Officer Francini, saw another echo on the screen apparently almost dead ahead, but very slightly on the starboard bow. It was closing rapidly. Calamai checked the radar screen himself and saw that Francini was right: it was fine on the starboard bow and steering a course roughly the reciprocal of the *Doria's*. He thought they would pass starboard to starboard, but too close for comfort, so he altered course 4° to port to widen the distance and at the same time he told the helmsman to steer 'nothing to starboard'. In so altering he officially broke the Rule of the Road which clearly states that when two ships are meeting end on, or nearly end on, they should both alter course to starboard. In fact if one ship reckons she can avoid a difficult situation by an early alteration of course to avoid approaching each other end on, or nearly end on, she is at liberty to do so, but — and this is the important point — any such alteration must be bold and in very good time. Calamai's alteration was neither.

Stockholm's OOW, Third Officer Carstens-Johannsen, generally known as Carstens, maintained at the subsequent enquiry that when he first picked up the *Doria's* echo, it was not on *Stockholm's* starboard bow, but was fine on his port bow. He considered that they were meeting end on, or nearly end on, and that any alteration of his course must be to starboard.

The two ships were then about 3½-5 miles apart (opinions differ). Calamai started to get worried, particularly as he knew that they must be getting close to each other, but he could not hear the other vessel's fog signal. It is not certain whether he appreciated how little time he had — between three and five minutes with their relative approach speed of nearly 40kt. He warned everybody on the bridge to keep a close look out and the words were hardly out of his mouth when they suddenly saw the other's side lights. They were expecting to see a green (starboard) light on their starboard bow, but to their horror a red (port) light appeared and she seemed to be crossing their bows. Calamai at once ordered 'Tutte sinestra' (hard-a-port) and sounded two blasts on the siren. He watched in horror as the other ship's bows rushed towards him. The *Doria* started to turn to port, but it was too late and the other ship's bow crashed into the *Doria's* starboard side abreast the bridge.

Now let us look at it from the *Stockholm's* point of view. She had sailed from her pier at 57th Street in New York at 11.30 and she had followed the French liner *Ile de France* down the Hudson River. It was a hot muggy day with a light haze but

114

no fog. The *Ile de France* drew ahead of her. At 20.00, when Third Officer Carstens came on watch, it was still quite clear. Capt Nordensen came on to the bridge at 21.00 for about half an hour and ordered a 3° alteration of course from 090° to 087° to avoid passing the Nantucket Light Vessel too far away. He then went to his cabin, leaving orders to be called in the event of fog, if another ship appeared to be coming within one mile, and when the Nantucket Light Vessel was abeam. Carstens checked the ship's position by radio bearings and found that a northerly set was taking the ship too far to the north, so he made a 2° alteration to 089° to allow for it. At about 23.00 he took another fix and found that the ship was still being set to the north, so he altered to 091°. It should be noted that the *Stockholm* intended to pass close to the south of the Nantucket Light Vessel and Carstens was trying to reach this position.

Shortly afterwards a radar echo appeared on his screen at 12 miles range; and when it reached 10 miles, he recorded it in the log, as a radar echo from an unknown ship 2° to port of the heading marker. He was still in clear weather and saw no need to reduce speed, which was about 18kt, but did not appreciate that the *Andrea Doria* was in fog — until just before the collision. He posted a look-out on the port side of the bridge with instructions to sing out as soon as he saw any lights. He had decided in his own mind that as soon as he saw the vessel's lights for himself, he would alter course to starboard, as he considered that the two ships were approaching end on, or nearly end on. He was becoming increasingly worried as he thought he should have seen the other vessel's lights, when the bridge lookout reported 'lights to port' and almost immediately after the crow's nest look-out also reported lights to port. Carstens went to the wing of the bridge to see for himself and saw the two masthead lights of the *Doria*, very close but still to port. He called to the helmsman 'starboard' and watched while the ship's head swung about 20° to starboard. He then ordered 'midships', immediately followed by 'steady as you go'. He was then called to the telephone in the wheel house: it was the look-out in the crow's nest again. He dealt with it as quickly as he could and then rushed to the port wing of the bridge again. To his horror he saw that the *Doria* was even closer and was presenting her green (starboard) light to him. He realised that she could not be passing him port to port, as he thought, and seemed to be crossing his bow. Carstens went hard-a-starboard and full astern but it was too late and the *Stockholm's* bow sliced into the *Doria*.

No order was given onboard the *Doria* to stop engines and she still had a considerable way on her. The *Stockholm's* bows were still in the *Doria* starboard side, but the way on the *Doria* shook it clear, and in so doing caused the bow to slither along the *Doria's* side causing tremendous sparks and a lot of damage. Eventually both ships came clear of each other and slowed to a standstill. *Stockholm*, whose engines were already stopped, lost all her anchor cables, but not the two anchors, which were caught up in the wreckage. The cables all ran out and effectively anchored the ship, having caught in an obstruction on the sea bed.

It is interesting to note that neither ship knew the identity of the other at this time. *Stockholm* broadcast on the distress frequency that she had been in collision with an unknown ship and asked any ship that had been in collision to identity herself. *Doria* almost at the same time made a distress signal giving her name, and thus solved the mystery. *Doria's* SOS also gave her position as 40° 30' North,

69° 55′ West, which was some 30 miles south of Nantucket Island and some 15 miles west of the Nantucket Light Vessel.

The *Stockholm* was badly damaged: her bows were pushed back about 60ft and her forward crew mess-deck had all but disappeared, but she was still afloat and the forward bulkhead was holding well. The *Doria* was in a bad way. The *Stockholm* had hit her in the starboard fuel tanks, which were nearly empty, so the water rushed into the starboard tanks. The port tanks were completely empty and filled only with air. This combination produced a great healing moment and the *Doria* at once started to list to starboard. The maximum heel she had been designed for was 15° but she soon reached 18° and later 22°.

The fuel tanks were arranged on each side of a passageway or tunnel. At the forward end of this tunnel was a small pump room containing valves for controlling the flooding of the tanks with sea water, if it became necessary to flood them to correct a list. The other end of the tunnel led into the generator room, but there was no watertight door fitted in the tunnel. The tunnel was pierced by the *Stockholm* and at once flooded, rendering it impossible to reach the small pump room and thus flood the port tanks to correct the heel. The generator room also became flooded, leading eventually to the loss of power.

The order was given for the port side boats to be swung out, but the list to starboard was too great to enable them to be lowered. This meant that only the starboard side boats could be used, and their total capacity was only about half the number of passengers and crew. The excessive list also meant that, when lowered, the boats were a long distance from the hull and had to be braced into the side to enable anyone to get into them, thus causing considerable delay.

It was obvious that external assistance from other ships was vital. *Doria's* SOS signal had been heard by a number of ships, the nearest of which was the *Cape Ann*. She was only 15 miles away but she carried only two boats. The US Navy Transport *Private William H. Thomas* was 19 miles away, and the tanker *Robert E. Hopkins* was a little further away. They all radioed that they were coming to the *Doria's* aid. The US Coast Guard was also alerted and did useful work organising the rescue and despatching US Coast Guard cutters and tugs.

The *Ile de France*, with by far the largest number of boats, was by this time some 45 miles out into the Atlantic, but she reversed her course and arrived at the scene at 02.00 and took up a position on *Doria's* starboard side. About 1,500 people still remained onboard the *Doria*, the other passengers having been sent piecemeal, in what boats were available, to the *Stockholm* and the *Cape Ann*. Regrettably the first three boats arrived at the *Stockholm* only half full, mainly with stewards and galley staff. The boats had to load from the *Doria's* stern which was fairly low in the water, but some panic prevailed with men rushing the rails and children being dropped into makeshift blanket drops and sails.

However, order was restored, with the arrival of the *Ile de France*. Passengers were assembled on the high port side and helped down the steeply sloping deck to the low side from where it was not very far for them to climb down ropes or ladders to the waiting boats. In some cases nets were used to lower the elderly or handicapped people. Some 30 boats had now arrived and they carried out a ferry service between the *Doria* and the four main rescue ships — the *Ile de France* (753 survivors rescued), the *Stockholm* (545 survivors), the US Navy Transport (158 survivors), the *Cape Ann* (129 survivors) and the destroyer escort which stayed until the end and embarked Capt Calamai and his officers (77 survivors). A total of 1,662 were rescued out of the 1,700 persons onboard. The major part of the rescue was completed by 04.00.

When all the passengers had been rescued, Calamai ordered what few crew members were still onboard to abandon ship, but called upon volunteers to remain behind until the tugs he had asked for arrived. He still hoped to move the ship into shallow water and beach her. A number remained, including all the officers, but the list was still increasing so Calamai was forced to let most of them go. At 05.30, when the list had reached 40°, Calamai told the officers that he himself intended remaining and they could go; but when the officers threatened to remain with him, he had to give up the idea of staying. The last boat with Calamai and his officers left shortly after 05.30, but they went to a Coast Guard cutter, the *Hornbeam*, because Calamai wanted to await the promised tugs. Towing was discussed but was found to be quite impracticable, so they were all transferred to the small destroyer *Allen* for passage to New York.

Doria's engineers had had a long struggle to keep the ship afloat. In spite of the

Left:
Stockholm's battered bow. Her bow had been reinforced against ice, but the force of the collision was too much for it. *Associated Press*

Below:
The *Andrea Doria* listed heavily before sinking. Note that the starboard lifeboats only could be used. *US Coast Guard*

risk of her capsizing at any moment, they continued to man the pumps and kept the lights going, but only gave up when the main generator room was flooded and the water had reached the engine room. They made one important mistake. When it was found to be impossible to flood the port tanks, it was decided to empty the starboard water ballast tanks, under the impression that when the tanks had been emptied of water, it would increase the buoyancy of the starboard side. Unfortunately it had the effect of increasing and not reducing the list, due to the removal of the much needed weight in the lower part of the ship.

The *Stockholm* had no passengers injured, but three seamen who had been in the forepart of the ship were missing, believed killed, and four seamen were hauled from the wreckage badly injured.

A short time after the *Doria* sank, the rescue craft were released. The *Ile de France* left first and circled the spot where the *Doria* had foundered, sounded her siren, half masted her colours and dipped her ensign in salute — a gesture much appreciated by the few Italians left to see it. She went back to New York, as did all the other rescue craft.

Of all the unbelievable injuries, heroic rescues and terrible deaths, perhaps the most amazing was the saga of a girl aged 14, called Linda Morgan. She had been asleep in a cabin onboard the *Doria* with her sister; her mother and father were in an adjacent cabin. The bow of the *Stockholm*, when smashing into the cabin, had miraculously got underneath Linda and she was deposited on to the forecastle of the *Stockholm* behind a sort of breakwater, 2½ft high and some 80ft from *Stockholm's* bows. The breakwater had protected her and she was still alive. A Spanish seaman and two Swedish sailors found her and to their amazement she spoke to him in Spanish and said 'Dondé esta Mama', where is mother? It turned out afterwards that she had been born in Mexico and lived all her life in Spain or Italy and that Spanish was her first language. The sailor thought that she must be a passenger onboard the *Stockholm*, but on checking with the purser no Linda Morgan was found in the passenger list. Eventually it transpired that she had been lifted bodily by the *Stockholm's* bow and when the two ships managed to break apart she remained onboard the *Stockholm*.

To return to the collision. An enquiry was held in due course and the inevitable legal battles arose, each shipping line trying to blame the other. The Italian Line sued for $1,800,000 and the Swedish America Line for $4,000,000.

The Italian Line's case was that the two ships were set to pass starboard to starboard, and in fact the *Doria* altered to port to allow more sea room. It should have been quite safe if the *Stockholm* had not later altered to starboard. They laid stress on the fact that Carstens was alone on the bridge (the Italians kept two officers on the bridge at all times), that he was only 26 years old, that he did not inform the Captain that he suspected fog might be obscuring the lights of the *Doria*, that he waited so long before taking any action because he wanted to see the other ship's lights for himself, and that in any case the *Stockholm* was not on the recommended track.

The Swedish America Line's case was that the *Doria* was proceeding too fast in fog. They had a good point here. The Rule of the Road states that 'a moderate speed should not be exceeded': with the visibility not much more than 200yd, something like 10kt might have been much more appropriate. The Swedes went on to argue that the *Stockholm* was not in fog and therefore her 18kt was a

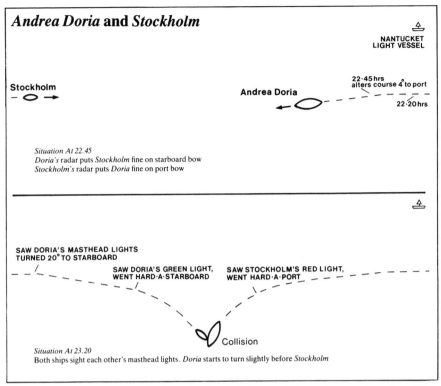

Andrea Doria and Stockholm

NANTUCKET
LIGHT VESSEL

Stockholm

Andrea Doria

22·45 hrs
alters course 4° to port

22·20 hrs

Situation At 22.45
Doria's radar puts Stockholm fine on starboard bow
Stockholm's radar puts Doria fine on port bow

SAW DORIA'S MASTHEAD LIGHTS
TURNED 20° TO STARBOARD

SAW DORIA'S GREEN LIGHT,
WENT HARD·A·STARBOARD

SAW STOCKHOLM'S RED LIGHT,
WENT HARD·A·PORT

Collision

Situation At 23.20
Both ships sight each other's masthead lights. Doria starts to turn slightly before Stockholm

perfectly reasonable speed, that the *Doria's* log could not be produced, neither could a plot of the bearings and range of the *Stockholm*. In fact it appeared that no plot had ever been made and that the log probably went down with the ship. The Swedes were on thin ice regarding a plot being produced because nobody could produce the plot kept by the *Stockholm* — Carstens swore he made a plot, but it had apparently been rubbed out.

Capt Nordensen strongly defended his Third Officer. Carstens had not called him since the ship was not in fog and in the short time available he had no chance of judging whether the other ship was in fog, particularly as her fog signal had not been heard. Nordensen said he had followed the same track, both inbound and outbound, for 36 years and that there were no regulations against it (quite true). He said that Carstens, for all his inexperience, had done nothing wrong. He had been quite right to wait until he saw the lights of the *Doria* before he altered course.

In his evidence Calamai admitted that he had had no formal training in the use of radar and that he knew nothing about the stability and ballasting arrangements of his ship; it was the responsibility of the Staff Captain and other officers.

The Court had been in session for three months when the two shipping lines agreed to settle out of court and dropped their claims against each other. Although the Italian Line did not admit it, the builder of the *Doria*, as was often so common, did not provide a sufficient margin of stability. The company had allowed for a 7° list, with an absolute maximum of 15°, and did so by arranging

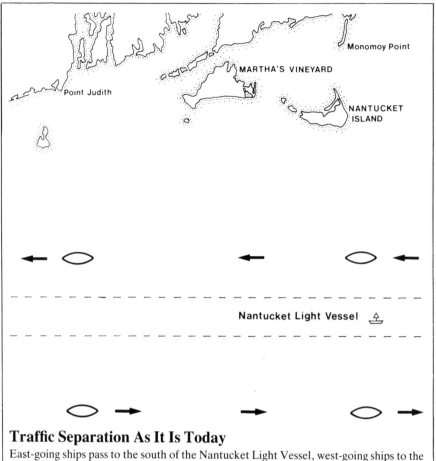

Traffic Separation As It Is Today

East-going ships pass to the south of the Nantucket Light Vessel, west-going ships to the north of it.

that when certain fuel tanks were empty, they should be flooded with sea water to counter any list. Engineers do not like to contaminate fuel tanks with water and then have to clean the tanks out by pumping the oil and water out into the barges in harbour for removal. They probably seldom admitted sea water into the fuel tanks, with the result that the *Doria* could not even withstand a 7° list. The owners were held responsible for not ensuring that ballasting was regularly and correctly carried out.

Two lessons learnt from the *Andria Doria* disaster were that separate ballast tanks, which never contained fuel, should be provided in future ships, and that remote control from a safe position should be provided for valves used in counter-flooding.

A number of navigational lessons too were learnt. Firstly, no ship should be allowed to go to sea without her deck officers fully understanding the use of radar. Nowadays all deck officers have to undergo courses in radar. In fact, modern radars are a great deal more foolproof than in 1956. For example, it is now possible to read off the true bearing of any radar echo, rather than having to read off the relative bearing. In both the *Doria's* and the *Stockholm's* cases, the relative bearing of the other ship was compared to the heading marker. This can lead to errors. For example, ships do sometimes get a few degrees off course and by comparing the other ship's relative bearing with the heading marker it is quite possible to think that she is dead ahead, but in fact she might be up to, say, 5° on one bow or the other.

It is comparatively easy to underestimate the short time available in which to avoid a collision. Take this case — the *Stockholm* was approaching the *Doria* at 18kt and the *Doria* was approaching the *Stockholm* at 21kt, a combined relative approach speed of 39kt. Navigational radars, particularly in those days, probably had a maximum range of 12 miles on another ship. Thus if one detects a ship 12 miles right ahead, there is only about 20 minutes before the two will meet. With large, cumbersome liners, the wheel would have to be put over about a minute before meeting to have much effect on the ship's track, thus we are left with an absolute maximum of 19 minutes. In fact the time is far shorter than that, and it is one of the rules for avoiding collision to act in good time and very decisively.

As we have seen, the Rule of the Road is that when two ships are meeting end on, or nearly end on, they both shall alter course to starboard. The *Doria* considered that by her radar the *Stockholm* was very fine on the starboard bow, a nearly end on position. Both ships should have altered to starboard. However, Calamai in the *Doria* was so convinced that they would pass starboard to starboard, but very close, that he altered 4° to port to widen the distance. In this he was also influenced by the Nantucket shallows, which were to starboard of him, and he did not wish to get too close to them. Had he had some training in the use of radar he would have realised that a 4° alteration of course would hardly show up in the short time available and, as Calamai was taking an action not in accordance with the Rule of the Road, he should certainly have made his intention doubly clear by making a bold alteration to port, so that it would show up clearly on *Stockholm's* radar screen. As it was, of course, *Stockholm* had appreciated that it was a case of two ships meeting nearly end on and in any case would have altered to starboard.

Carstens, the *Stockholm's* OOW, apparently did not put his full faith in the radar and wanted to see the other ship's lights before altering course. Unfortunately he did not realise that the *Doria* was in fog, and her lights did not appear until it was too late. It could be argued, of course, that when the *Stockholm* picked up the *Doria* fine on her port bow she should have made a bold alteration of course to starboard straightaway; ie when she was still 10 to 12 miles distant, and *Doria* should have done the same.

The collision has been referred to as the 'radar assisted collision'. This is perhaps not quite fair, but officers were not so familiar with radar as they are now and failed to appreciate its limitations. In addition, apparently neither ship plotted the radar bearings and ranges.

The author himself was witness to a similar situation towards the end of the war, when ships were steaming without lights. The liner in which he was travelling detected on the radar an echo on her starboard bow. The OOW watched it carefully, but failed to observe that it was keeping a steady bearing, and solemnly continued watching the rapidly approaching echo until the two ships collided. The other ship had no radar and was unaware of the liner's presence. The other ship sank with a small loss of life. It was a typical case of ignorance of the use and value of radar.

Nowadays true motion radars have been introduced which enables the OOW to see the actual course and speed of the other ship, instead of the relative motions. In addition, by international convention, Automatic Radar Plotting Aids have to be fitted in all ships over 10,000 tons built after 1984 and in all existing vessels over 15,000 tons by 1 September 1988. The device will automatically develop a plot of its own and other ships' courses and speeds and it will at once become apparent when risk of collision occurs. Indeed many equipments sound alarms when such a situation arises. In future there should be no excuse for making mistakes similar to those made in this case.

The Nantucket Light Vessel, some 159 miles from the entrance to Long Island Sound, has long been the focal point for both inbound and outbound traffic for New York. In 1956 all ships, whether inbound or outbound, passed south of the Light Vessel. A voluntary agreement between some of the major shipping lines (but not all) recommended outward bound passenger liners to pass about 20 miles south of the Light Vessel and inbound ones close to the south of it. Neither the Swedish America Line nor the Italian Line were parties to this agreement, which in any case was not compulsory. In fact Scandinavian vessels, because they had to set a course further north than most ships to clear Scotland, usually passed very close to the Light Vessel on the outward voyage. In addition, if they had had to keep 20 miles to the south of her (as recommended) they would have had to cross all the inbound traffic, which might have been dangerous. As Capt Nordersen said, he had used the same track (close to the Light Vessel) safely for 36 years.

However, a traffic separation scheme in the area was introduced in 1977 for vessels leaving and approaching New York. Eastbound vessels must keep to a lane south of the Nantucket Light Vessel, and westbound traffic must keep to a lane to the north of the Light Vessel. The separation zone between the two lanes is three miles wide with the Nantucket Light Vessel in the middle of it, and each lane is five miles wide. By this means it is hoped that the two streams of traffic will be well separated and there should be no risk of collision. On the whole it is working well.

The sinking of the *Andrea Doria* was the first big peacetime passenger liner disaster since the loss of the *Titanic* in 1912. In terms of lives lost the *Titanic* disaster vastly outnumbered the figure for the *Doria* where only 44 lives were lost plus three from the *Stockholm*.

After the *Stockholm* had been repaired in the Bethlehem Steel Shipyard in Brooklyn, the Swedish America Line expressed its confidence in the officers by appointing Capt Nordensen to command the Line's new flagship, the 23,500-ton *Gripsholm*, with which he remained until 1958 when he retired on reaching retirement age of 65. Third Officer Carstens was also appointed to the same ship until 1958 when he left the Line to take up a job as Chief Mate of a small freighter of the Bromstom concern. Capt Calamai never went to sea again. He was kept on the books of the Italian Line until he reached the compulsory retiring age of 60 in 1957. The *Stockholm* was sold in 1960 to the East German Trade Union Federation and renamed the *Volkerfreudschaft*. She is now laid up in Southampton (UK) awaiting a buyer.

14

The Herald *Disaster*

'My God, she's going over' cried a man seated at a table in the cafeteria of the Townsend Thoresen car ferry, the *Herald of Free Enterprise*. A few seconds later he, together with all the other passengers in the cafeteria, was shot over to the port side of the saloon and ended up with the furniture, the crockery, the glass and the hand luggage against the plate glass windows which covered the side of the compartment. Nobody had any idea as to what had happened until the sea started rushing in, engulfing them all in bitterly cold water. The cafeteria had been full and all the passengers ended up in a screaming mass, one on top of the other with the glass windows below them. Many people were drowned immediately, while others grabbed various fittings secured to what had been the deck of the cafeteria and were trying to pull themselves up out of the water which was rapidly flooding the entire compartment.

The chaos was indescribable — men, women and children all fighting to try and keep their heads above water, many of them being crushed beneath the weight of the bodies on top of them. To add to the confusion, all the lights went out, and it was pitch dark. People not in the bars and cafeteria were thrown violently from one side of the ship to the other; some were catapulted right overboard, but the water was so cold that a number of them died almost immediately. People on the lower decks below the saloons stood little chance of escape and were drowned; the cross passages became vertical tunnels and it was impossible to get up them. Thus was the scene in the worst ferry disaster ever known in the Western world.

The *Herald* was one of two similar ships of the Townsend Thoresen line, each displacing just under 8,000 tons. The *Herald* normally plied between Dover and Calais, but on Friday 6 March 1987 her normal route had been changed because one of the other ships of the line was out of service. She had sailed early that morning from Dover to Zeebrugge in Belgium, a 2½-hour voyage. She had only about half of her 1,200 passenger capacity filled, mostly with day trippers on shopping sprees. It was to be a gala day for some of them, for the P&O company, the owner of Townsend Thoresen, was running a special cheap day excursion to Belgium. Many of the passengers were women and children, but for the return voyage the ship picked up about 100 Servicemen from the British Army stationed in Germany going home on leave, many of them with their private cars and their families.

Zeebrugge is a small harbour and the ferries proceed into their berth bows first. The massive bow doors are opened and the ramps put into position so that the vehicles and the foot passengers may go ashore. When the ship comes to leave, she has to vacate the berth stern first and put her stern into a small basin to give her enough room to go ahead into the swept channel between the breakwaters. Zeebrugge is deceptive because the harbour looks quite large, but in fact almost three-quarters of it is silted up with sand and mud, so ships have very little room to manoeuvre.

To ensure that the ferries are more or less level with the height of the quay at their berth, they are provided with water ballast tanks. By flooding or discharging these the height of the bows above the water — and thus the height of the disembarking platforms — can be varied to suit the tide.

After an enjoyable day on shore, the passengers, laden with their shopping, started to dribble back onboard around 17.00, and the vehicles started moving up the ramps into the car decks onboard the ship. There were more vehicles than on the outward voyage; these included a number of heavy freight lorries which mostly embarked last, thus adding to the weight in the bows and forcing them still further under the water. It now appears that the ship was down by the bows somewhat more than usual, but strangely the bow ballast tanks were not emptied to bring her on to a level keel.

Once onboard, most of the passengers made for the saloons and particularly the cafeteria; these were all in the highest part of the ship. The ship was late in leaving her berth, and it was not until 18.30 that she started to move astern into the turning basin. It took her nearly 10 minutes to turn, but by 18.42 she was going ahead out of the harbour. At 18.46 the Belgian Coastguard received a signal from a German coaster that the *Herald* appeared to be listing heavily, and only one minute later she turned right over on to her port side, with her upperworks lying parallel to the water and already half submerged and in total darkness. Dover Coastguard too was informed and a helicopter was sent from the UK. By 19.00 a massive search and rescue operation was underway, and soon two warships, five helicopters and a fleet of small craft were deployed around the stricken vessel, now lying stopped just outside the dredged channel with a list of about 90° to port. Divers were flown over by helicopter, from the UK.

It soon became apparent that the ship had run aground on a sandbank and this had undoubtedly prevented her from turning right over. There had been no time to lower any lifeboats; those on the port side had been smashed to pieces in any case. There was little time to put on lifebelts, and those that were dropped to people in the water were virtually useless as the water was so cold that fingers were to numb to adjust the tapes. The starboard side of the ship now became the upper deck and passengers started to gather there. Some had managed to drag themselves up by their own means, but many had grasped the ropes thrown down to them by members of the crew. Most of the passengers who could be seen were taken off by tugs and other small boats who had managed to get alongside. Others in the water were lifted out by helicopter.

The Captain, David Lewry, had been on the bridge and shot right across it, hitting the side of the bridge with some force. He injured his lungs, but, still in great pain, he at first insisted on remaining with his ship. Eventually however he was pursuaded by his officers that he could do no good there and was taken off by a tug.

The few passengers that had already gone below decks had no chance at all. Nearly all the lower decks on the port side were flooded and they had no means of escape. Few of these unfortunates survived to tell the tale, but luckily not many passengers had penetrated below decks when the disaster struck.

The surviving members of the crew behaved magnificently. Not only did they break the heavy glass windows on the now upper side of the ship with axes taken from the remaining lifeboats, but they did sterling work in lowering knotted ropes, also taken from the lifeboats, to the tangled mass of passengers now stranded on the inside of the windows on the port side of the saloons. Those that had the strength grabbed them and the crew hauled them out. Regrettably little chivalry was shown by some male passengers and there were a number of incidents of men knocking women and even children off ropes they were endeavouring to climb.

One horrible tale, typical of many, was told by a man aged 51. He was in one of the saloons which had filled with water, and was supporting his wife as best he could. He saw some men on a ledge just above the level of the water and he asked them to help his wife on to the ledge. They replied 'sorry mate, there's no room up here'. He could see plainly that there was plenty of room for one more person, and he endeavoured to plead with them, but the men went on talking together and smoking and paid no attention to him. His wife slid out of his arms and was drowned. He himself made a supreme effort and was just reaching safety when a man behind him dragged him back into the water and clawed his way over the top of him to safety.

On the whole, though, the passengers behaved well and there were many stories of great unselfishness at the risk of people's own lives, like Private Messon of the British Army in Germany. He was suffering from a spinal injury and was in a wheelchair. He saw that his baby daughter was in danger of drowning, so he clenched her clothing in this teeth in order to ferry her to safety in his wheelchair. 'All of a sudden' he said, 'the ship went over. I reached out and grabbed my wife, Kathleen, by the arm, but she slipped out of my grasp and was swept away by the water. I never saw her again, but I did manage to rescue my little daughter'.

Perhaps, however, of all the stories of bravery and unselfishness, one stands above all others. Andrew Parker, a bank clerk of 33 years, was on a day trip with his wife Eleanor and their daughter Janice. They were all three thrown across the lounge in which they were sitting, together with all the other passengers. Fifteen-stone Mr Parker landed on top of the pile of passengers, but he managed to pull himself and his wife and daughter on to a metal ledge or platform above the water. There was another similar platform on the other side of the saloon from which a broken window led to the now 'upper deck' (the starboard side) and from which escape could be made, but there was a nearly, 5ft gap between the two platforms. By this time Mr Parker had pulled some 20 passengers on to his platform. Without a moment's thought for himself, he managed to stretch his 6ft 3in frame across the gap and told his daughter, aged 12, to clamber over him. She was followed by his wife and by the other passengers on the platform, one by one. All three of the Parkers got out of the broken window and were rescued, but were separated and believed each was the only one alive. In fact they were reunited the next day.

One of the main problems of the rescue was the difficulty of keeping count of those who had been saved. The survivors were all brought ashore at different points round the harbour, and those rescued by helicopter were landed at various assembly points. From all these points they were distributed to the various hospitals which had offered help. As a result the Belgian authorities found it very difficult to keep a proper tally of those rescued. Thus, in the long run, it became almost impossible to make an accurate record of those who had died, particularly as the ship had no passenger list.

The seven Royal Navy and 12 Belgium Navy divers were put onboard by helicopter as soon as possible, but they faced a very difficult task, working in pitch darkness and only able to find bodies by feeling for them with their hands. The ship was full of mud and sand and was lying on her side; the divers were only able to enter the partly flooded upper part of the ship as it was too dangerous to go further down. They were faced with pathetic spectacles. One diver found a little girl still clasping her doll, another found a couple grasped in each other's arms. Most of the bodies were unrecognisable as they were so covered in mud.

The divers were able to search the upper part of the ship in two days and recovered a large number of bodies, but they had seen many others on the lower decks. They were unable to recover them until the water and mud was pumped out of the ship, which could not be done until she was upright and afloat.

The salvage operation was to be a tremendous task and entailed driving wedges into the sea bed, to which would be attached wire hawsers running from the ship. These would be used to pull her upright while a crane attached to her port side would help in the lift. After a mishap which delayed work for two days, she was finally pulled upright and floated on an even keel. Even then she listed over again, but fortunately only a few degrees. She was then towed into the outer harbour at Zeebrugge on 7 April, almost exactly a month since the disaster.

Again the divers searched, and after two days they had recovered 111 bodies although they knew there must be some more on the lower decks which were still inaccessible. The salvage team reported that it would be some time before the mud and silt was pumped out, so again the divers' operations were suspended.

Soon after the disaster it was clear to all concerned that the bow doors to the car decks had not been closed when the ship left her berth, and that the flooding of the ship was caused by water entering the car decks. These decks have no longitudinal bulkheads, thus there was a mass of free water on the decks. At first it caused only a slight list to the port side but this increased until she went over to about 90° from the horizontal. In fact she was only prevented from turning turtle completely by a sandbank, because the ship suddenly veered to starboard and got out of the dredged channel.

The Court of Enquiry opened on 27 April in the Central Hall, Westminster, before Mr Justice Sheen, the Commissioner of Wrecks. On the first day the Counsel for the Ministry of Transport, Mr David Steel QC, spelt out the Government's case. He told the court that he would bring evidence to show that there were sloppy procedures onboard the ship 'which were not only dangerous, but were a reflection on the sloppy practices within the Townsend Thoresen management as a whole.' He went on to tell the court that the ship had capsized because no effort had been made to close the bow doors. 'It would be wrong', he said, 'to blame just one person, as operating instructions onboard the ship left ample room for error.' 'It was', he said, 'apparently the job of the Assistant Bosun, Mr Mark Stanley; however, a system had developed whereby the doors were often shut by somebody else. In fact Mr Stanley had told him that he often went to shut the doors only find them already shut'.

On this occasion the Assistant Bosun had been asked to carry out other duties and was eventually dismissed by his superior, the Bosun himself, so he went to his cabin, lay down on his bunk and went to sleep.

The Chief Officer, Mr Sabel, was on the car deck and it was his job to confirm

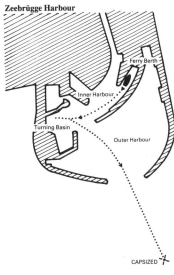

Zeebrügge Harbour

Ferry Berth

Inner Harbour

Turning Basin

Outer Harbour

CAPSIZED

Above:
One mile off Zeebrügge on 7 March 1987, the day after the tragedy, rescue work continues on the red-hulled Townsend Thoresen ferry *Herald of Free Enterprise*. Note the open bow doors. *Popperfoto*

that the doors were properly shut. It transpired, said Mr Steel, that it was NOT the custom to report the doors shut to the bridge, but only to report if they were open. The rule thus left the Captain with no idea as to whether the doors were open or shut.

Mr Steel then went on to deal with the entry of the water into the car deck. On this occasion the water in the ballast tank was not pumped out before the ship put to sea, thus she was bows heavy and this led to a tendency for her to bury her bows into the sea. Mr Steel added that Captain Lewry had written to Townsend Thoresen management six months before, pointing out this tendency, and previously two other Captains had written similar memos to the management, but the memos had not even been acknowledged and nothing had been done about it.

As regards the bow doors themselves, Mr Steel quite rightly made the point that it would be a simple matter to install a warning light on the bridge which would show the position of the doors, or closed circuit TV could be used. There was no hard and fast rules that the doors must be shut before the ship left her berth, and indeed there was plenty of time to close them whilst she was manoeuvring to turn round to face the exit from the harbour. Apparently, said Mr Steel, tests had shown that there was a critical speed of 15kt beyond which the ship raised a bow wave which would be high enough to come inboard if the bow doors were open, but if the ship was already down by the bows this speed might be lower.

On the second day of the Enquiry, Mr Anthony Clarke QC, Counsel for Townsend Thoresen, announced that the Company accepted the entire blame for the affair, partly due to management failure, and partly because of failures by its employees — the crew. It was a generous gesture and it was hoped it would shorten the proceedings (which it apparently did not). Mr Steel was forced to call all his witnesses to prove the remarks he made in his opening statement.

Yes, the Assistant Bosun had been asleep in his cabin. Yes, there were really no clear orders as to who was to close the doors, but it was generally accepted that it was the Assistant Bosun's job. Mr Sabel, the Chief Officer, told the court that it was his job to see that the doors were closed, but it was also in the standing orders that when Harbour Stations was ordered, his place of duty was on the bridge. In fact when this order was given over the Tannoy system, he went on to the bridge and omitted to see that the bow doors were closed, although he said he had ensured a man (whom he could not name) was standing by to close the doors.

Captain Lewry, in his evidence, admitted that, with afterthought, it was a dangerous practice not to have a positive assurance that the bow doors were shut. When told that the sistership to the *Herald* had once gone to sea for four hours with the bow doors open, he said that nobody had ever told him of it.

Mr Steel raised the question of memos regarding the bow doors sent by various Masters to the management, none of which seemed to have been answered, with one exception which turned down the request that warning lights should be fitted on the bridge. Mr Steel then asked a Director of the Company if anybody had approached the management on the question of warning lights. The Director replied that nobody had. Mr Steel then produced a memo from one of the Masters actually requesting a system of warning lights. The Director had to admit that he had lied, but said he did not know why he had done so.

The Enquiry lasted seven weeks and on conclusion Mr Justice Sheen said that it would be several weeks before the Court could issue its report. Counsel for the Ministry of Transport said that it was not the intention of the Department of Transport to prosecute in this case, but that the Enquiry might find that the ferry's owners and masters should face criminal charges.

The final two days of the Enquiry were devoted to speeches by Counsel. The Counsel for the Ministry urged that early action should be taken to improve the safety standards in ferries. The Counsel for the passengers gave a list of 10 points which he asked the Court to consider. They mostly dealt with the safety of passengers onboard and included such things as the provision of first aid lockers, ladders, axes, torches, portable lifting gear, better emergency lighting, provision of gaps in glass partitions, detailed guidelines issued to each passenger and simpler lifejackets. He also wanted immediate action.

Finally, it was stated that in all 188 persons lost their lives in the disaster.

So ended this sorry episode in Britain's maritime history. An episode which could so easily have been avoided with only the minimum of obvious safety precautions and regulations, which, above all, would not allow car ferries even to leave its berth in harbour with a wide gaping hole in the bows through which the sea could so easily enter.

15

Queen Mary *and* *HMS* Curacoa

On 2 October 1942 the cruiser *Curacoa* and the liner *Queen Mary*, then employed as a trooper, were in collision with the result that the *Curacoa* sank. Although the collision took place during the war, enemy action had no part in it, hence it is included here.

The *Queen Mary* and the *Queen Elizabeth* were both very large ships of over 80,000 tons. By ripping out most of the luxurious accommodation, these monster ships could carry some 10,000 servicemen, sleeping in bunks in relays. They were thus used during the war as fast troop carriers and travelled unescorted to and fro across the Atlantic, except when nearing the British Isles where German U-boats were concentrated and they were in range of German long range bombers. Their route across the Atlantic was the great circle route from America to just south of Iceland, then south down the west coast of Scotland to the Clyde. An escort was provided from north of Ireland to the Clyde.

On the occasion of the collision the *Queen Mary*, using her maximum possible speed (28.5kt), was to meet her escort off Northern Ireland. The escort consisted of HMS *Curacoa* (4,200 tons), an escort close range anti-aircraft cruiser and a flotilla of destroyers.

At 09.00 on 2 October *Curacoa* sighted the grey funnels of the *Queen Mary*, low on the horizon and approaching from the west; her Captain, Capt Wilfred Boutwood, signalled his destroyers to take up a bent line screen ahead of her. He himself decided to take up station about five miles ahead of the *Queen Mary* inside the destroyer screen.

Capt Boutwood was a most experienced Captain and had carried out the escort duty for both the *Queen Mary* and the *Queen Elizabeth* many times before. Ideally, in order to defend the *Mary* from air attack, he should have been reasonably close astern of her, but she was making 28.5kt and his maximum speed was only 25kt so, to prolong the time he spent with her, he thought it better to start ahead and gradually drop astern. All ships were in station by about 10.30 and at this time Boutwood sent a signal to Capt Illingworth, the Captain of the *Queen Mary*, which read: 'What is your present course and speed please?' Illingworth replied: 'Mean course 108 degrees, am zigzagging, speed 26.5 knots.' Illingworth had reduced speed by 2kt to assist the destroyers to keep up. In fact the mean course was 106° — the *Mary's* gyro compass was 2° high.

The number of the zigzag was not given, but Boutwood had met Illingworth ashore in the Clyde and the latter had told him that he always used zigzag No 8 as it was the most suitable for large ships. Even so, Boutwood did not know which leg of the zigzag the *Mary* was on. No 8 zigzag was as follows: Starting at the base course of 106°, it consisted of four minutes on 106°, eight minutes on 081°, eight minutes on 131°, back to the base course for four minutes, then to 131° for eight minutes, then to 081° for eight minutes, and finally back to 106°, the base course.

After that the whole cycle was repeated.

It will be seen that not knowing which leg of the zigzag the *Mary* was on presented difficulties for Boutwood. His AA cruiser did not have very long range armament and he could best afford protection by keeping close to the *Mary*. It was not easy to observe the *Mary's* course and he was never sure which leg of the zigzag she was on. For example, if she was approaching turn 4 she would be altering 25° to port. On the other hand, if she was approaching turn 7 she would be altering 25° to starboard. As he was not yet astern of the *Mary* he might be in trouble if he had made a mistake about which leg she was on. In addition he had no excess of speed to get out of the way.

At 12.30 he made another signal to the *Mary*: 'I am doing my best speed 25 knots on course 108 degrees. When you are ahead of me I will edge in astern of you.' Shortly after 13.00 he realised that he was too far to the south so he altered to 105° to try and close the *Mary*, but seeing that this did not take him close enough he altered again to 100°. Not long after that, as he had altered sufficiently, he altered to the mean course which he still thought was 108°, but in fact was 106°. He then saw that he was at last inside the liner's zigzag pattern, as on her next starboard leg she crossed his track astern of him.

The time was then about 13.30 and the *Mary* was on the starboard leg of the zigzag steering 131°, but at 13.32 she was due to alter course to 081°, 50° to port. Only two minutes before the *Mary* had passed astern of the *Curacoa*, and the latter was now on the *Mary's* port side. However, the Officer of the Watch in the *Mary* obeyed the zigzag instructions and ordered her wheel to be put to port and the ship started swinging to port, whilst the bearing of the cruiser grew ahead.

The OOW onboard the *Mary* was Senior First Officer Robinson, so let us now look at the situation from his point of view. He knew that the *Curacoa* was now on his port side, but he saw no reason why he should not alter towards her as she could easily get out of the way. As the *Mary* started to swing, Junior First Officer Wright came on to the bridge to relieve Robinson for lunch. Robinson told Wright what he was doing, but on looking again he saw that the two ships had got much closer and the *Curacoa* was not apparently getting out of the way as he expected. He ordered the quartermaster to check the swing and to steady on a course of 101° instead of the new correct course of 081°. The *Curacoa* was then on the *Mary's* port bow about four cables distant. He then asked Wright if he had got the ship and went below to his lunch.

Wright, after a bit, decided that he would try and get on to the prescribed course of 081° and ordered 'Port-a-little'. He then changed his mind and steadied the ship up on 086°. However, not liking the situation at all, he ordered 'Hard-a-Starboard'. The Captain, hearing the order, came out of the chartroom and asked what was the matter. Wright told him they were getting too close to the cruiser. The Captain studied the situation and then said 'No, that's alright. Put your helm amidships and come back on the port leg of the zigzag'. Having lost a bit of headway by Wright's manoeuvres, this was a safe move and the *Mary* then steadied up on her correct course of 081°, passing close astern of the *Curacoa*. The Captain then turned to Wright and said 'You needn't worry about that fellow, they know all about escorting, he will keep out of your way'. Two minutes later Wright altered course again, in accordance with the zigzag plan, to the mean

Top:
The *Queen Mary* was a troopship in World War 2 and was repainted in camouflage
colours. *Real Photos (S1567)*

Above:
The cruiser HMS *Coventry*, sister ship of HMS *Curacoa*, seen at Portsmouth in 1930.
Real Photos (S1160)

course of 106°. *Curacoa* was still ahead and to starboard and almost on an exactly parallel course.

The time was 13.40. The next alteration of the zigzag was at 13.44 and was to port, which opened the distance from the *Curacoa*. Then at 13.52, in accordance with the zigzag plan, the *Mary* altered 50° to starboard, from 081° to 131°, and was once more approaching the *Curacoa*, which, one would have thought, having had one near collision, might by this time have got well out of the way.

At 14.00 the plan required another alteration to port back to the mean course of 106°, and this was duly carried out. At 14.04 the plan showed another to starboard of 25° degrees to 131°. *Curacoa* was then about 45° on the *Mary's* starboard bow. At that moment Robinson returned to the bridge to take over the watch again after his lunch. Wright gave the order to alter to 131°, but made no mention of *Curacoa's* close proximity, but he did tell Robinson about the Captain's remarks that she would always keep clear of them. He saw the Captain before he went off watch but did not mention it to him either. The ship steadied on 131°.

Robinson took one look at the *Curacoa* and decided that she was too close. Deciding to forget the zigzag for a bit, he ordered the quartermaster 'Port-a-little' in order to open the distance. He quite thought the cruiser would also open the distance by turning to starboard. Very shortly afterwards he had another look and saw that she had not done so and was dangerously close, so he ordered 'Hard-a-port'. It was too late and the giant bows of the *Mary* caught the *Curacoa* about a third of her length from aft and sliced her clean in two. The *Curacoa* was hit on her port side as she was crossing the *Mary's* track from starboard to port. Some observers thought that at the last moment the *Curacoa* had altered course to port, but this may have been caused by the interaction of two ships very close together.

The effect of a monster ship at 26.5kt hitting a small ship of 4,000 tons has to be seen to be believed. The *Mary's* bows went straight through her like a knife. She was slewed right round and pushed under the water. When the *Mary* had passed, the two sections of the cruiser was still afloat but obviously sinking. On the *Mary's* port side was the forward section and on her other side was the stern section, end up and sinking fast. The forward section was heeled over but righting itself slowly. Boats and debris were everywhere and men could be seen jumping off both sections.

Onboard the *Mary* there was a bump and Capt Illingworth rushed out of the chartroom and asked if it was a bomb. 'No Sir' replied the quartermaster, 'we hit the cruiser'. Illingworth sent for the carpenter and together they inspected the damage. Speed was reduced to 10kt, but the great ship did not stop to rescue survivors because of the danger from German U-boats. However, Illingworth did signal one of the destroyers, HMS *Bulldog*, as follows: 'It would appear that *Curacoa* attempted to cross my bows when collision occurred. Am reducing speed to 10kt to ascertain extent of damage and have ceased zigzag. Will keep you informed.' *Bulldog* and other destroyers proceeded to pick up survivors.

The damage to the *Mary* was extensive. The stem was crushed in and the plates buckled round the bow, almost closing the hole, which was on the waterline. A collision mat was rigged across the bows and speed was increased to 13kt. Later Illingworth signalled to *Bulldog*: 'After consideration I can only conclude

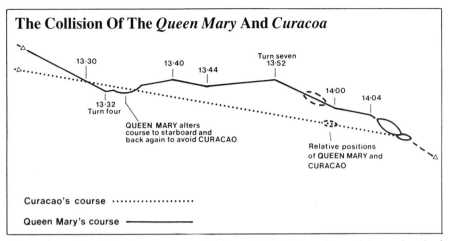

The Collision Of The *Queen Mary* And *Curacoa*

13·30

13·40

13·44

Turn seven
13·52

14·00

14·04

13·32
Turn four

QUEEN MARY alters
course to starboard and
back again to avoid CURACAO

Relative positions
of QUEEN MARY and
CURACAO

Curacao's course ·····················

Queen Mary's course ──────────

Curacoa put her helm the wrong way'. Meanwhile both sections of the cruiser had sunk, one after the other.

Over 300 officers and men, the greater part of the crew, were lost in the *Curacoa*, including all the officers on the bridge with the exception of Capt Boutwood, who became a key witness at the subsequent enquiries.

The official enquiry was not held until June 1945. It was presided over by Mr Justice Pilcher, with two Trinity House Masters as assessors. The object of the enquiry was to apportion blame. If any of the blame fell on the *Queen Mary*, her owners, Cunard, would have to pay compensation for all those who had lost their lives. If the *Mary* was held to be blameless, the relatives of the dead men would only receive naval widows' pensions and any other compensation ordered by the Admiralty.

Cunard's case was that it was standard practice for warships escorting merchantmen to keep out of the way and that therefore the *Queen Mary's* crew were entitled to expect *Curacoa* to keep clear.

It should be remarked that Illingworth could only assume that Boutwood knew that zigzag No 8 would be in use because no signal had been made to inform him. It was not well brought out at the enquiry that it is standard practice in the Royal Navy that when a ship joins other ships zigzagging, the senior officer of such ships signals the number of the zigzag in use to the joining ship, and to indicate what leg of the zigzag he is on. This is easily done as the zigzag turns are all numbered and all that it would be necessary to say would be 'Zigzag No ... in use. At present we are between positions No ... and No ... . Mean course is ...'. Captain Boutwood had to ask for the mean course (and speed) and he was never given the number of the zigzag or which leg the *Mary* was on, but perhaps Illingworth thought that his much earlier conversation with Boutwood was sufficient. However, unless Boutwood was dead astern of the *Mary* he would have found it very difficult to predict the *Mary's* alterations of course. Capt Illingworth could have been blamed for not signalling all the details of the zigzag, and Capt Boutwood could have been blamed for not asking for them.

The enquiry got somewhat complicated by the introduction of the Rule of the Road as regards the overtaking ship. The *Mary* could have been deemed as an overtaking ship and should have given way. Under the circumstances she could not really be regarded as an overtaking ship and the intitial enquiry thought so too, but the subsequent enquiry took a different view.

Capt Boutwood was put into the witness box, but he did not add much to what was already known. He did say that the *Mary* was not steering a very steady course. Talking of the last minute or so immediately before the collision, he said that he did give an order of 'Starboard 15' when he thought the liner was getting too close and at the same time took control of the ship. He could not remember what subsequent steering orders he gave, but he asserted that he made every effort to save his ship. After the collision he quickly realised that there was no hope of saving the ship and he told all the officers who were on the bridge with him to go below, collect what ratings they could find, and get the life saving equipment ready. He did not himself give the order to abandon ship, but he heard somebody else give it and he fully agreed with it. He then found himself standing somewhere on the fore part of the ship until she finally dipped, 'and I dipped with her'.

Asked what happened after the 'Starboard 15' order was given, he said: 'Not very long before the collision I am strongly of the opinion that I put my wheel amidships and possibly reversed it in order to check my swing. I am absolutely certain that just before the impact I had in mind the possibility of averting disaster by going hard-a-port in order to swing myself clear, but it was quite out of the question in the time available'. He mentioned that, throughout, the *Mary* was not carrying out zigzag No 8. He went on to say that he never thought of asking her what zigzag she was doing.

The question of interaction of two ships in close proximity was raised and tests were carried out in the National Physics Laboratory. The assumption was that the large volume of water pushed aside by the *Mary's* bows had swung the *Curacoa* stern to starboard and her bows to port. The experts differed on the matter and thought that only a little opposite helm would overcome any ship interaction. The point was left open by the Court, but nowadays a great deal more is known about the interaction of two ships very close together, and it would appear that this might well have been the case.

Mr Justice Pilcher gave judgement as follows: He concluded that after 13.40 the *Mary* carried on with her zigzag normally, using zigzag plan No 8, and that Capt Boutwood's assumption that she was not using the plan was incorrect.

He thought that the forces of interaction had played a part in swinging the *Curacoa* in front of the *Mary* at the last moment. In his opinion the cruiser had complete liberty of action and it was clearly her duty to keep out of the way of the much larger liner. He criticised the look-out kept by the *Curacoa* and the fact that she did not ask what zigzag was being carried out. He ended: 'I find the liner free from blame and the collision was solely due to the negligence of the cruiser'. This was a verdict with which most mariners would agree.

However, the Admiralty at once appealed, but the appeal was not heard until nearly two years later. The appeal was heard in the Supreme Court of Judication before Lord Justices Scott, Bucknell and Wrottesley, assisted by Rear-Adm Hamilton and Capt Townshend RNR as assessors. The Justices disagreed on a number of points.

Lord Justice Scott thought that in the special circumstances of an operation involving a naval and a merchant ship, the normal rule of the road regarding the overtaking ship could not apply and that when a risk of collision became imminent, as in this case, the *Mary* became the 'stand on' ship and the *Curacoa* the 'give way' ship. He pointed out that the *Curacoa* was a far more manoeuvrable ship than the *Mary*. He went on to say that *Curacoa's* contention that the *Mary* abandoned zigzag No 8 showed that *Curacoa* was not watching her as closely as she should have done and in fact the zigzag was not abandoned. 'It was', he said, 'Captain Boutwood's failure to realise that at 14.06 the *Mary* had just altered to starboard which was the real cause of the collision. For all that', he went on, 'the *Mary* had supplied very little information regarding the zigzag, and it would have been sensible to have given one blast on the siren when she put the wheel over to starboard; at least it would have woken up the *Curacoa's* officer of the watch.'

Lord Scott said he had a momentary doubt as to whether the *Mary* had left it too late before taking any avoiding action, but in the end he considered that she had not and that Robinson's action was entirely consistent with good seamanship. Lord Scott ended by saying 'I have said nothing about the question of interaction, on which so much time was spent in the lower court, because I am satisfied that it had nothing to do with causing the collision.'

Lord Bucknell disagreed with a number of points. Whilst he agreed that it was only prudent for the *Curacoa* to keep out of the way of the much larger ship, he did not think that in itself was sufficient to release the *Mary* from all obligations to obey the overtaking rule, unless there was either a rule, a recognised procedure, or a definite understanding between the two Captains. He agreed that even if the *Mary* was the 'stand on' vessel, she should take avoiding action if collision appeared imminent, but she took such action too late and he attributed much of the blame for this to Capt Illingworth's remarks to Wright that the *Curacoa* would keep out of the way. He thought that the forces of interaction did come into play at the last moment and that the *Curacoa's* stern was pushed to starboard by the force of the water from the *Mary's* bows. He ended by saying: 'In my view the blame should be apportioned as follows — two thirds to the *Curacoa* and one third to the *Queen Mary*.

Lord Wrottesley agreed with Lord Bucknell and the verdict was carried as proposed by Lord Bucknell, two to one. However, this was still not the end of the matter and both parties appealed to the House of Lords. The appeal was not heard until February 1949 and Their Lordships upheld the verdict of the Appeal Court. Thus, after six years, Cunard still had to pay compensation for the loss of expectation of life to the next of kin of more than 300 officers and men lost in the collision.

The verdict was not well received by the Merchant Navy as a whole and indeed by many naval officers, who felt that the *Curacoa* was largely to blame. The whole case was well summed up by the *Merchant Navy Journal* which said:

'Those on the bridge of the *Queen Mary* at the time of the collision will perhaps find some consolation in the thought that it has taken the efforts of the best brains engaged in the practice of administration of Admiralty Law just about as many weeks as they had seconds in which to decide what was the correct action to be taken in the circumstances.'

16

Egypt *and* Seine

The *Egypt* and *Seine* collision occurred in May 1922 and once again was due to fog, but it gained a great deal of notoriety because of the alleged bad behaviour of the *Egypt*'s Asian crew.

The *Egypt* was a P&O liner, commanded by British officers but with a largely Asian crew, mainly Lascars. These were divided into two groups: the deck hands worked under a Serang, one of their own tribe, who was responsible for their behaviour and discipline. He was roughly equivalent to the Boatswain (Bosun) and he was assisted by Tindals, equivalent to Leading Seamen. Below decks, the engine room and firemen staff were also Asians and they too had their own Serang.

The P&O officers were a very highly trained body of men, almost as disciplined as Royal Navy officers. P&O took great trouble to ensure that it got only the highest grade of men and recruited them from the training ship HMS *Worcester*. Their morale was high and they tended to regard themselves as somewhat above other Merchant Navy officers.

Egypt was on the Indian run, but she was an old ship having been launched at Greenock in 1897. At 300ft long she displaced only 7,941 tons, her reciprocating engines giving her a cruising speed of 15kt and a full speed of 18kt. She had served in World War 1 as a hospital ship and after the war had been refitted and turned back into a liner by Bombay Dockyard. She was capable of carrying 301 first class passengers and 208 second class, plus a large crew of 293, of which some 85 were European and the remainder Asian.

Under the command of Capt Collyer, who had commanded many P&O ships since 1909, she sailed from the Thames on 19 May 1922 carrying only 44 passengers, which could hardly have been very profitable. However, in addition to the passengers she had secretly embarked a very valuable cargo of gold bars and boxes of gold sovereigns, worth over £1 million.

In the light of what happened, it is necessary to describe in some detail the situation as regards boats onboard. She had 16 boats capable of holding 380 persons, enough for all the passengers if she was full, but not enough for the crew as well; she probably carried life rafts in addition. The P&O company's regulations stated that the boats were to be secured outboard at sea whenever possible, but otherwise they should be stowed either inboard or outboard at the Captain's discretion. The boats were hoisted at davits and these could be turned back so that the boats were just above the deck, or they could remain turned out so that the boats were ready for lowering. The outboard position was the safer in an emergency as it took some time to wind the davits out. When the boats were turned out it meant securing them to a spar, running between the davits, to prevent them swinging about when the ship was rolling.

When the *Egypt* sailed she had four of her boats turned out because bad weather was expected in the Bay of Biscay; two were on the starboard side and two on the port. P&O also laid down that the crew were to be exercised at fire and boat stations once a week and it was Board of Trade regulations (after the *Titanic* disaster) that the passengers should go to boat stations once a week, the first time being as soon as possible after the ship sailed. The collision occurred in the evening of 20 May and the ship had sailed on 19 May. Thus there had been one clear working day on which boat stations could have been exercised, but no boat drill was carried out.

The voyage went well at first and by 02.00 the *Egypt* was well on her way down Channel, but at that time she ran into some fog patches and 'stand by' was rung down to the engine room. The Captain was called and stayed on the bridge for the remainder of the night. In the afternoon of 20 May the weather had cleared sufficiently for the navigator to take a fix from land marks on the northern French coast and at 17.30 course was altered to a more southerly direction for Ushant.

At 16.00 Second Officer Cameron had come on watch and he had Third Officer Brown to assist him. The visibility was patchy, but in a clear spell at about 18.45, Cameron went below for his evening meal, leaving Brown in charge. Almost immediately the fog came down again, but this time much thicker. Brown rang down to the engine room to 'stand by' and the Captain, hearing this, came up on to the bridge. As he arrived, both he and Brown heard a fog whistle just forward of the port beam. Collyer stopped the ship. Two minutes later they heard it again, but much louder, so Collyer ordered a prolonged blast on the siren. No sooner had it died away than both he and Brown saw a white bow wave of a ship approaching them at some speed and they could just make out the shape of the ship behind it. The Captain ordered 'hard-a-port', thus swinging his bow to starboard, hoping to make the now inevitable collision more of a glancing blow, but the ship struck them between the two forward boats on the port side. It was a very heavy blow and it threw the *Egypt* over to starboard as the unknown ship's bows tore into the port side. The ship was in fact the *Seine*, a French ship, and she had specially strengthened bows for pushing through ice. It was these which ploughed into the *Egypt* with tremendous force, buckling everything in its path and with sparks flying in all directions.

The shock was clearly felt in the engine room and the Asian firemen and trimmers came pouring out, shouting and screaming. The Engineer Officer of the Watch did his best to push them back and in fact did stem the rush for a minute or so, but the moment he turned away from them to obey the telegraph, they rushed out again shouting that the sea was coming in. The OOW went to look and saw that indeed it was and had already reached a position between the boilers. The engine and boiler rooms were evacuated.

In the saloon, dinner was about to be served when the ship careered over to starboard then immediately careered back and took up a heavy list to port, due to the weight of water that was entering. Capt Douglas Carr, of the Prince of Wales Own Rajputana Infantry, who was destined to play a further role in the drama, rushed out on deck and saw the *Seine* drifting away in the fog with badly damaged bows. Realising the the *Egypt* must be doomed, he rushed down to his cabin, changed into something warmer, put on an overcoat, stuffed his revolver into a pocket and rushed up on deck again.

Chief Officer Cartwright and the Bosun were looking over the side to try and

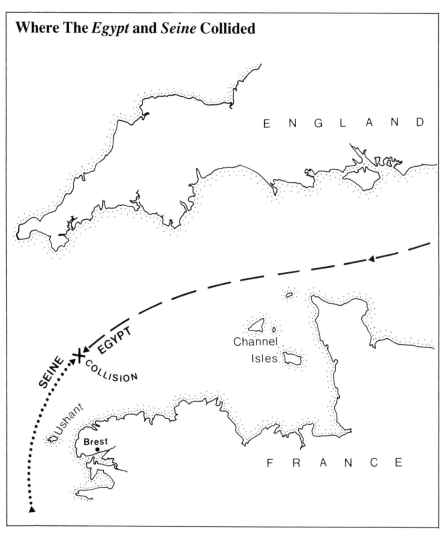

Where The *Egypt* and *Seine* Collided

ENGLAND

Channel
Isles

SEINE

EGYPT

COLLISION

Ushant

Brest

FRANCE

estimate the size of the hole. They could see little but they observed coal floating out of the hole, so they knew that a coal bunker must have been penetrated. Cartwright told the Bosun to close what watertight doors he could and then to go to his boat station, and he himself went off to report to the Captain. At that moment the siren gave four blasts, the signal for boat stations, but the steam ran out before the signal could be repeated.

Capt Collyer ordered the wireless operator to transmit an SOS signal and Brown was sent away to work out the position. Before he could do so, the SOS was transmitted with the noon position on it. It was picked up by two ships, the Royal Mail liner *Andes* and a ship called the *Cahiracon*, but neither was able to reach the *Egypt* before she sank. A few minutes later the SOS was repeated with the correct position on it, but it made no difference to later events.

138

By this time the Asians on deck had been joined by many others. They all appeared to be in complete disorder, some throwing themselves over the side, but most of them went to the boats on the starboard side as it was the high side and further from the water. Second Officer Cameron went first to his own boat on the starboard side but, seeing that it would be impossible to launch it because of the ever-increasing list, he went to one of the boats which was already turned out and was loaded with Asians even though it was still at the davit head. He told them to get out and, with the help of a Lascar who had not panicked, he managed to lower the boat to the level of the deck. Other officers succeeded in getting some of the Asians out of the starboard boats and over to the port side where the boats were being lowered quite easily. The starboard side boat full of Asians continued to be lowered but got caught on the accommodation ladder and could not be lowered further. Cameron then went to the port side and there found Chief Officer Cartwright pulling Asians out of one of the boats. He told Cameron to take the boat when it was clear, pick up a few of the crew and go round to the after well deck, which was nearly awash, and take off the women and children. Cameron seized some of the crew, among them the Serang; which was unfortunate as the Serang was the only person who could instill some order into the Asians. The boat was hurriedly lowered as the ship was listing more than ever and it was feared she might capsize on top of the few boats on the port side. Cameron's boat pulled away, but he could not get it alongside the after well deck, apparently because the crew had not the strength to pull the oars correctly, so he went off in search of the *Seine* which could still be heard whistling. The passengers who had been mustered on the well deck were left with the water already up to their knees.

Meanwhile, the other boat on the port side which was already turned out was lowered with little difficulty, but it was sent away with only very few passengers in it. As things got worse and the list even greater, confusion turned to panic. The passengers had very little idea of what was going on and to them it appeared that what boats were available were being filled with Asians. They could see the officers trying to get the men out of the boats, but the second their backs were turned, the Lascars kept crowding back. People were throwing anything that could float overboard and jumping in after them, hoping to cling to them. Although it was May the water was bitterly cold. The boats' falls kept jamming and often the boats were crowded with Asians.

It was then that Capt Carr started to take a hand. He told one of the officers, French, that he had seen four boats pull away from the ship full of members of the crew (and not only Asians) but no passengers. French told him that it was impossible to hold them back and Carr then told him that he would shoot them. French reasoned with him and persuaded Carr to hand him his revolver. French waved it in the air and this produced some effect among the Asians to make room for some of the passengers, but it was short lived and the Asians jumped back into the boat again. Carr pointed out that sterner measures were necessary, so French gave him back his revolver and told him to enter a boat together with a European quartermaster in order to take charge of it.

French then walked forward and met another crowd of Asians who obviously intended to rush the boat. He bravely attacked them and managed to clear them away. On his way forward he met a nun, Sister Rhoda, praying on the deck. He offered to help her find a place in one of the boats, but she refused, saying that she was in God's hands. She was drowned a few minutes later.

Other Asians had arrived and started sliding down the lifelines into the already overcrowded boats. Carr decided that he must stop this fresh inrush so he produced his revolver and fired a shot into the air to frighten them. Unfortunately the bullet struck an Asian scrambling down a lifeline. It wounded him and he lost his grip and fell into the boat, alive but very shaken. Carr then fired another shot into the air, but this hit another Asian sliding down a lifeline. He, too, was wounded but managed to climb back onboard the ship. However, a few minutes later he grabbed a lifeline again and slid down it into a boat. It seems odd that an experienced Army officer intending to fire only into the air should so have misjudged his aim as to wound two Asians, one after the other.

The ship was now sinking fast and nothing could induce the Asians in the boats to come back alongside to embark the passengers. It appeared that they were frightened that the ship would capsize on top of them, as they were forced to use the port side because the other side was too high out of the water. Third Officer Brown was trying to induce the remaining passengers to slide down the lifelines into the water and eventually had to push them overboard when they refused.

Twenty minutes after the collision the ship started sinking by the stern and everybody who could do so jumped into the water. Capt Collyer was the last to leave and he walked along the starboard side, which was now horizontal, until he reached the bilge keel when he had to jump into the sea. In falling he struck his head and injured his knee, but one of the boats rescued him and he at once took charge although he was in great pain.

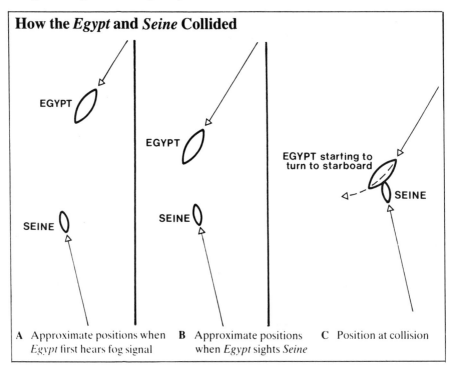

How the *Egypt* and *Seine* Collided

A Approximate positions when *Egypt* first hears fog signal **B** Approximate positions when *Egypt* sights *Seine* **C** Position at collision

Some boats on the starboard side had been cut loose by the Chief Officer, helped by French and another officer. They floated clear as the ship sank and some members of the crew scrambled into them and started picking up passengers in the water.

Cameron's boat had been unable to find the *Seine* and came back again. The Chief Officer was picked up by her together with some others. Cameron then went off again to look for the *Seine* and eventually found her stopped in the water. Cameron climbed onboard and went up to the bridge where he found the Captain making no effort to do anything and with the wheel unmanned. Cameron put one of the *Egypt's* quartermasters at the wheel and himself rang down slow ahead to set off to rescue as many people as he could. The *Seine's* bows were in a terrible mess but she was capable of steaming. Cameron stopped her in the middle of a crowd of people in the water and she lowered some boats and succeeded in rescuing quite a number of persons, most of them clinging to spars and bits of wood, but they told of many others who had succumbed to the cold and slipped away.

Eventually the search had to be called off. Out of 338 persons onboard the *Egypt*, 252 were rescued which, considering the confusion and the panic was a very good proportion. All the deck officers were saved and so were eight of the European engine room staff and 35 of the catering staff including three of the five stewardesses onboard. Of the Asian staff, 36 of the deck staff, 63 of the engine room and 60 of the catering staff were saved. The valuable cargo of gold bars and sovereigns went down with the ship, but they were later salvaged.

A Board of Trade Enquiry into the loss was held two months later and lasted 10 days. The *Seine* and her owners, not being British, were not required to attend and sent nobody at all. It was a straightforward enquiry but it ended in an argument as to the behaviour of the Asian staff which was bedevilled by a Trade Union official, Mr Joseph Cotter, who appeared for the Amalgamated Marine Workers Union. He was determined to throw all the blame on the Asians and in this he was fully supported by the press, which came out with wild stories about their cowardly behaviour, much of which was nonsense. The ship's officers on the other hand tended to support their Asians.

Capt Collyer, who had still not fully recovered from his injuries, was allowed to sit to give his evidence. He admitted that the passengers had received no instructions as what to do in the event of it being necessary to abandon the ship, but pointed out that they had only one full day onboard. They should have been given their boat allocations by the Purser, but this, too, had not been done. No boat drill had been carried out in the short time available.

Mr Cotter rose to ask him, 'In the case of an accident and the necessity to save human lives would you rather have a British or a Lascar crew?' Capt Collyer replied 'Even if the crew had been entirely white the accident and the loss of life would have been the same. Most of the loss of life could be put down to the abnormal list of the ship.' Cotter asked him again 'But a British crew is not built of the same kind of stuff as are Lascars? Is not the British seaman built of sterner stuff?' Collyer replied, 'I do not know. I have been in accidents before, when I have had a white crew, and there is not much to choose between a Lascar crew, if they are properly led, and a white one.' However, the passengers all testified to the panic of the Asian crew and the comparative calmness of the white crew and their officers. Capt Carr, the gallant Army officer, was then called and was asked whether his revolver made more impression on the Asians than the language he used, in both English and Hindustani. He replied 'Most certainly'. His wounding of the two Asians clambering down the lifelines was glossed over by the court as an unfortunate mistake.

The arguments went on between the officers of the *Egypt* and the Board of Trade for some time, with Mr Cotter putting his oar in occasionally. The officers loyally supported their Asian crew and Mr Cotter got nowhere. In spite of this, the public and the press were convinced that the Asians had behaved very badly. The only thing that did emerge clearly was that the collision was so sudden and did so much damage that the normal rules for abandoning ship could not be followed: it was practically a case of every man for himself. The *Egypt* sank only 20min after the actual collision, and most of the starboard boats were out of action because of the list.

The Commissioner of Wrecks, Butler Aspinall, summed up at length. The main points he made were:

(a) If the starboard boats could not be lowered because of the list to port, there should have been more hands to help in lowering the port boats.
(b) Some of the non-European crew were seized with panic.
(c) If the boats had been properly handled, many others might have been saved.
(d) *Egypt*'s speed at the moment of collision was 12.5kt — not excessive in a patchy fog.
(e) The behaviour of the non-European crew left something to be desired, but this was largely due to the absence of the Serang (who had been taken off in Cameron's boat).
(f) The court found it 'difficult to understand' why it was that Mr Cameron's boat had been unable to get alongside the *Egypt*. Had it done so, it might have been the means of saving many more lives.

Finally, the court suspended Capt Collyer's Certificate of Competency for six months and severely reprimanded Chief Officer Cartwright.

There was quite a public uproar at the court's findings and a considerable amount of correspondence in the press. Most people supported Capt Collyer and the Chief Officer, and the general opinion was that the censure on these two officers was too harsh. Adm Francis Noel, in a letter to the *Morning Post*, wrote: 'Captain Collyer deserves, and will receive much sympathy. There was no personal failure on his part; on the contrary, when suddenly confronted with disaster, he acted up to the best tradition of English seamanship.'

However, in spite of all the support he got, Capt Collyer was prematurely retired on full pension. Chief Officer Cartwright was later promoted and got a command. The other officers, with the exception of Cameron, continued with the P&O company for the rest of their careers.

As to the collision itself, the *Seine* seems to have got away without censure, but it appears that had she stopped engines at the same time as the *Egypt* did, it is possible that the collision might never have taken place. As it was, she seemed to be proceeding at a considerable speed when she struck the *Egypt*.

142

Torrey Canyon

This is the story of the *Torrey Canyon*, a supertanker which ran aground in the Scilly Isles in March 1967 and spilt all her oil, causing colossal pollution.

The *Torrey Canyon* was 974ft long which meant she was one of the largest ships in the world in 1967. She was powered by two steam turbines of 25,290hp driving a single propeller, giving her a cruising speed of 16kt. She had started life at only 810ft long, but was 'jumbo-ed' in Japan by Sasebo Heavy Industries which built an entirely new midship section and bow. The ship was then cut in two, leaving the after end to be joined on to the new midship section and bows while the upperworks and bridge were transferred from the old ship to the new. 'Jumbo-ing' of smaller tankers had become quite common with the advent of even larger tankers in the 1960s.

The rebuilt *Torrey Canyon* was able to carry 117,000 tonnes of oil, nearly double her original capacity of 67,000 tonnes. The property of a US company incorporated in Liberia and nominally doing business in Bermuda, she was under a long term 'time charter' to Union Oil, manned by an Italian crew and flying the Liberian flag. At the time of the accident she was on charter to BP for a single voyage from the Persian Gulf to Milford Haven in Wales.

Her Captain was Pastrengo Rugiati, an experienced tanker skipper who had been in command of tankers since 1947. Born in the island of Elba, he was educated at the Merchant Navy Academy in Leghorn. He took command of the *Torrey Canyon* on 22 March 1966.

On 17 March 1967 the *Torrey Canyon* was approaching the Scilly Isles from the South. Before turning in, Capt Rugiati left instructions that he was to be called at 06.00 when he expected that the Scilly Isles would be showing on his radar off the starboard bow. He had set a course of 018° to pass some five miles to the west of the Scillies, which themselves are some 25 miles west of Land's End. He had checked his position at noon that day and found that it agreed with the dead reckoning. The ship was on the autopilot.

The Chief Officer, who was keeping the morning watch, telephoned Rugiati at 06.00 on 18 March and told him that the radar had not yet picked up the Scillies. Three-quarters of an hour later he telephoned the Captain again and told him that the radar had now picked up the Scillies, but that they were on the port bow instead of the starboard, and that he had altered course 12° to port which put the Bishop's Rock (at the southern tip of St Mary's island) right ahead. He obviously expected that the Captain would be up shortly and could then make up his mind as to which side of the Scillies he would pass. Rugiati asked if by holding the course of 018° would the ship pass to the eastward of the Scillies. When the Chief Officer said that it would, Rugiati told him to go back to 018°.

Some time previously, Rugiati had received a radio signal from the BP agent at

Milford Haven telling him that if he did not manage to catch the high tide at 23.00 on the night of 18th he would be unable to enter harbour to discharge his cargo for five days as, owing to his deep draught, the neap tides would not reach a sufficient height until then. This worried Rugiati. Although Milford Haven was only about 150 miles distant, he had to do some adjusting of his cargo to lighten his draught amidships even to go into harbour on the next high tide at 23.00. Tankers tend to sag in the middle when they are fully laden and he had to transfer some oil from the midships tanks to the tanks forward and aft. The process takes about five hours and has to be done in calm waters or the rolling of the ship might cause a spillage. The Chief Officer afterwards asserted that the sea was calm enough to do it whilst on passage to Milford Haven, but Rugiati was adamant. This meant that the ship must arrive in Milford Haven at 18.00 at the latest if she was to enter harbour on the tide. The time was then about 07.30 and to cover 150 miles at 16kt would take the ship 9½ hours. Rugiati therefore calculated that if no time was wasted he would arrive about 17.00.

He felt that it was imperative to catch the tide as Union Oil would not take kindly to him wasting five days at anchor off Milford Haven. There were also other considerations. A small change of members of the crew was to take place on arrival : the relief crew had already arrived in Milford Haven and they would have to stay there (doubtless in expensive hotels) for five days. Furthermore, the men about to be relieved were going on leave and he did not want them to be delayed.

From where he was the most direct route to Milford Haven was to pass east of the Scillies. The course of 018° would suffice but it did pass rather close to the Seven Stones Reef which, since it was near high water at the time, was covered. At the subsequent enquiry Rugiati stated that he changed his mind and decided to pass between the Scillies and the Seven Stones Reef. His intention was that when he was about half-way between the Scillies and the Seven Stones he would alter course to port to about 325°, and when the Seven Stones was clear, he would alter back again to about 018°. The ship was still on the autopilot and he decided to alter course but keep the autopilot engaged. The most he could alter course in such circumstances was 3°. By altering the autopilot's heading he made one alteration of 3°, and another of 2° which put him on a heading of 013°. He had wanted to turn much further, to 325°, but there were a number of fishing vessels in the way and he was prevented from a further turn to port by them and their nets. Meanwhile the Officer of the Watch had taken a number of fixes which put the ship much further south than in fact she was. However, the OOW admitted at the time that he was uncertain about them as he had difficulty in identifying the points of land that he had chosen. It subsequently transpired that he was wrong and the ship was very close to the Seven Stones Reef. What had happened was there had been a strong northeasterly set during the night, a common occurrence between Ushant and the Scillies. It accounted for picking up the Scillies by radar on the port bow instead of the starboard and the northerly element of the set had put the ship further north than her officers thought.

Rugiati by now was a very worried man. At 08.42 he switched the autopilot from auto to manual and himself brought the ship round to 000° and said that he then returned the autopilot to auto. At 08.48 the OOW took another fix, this time using the Seven Stones Lightship which was clearly visible. To his horror, on plotting it, he found that the ship was only 2.78 miles southwest of it, which put

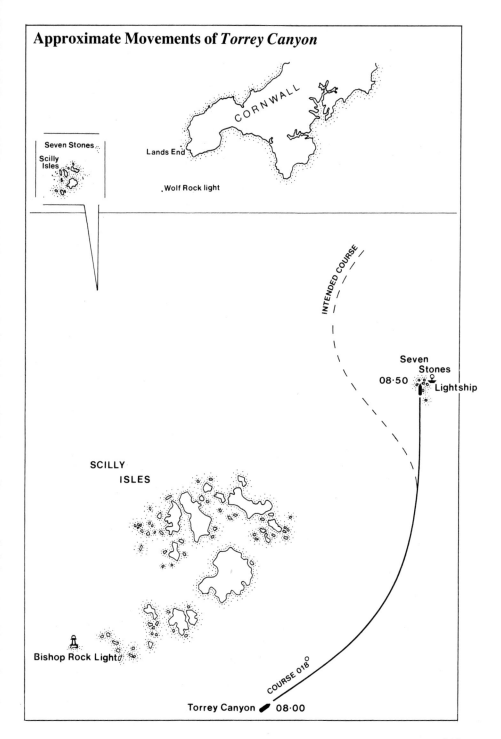

Approximate Movements of *Torrey Canyon*

Seven Stones

Scilly Isles

CORNWALL

Lands End

. Wolf Rock light

INTENDED COURSE

Seven
Stones

08·50   Lightship

SCILLY
ISLES

Bishop Rock Light

COURSE 018°

Torrey Canyon   08·00

her right amongst the rocks of the Seven Stones Reef. On hearing from the OOW where he was, Rugiati shouted to the helmsman to come hard left. The helmsman put the wheel over but the ship did not respond. Rugiati rushed to it and saw that the selector switch at the autopilot was to 'control', a position which disengaged the wheel. He threw the switch to manual and helped the helmsman to put the wheel over: the ship began to swing to port and had reached a heading of 350° when she struck the Pollard Rock — one of the northernmost of the Seven Stones and came to a sudden stop. The ship must already have missed a number of other rocks on the way.

Before going on to discuss the resulting pollution, it is necessary to investigate further Rugiati's behaviour. Only five days after the stranding, the Liberian Deputy Commissioner of Maritime Affairs appointed a Board of Investigation chaired by James Malcolmson, a retired naval architect and a native of Northern Ireland. The second and third members were Kenneth Volt, an American specialist in martime law, and Roy Melita, a 51-year old merchant service officer of Italian origin. The Board met in Genoa and later in London, and the Department of the Treasury in Monrovia published the Board's report and issued a Press Release on the matter.

The Board concluded that 'the Master alone is responsible for this casualty'. It went on to say:

'Considering the fact that the Master's experience in the waters to the east of the Scilly Islands was very limited, that the *Torrey Canyon* was an extremely large and deeply loaded tanker, the Board feels that the decision to pass to the east of the Islands exposed the vessel to an unnecessary risk which could have easily been avoided. Furthermore, when he was advised shortly before 07.00 that the vessel was to the east of the projected track, in the Board's opinion, the Master should have gone to the bridge, conferred with the Chief Officer, before making his decision how he would pass the Scilly Islands.'

In addition, the Board continued:

'The Master was negligent in the following respects:
'He took the ship between the Seven Stones and the Scillies, rather than between the Seven Stones and Land's End. Despite the presence of fishing vessels and nets, he kept the ship on automatic steering, failing to put her in hand steering.

'He failed to reduce speed at any time prior to the stranding and especially at 08.40 when he reckoned he was nearer to the Seven Stones than he had previously thought and when a turn to 325° was prevented by the presence of a fishing vessel on his port side.

'He had not established any regular or routine practice for the operation of the steering wheel selection lever.'

With regard to passing to the east of the Scillies, the current Admiralty Channel Pilot at that time read:

'The actual width of the channel between the nearest of the Scilly Islands and

Land's End is 21 miles, but as the route taken by all large vessels must be westward of Longships and should be eastward of Seven Stones Lightship, the navigable channel can only be considered as 12 miles wide.'

However, the *Torrey Canyon* did not have this book onboard. Rugiati was asked by the Board, 'What sailing directions do you use in navigating these waters? What books?' His reply was '*Brown's Almanac*'. This was a palpably absurd reply as *Brown's Almanac* contains no sailing directions — it is a book of celestial details and tidal data — but the Board did not follow this up. Perhaps the members did not know what the book contained.

Curiously, the Board seems to have asked no questions as to why Rugiati changed his mind about passing the Scillies to the east and endeavoured to pass between the islands and the Seven Stones, particularly as it would have added an hour or so to the voyage and, as we have already seen, he was in a hurry. It was a most extraordinary thing to do, especially as he could clearly see the fishing vessels in the gap. Only Rugiati can tell what prompted him to take such a hazardous course.

Finally, the Board ended with a recommendation that Capt Rugiati's licence should be revoked because of his negligence and the severity of the incident. This recommendation was in due course carried out.

It is interesting to note that Capt Rugiati was not the only seafarer to be deceived by the strong northeasterly set which put the *Torrey Canyon* further to the north and east than he expected. The strong set is a well known phenomenon at certain times of the year. It runs between Ushant and the Scillies and has accounted for many of the 257 known wrecks on the troublesome rocks and islands of the Scillies. Perhaps the best known, and the one which caused the biggest loss of life, was in 1787 when Adm Sir Cloudsley Shovell led a British fleet of 18 ships on to the Outer Gilstone Ledge at the extreme southwest corner of the islands. The fleet had experienced bad weather for the past few days and no sights had been possible during the latter part of the voyage from the Mediterranean; neither had the ships seen the shore. So bad was the weather that the Admiral made a signal to heave to and for the Masters (navigators) of all ships to repair onboard his flagship, the *Association*. He asked them to give their estimates as to where the fleet was. Their general opinion was that they were off Ushant. The fleet therefore proceeded under this assumption, with the Admiral leading in his flagship. In fact, due to the northeasterly set (not so well known in those days), the ships were only 10 miles southwest of the Scillies. Within two hours of setting sail again, the fleet, in darkness and with a gale blowing, ran on to the Gilstone Reef in the southwest corner of the Scillies. There was complete confusion. The leading ships had no time to alter course and they crashed into the rocks, ripping the bottoms out of them. The remainder turned away, but in all directions and complete chaos reigned. Four ships were lost and 1,800 men perished, including Sir Cloudsley Shovell and his Flag Captain.

The *Torrey Canyon* had good visibility, modern navigational aids, daylight, radar and there was no gale. Small wonder that the Board of Investigation found that only human error was to blame.

Immediately after the *Torrey Canyon* hit the Pollard Rock, Rugiati ordered 'full astern' but it made little difference: the ship was grinding heavily on the rocks and her bottom was being torn out of her. Rugiati sent out a distress call. Several ships picked it up and among them was the Dutch tug *Utrecht* and St Mary's lifeboat station in the Scillies. The *Utrecht* arrived first. She belonged to the salvage company Wijsmuller of Holland. The duty officer at the company's headquarters in Ijmuiden at once rang the *Torrey Canyon's* agent in the USA, a firm called Pacific Coast Transport, and suggested that they should endeavour to salvage her under a Lloyds Open Agreement. The agent rang Union Oil.

Meanwhile the *Utrecht* had arrived at the scene. With the assistance of the St Mary's lifeboat, which had also arrived, she put two radio operators onboard the *Torrey Canyon* at about 12.40. They carried with them a Lloyds Agreement, known as the No Cure-No Pay agreement, and invited Rugiati to sign it. He took some hours, saying that he was reading the small print, but was probably contacting the head office of Union Oil in America. Of course Union Oil knew all about it and the company's approval did not take very long. Rugiati signed.

Earlier the St Mary's lifeboat had got alongside the *Torrey Canyon* — not without considerable difficulty because of the large swell — to confer with Rugiati. The Coxswain, Mathew Lethbridge, realised that Rugiati was waiting for tugs, discovered that there were no injured persons onboard and that Rugiati did not want to evacuate the crew at that time. He reported that the ship was leaking badly from the bridge forward and he thought that she might break in two. Meanwhile a helicopter from the naval air station at Culdrose succeeded in winching Lt Michael Clark on to the ship. He reported on naval channels that a large part of the ship had been opened and oil was streaming out. He estimated that the slick was six miles long and that the ship was down by the bows and rolling and pounding. The Navy sent the destroyer *Barrosa* to the scene, and also a minesweeper, the *Clarkeston*, with 1,000gal of detergent onboard. It also arranged for the tug *Sea Giant* to arrive the next day with 3,000gal more of detergent.

Others then tried to take a hand in getting some action from the Government, which up to date had done nothing, perhaps because it was the Easter weekend. The MP for St Ives, Mr John Nott (who later became Minister for Defence), telephoned various Ministries, but it was a Saturday afternoon and he was unable to achieve much. The Council for the Isles of Scilly sent a telegraph to the Prime Minister, Harold Wilson, who should have been very interested as he had a holiday home in the Scillies. He arrived at his home a day later for the holiday. The next day the Sunday newspapers were full of the story, but their information was sketchy.

The *Utrecht* tried to pass a tow to the *Torrey Canyon* on the Saturday, but failed. A further attempt on the Sunday got the tow secured but it parted as soon as *Utrecht* went ahead. Wijsmuller, the salvage company, arranged for more tugs to be despatched, still hoping that they might succeed in salvaging her, but as time went by the salvage appeared more and more unlikely. The ship was still down by the bows and the wind was rising again.

At 12.30 on the Sunday, Rugiati sent a signal which read: 'Master and three crew and two operators from tug *Utrecht* staying onboard. All others leaving.' The St Mary's lifeboat came alongside, and with conditions rapidly worsening, with a 15-20ft swell, succeeded in transferring nine men to the lifeboat. Eight jumped into the boat but the ninth man fell into the sea and was only rescued by Coxswain Lethbridge's superb handling of the lifeboat. Rugiati then asked for a helicopter to evacuate nine more men. Culdrose immediately despatched two helicopters. The first winched up five men and the second four. Thus there was left onboard Rugiati, the Chief Officer, the First Engineer, the First Mate and the original two radio operators from the *Utrecht*.

Meanwhile the Vice-President of Union Oil M. S. Thomson, and Capt Darell Povey, a retired tanker captain and now a consultant to Union Oil, were flying from America and arrived in the UK on Monday. They thought that they should make every effort to save the ship as they were responsible to the insurers, so they went at once to the Scillies. Various other experts arrived on the Monday. Wijsmuller had sent Hans Stal, its senior salvage expert, to take charge BP sent its Marine Superintendent, Captain King, and the Admiralty sent the civilian head of salvage, Peter Flatt. Culdrose helicopters made numerous trips to deliver and take off the various functionaries.

A conference was held with the Navy in Plymouth and it appeared obvious to those who still wished to salvage the ship that the Navy wanted to destroy the ship and fire the remaining oil. However, they persuaded the Navy to stay its hand. There were also legal problems as to whether anybody had the right to destroy a ship in international waters. Meanwhile detergents continued to arrive at the scene. All kinds of ships were requisitioned and by Monday afternoon there were no less than 18 ships busily spraying the sea with detergents, although to many it appeared useless.

On Monday afternoon the House of Commons debated the situation. Mr Healey, the Minister of Defence, first reviewed the situation and told the House what the Government had or had not done. Then Dr Dunwoody, the Labour member for Falmouth, asked this question:

'Would not my Rt Hon Friend agree that there is great concern in the South West that much of the oil appears deliberately pumped out of the vessel in order to attempt to refloat it from the reef? Could he assure the House that it does not continue? As there are nearly 100,000 tons of oil inside the wreck, could serious consideration be given to the possibility of setting fire to the wreck and destroying the oil on the reef?'

Healey replied:

'On the question of pumping out the oil, I must point out to my Hon Friend that if the ship breaks up on the reef, all the cargo onboard is bound to be dispersed, so it is quite natural that the owners should have considered the possibility of floating it off, even if it does mean releasing some of the oil.'

'On the question of firing the ship, we have representatives of the company from New York in Plymouth and they have visited the ship. We are not in a position to be able to set fire to the ship until they give their agreement that this can be done. The vessel is on the high seas at the present time. However, I must tell the House that many technical and practical problems arise in firing the ship. Even if we take this step, there may be sometime before the danger is removed.'

The idea of transferring the oil to other tankers was considered and turned down as being too hazardous to bring the ships close enough to the *Torrey Canyon*. The Union Oil representatives still thought that the ship could be refloated . . .

By Monday evening the oil slick had reached to within a few miles of Land's End and the wind and tide were still considerable, but a Navy spokesman said that any significant change in the direction of the wind could blow the oil back again to the Scillies. Wijsmuller had provided compressors in order to give the ship some stability and buoyancy by forcing air out of the tanks. The air would expel the oil and sea water, and the compressors worked all night — so Dr Dunwoody had been right.

Whilst the Government was hoping for the best, it did instruct Mr Foley to take all precautions against the oil reaching the Channel beaches. Foley at once met with the local authorities, asked the Army to get ready to deploy and also announced that the Government would consider sympathetically the financial position of the local authorities. Tuesday dawned fine and the list of the ship was noticeably less, while Capt Stal and 14 other Wijsmuller men were preparing for another attempt to float the ship off at high water in the afternoon. However, all concerned were becoming increasingly alarmed by the possible risk of a gas explosion. There was so much gas around that the slightest spark might set it off.

Sure enough, just after 12.00 there was a terrific explosion in the engine room. It blew out the skylight and blew the adjacent swimming pool to pieces. Pieces of metal were flying about the deck and a number of men were injured (fortunately not seriously) and two others were blown overboard. One man, Van Wijk, from the tug alongside, was rescued from the sea by a young Dutchman. More serious, however, was the fate of Capt Stal. He too was blown overboard, but was probably unconscious when he entered the sea. Another Dutchman from the salvage company, Van Rixel, went to save his boss, grabbed him and got him to a ladder at the ship's side, but could not get him on to the ladder. Again Van Wijk jumped in to help. Capt Percy of Union Oil saw what was happening. He was 66 years old but he climbed down the ladder and went into the sea. Between the three of them they managed to get Capt Stal on to the *Torrey Canyon's* deck. A doctor, requested from Culdrose by the tug *Titan*, arrived and examined him and said that he should be transferred to a hospital ashore as soon as possible. He was put onboard the tug *Titan* for passage ashore, but very unfortunately he died before the tug reached Penzance. He thus became the only casualty in the whole disaster. It was never established what exactly caused the explosion.

Rugiati then decided to give up his heroic struggle to save his ship and asked to be lifted off, together with the other men still onboard. This was done in the afternoon of Tuesday 21 March. It left the ship entirely in the hands of the Wijsmuller Salvage Co.

After the explosion, three men from the Wijsmuller company examined the ship and said that, in their opinion, there was still a fair chance of saving the ship. The two Union Oil men also went onboard on Wednesday and said that they thought the salvage operations should continue, but Peter Flett, the Admiralty salvage expert, stated that 'we knew that she couldn't last very long'.

The Prime Minister himself, in response to a request from Wijsmuller, authorised the use of a BEA Sikorsky 61H high lift helicopter to assist by transferring heavy equipment, mostly compressors, to the *Torrey Canyon*. It had to move three compressors from the stern to the bows of the tanker and to transfer two other compressors from ships standing by the tanker. For three days the big helicopter worked at the job, which got progressively more difficult as the wind rose.

A decision was taken onboard the *Torrey Canyon* by the Wijsmuller company to make one last attempt to tow her off at the next spring tides due on Saturday 26, Sunday 27 and Monday 28 March. A problem arose as to where to take her, should she come off. The British Government, always fearful of more pollution, told the Dutch Government that it would probably forbid her to enter any British port. Even at the time of the final attempt it was uncertain where she should go, but probably Wijsmuller had in mind to tow her out to sea and transfer the oil to other tankers, weather permitting.

In the meantime the Government had called in Sir Solly Zuckerman, the chief scientific adviser. He gathered a number of experts around him and formed a committee. On the assumption that she would come off, their first consideration was what to do with her oil still remaining onboard, but no clear decision seems to have been arrived at.

The first of the oil reached the Cornish coast during the night of Friday 25th and Saturday 26th, the wind having changed to the southwest on Friday. Fortunately there had been a few days in which to make preparations to meet it and troops and equipment were standing by to spray detergents. The Navy was given the responsibility for spraying detergent to within 300yd from the shore, with the local authorities taking over from there, using small private boats.

Wijsmuller's final effort was to be made on Saturday 26th. Three tugs were to do the pulling, the compressors were turned full on and the tide gave 5-6ft more water above the rocks than when the ship had stranded. Unfortunately the attempt failed. It was found that a pinnacle of rock had entered right into the hull and was firmly inside the ship and no amount of pulling the ship would dislodge it. However Wijsmuller refused to admit failure and were determined to try again on Sunday. The tug *Utrecht* was to be used alone, but by Sunday it was blowing a gale and it was late afternoon before the tow could be secured. The second attempt also failed, as most observers knew it must.

On Sunday afternoon another meeting took place at Culdrose. Quite a lot of time was wasted discussing what to do if the *Torrey Canyon* got off. By this time it was known in the Scillies that this was impossible, but the news had not yet reached Culdrose. At least the Prime Minister was able to report that he had already taken steps to cope with the pollution of the coastline, thus allaying the public's anxiety and strenthening the impression that the Government really had the situation in hand (which it had not). A promise was also made to the local authorities that they would not have to pay for the troops' services, accommodation and rations, and that the Government would reimburse three-quarters of any additional expenditure they had to meet.

On conclusion of the meeting, the Prime Minister was flown back to his holiday home in the Scillies by a naval helicopter piloted by Lt-Cdr Mike Freemantle. On his return trip the destroyer *Delight* radioed the Lieutenant-Commander and said she believed that the stern of the *Torrey Canyon* was deeper in the water: would he check this? He flew over the ship and noticed that not only was the stern deeper in the water, but so were the bows. As he watched, a bend appeared in the hull and, during the next few minutes, it became further pronounced until there was a most peculiar hump in the middle and oil began pouring out. The *Torrey Canyon* had broken her back and was spilling all that remained of her oil.

David Fairhall, the Defence Correspondent of the *Guardian* newspaper, had predicted almost a week before that she would do this. Writing on the previous Monday evening for Tuesday's paper, he had noted the strong winds predicted by the Met Office and concluded 'under this sort of pounding the ship might possibly break her back'. Fairhall subsequently (with Philip Jordan, also of the *Guardian*) wrote a vivid account of the stranding of the *Amoco Cadiz* and the consequent pollution of the Brittany Coast which occurred at Easter off Ushant 11 years later.

Union Oil finally accepted the loss on Tuesday 28 March and Wijsmuller withdrew all its tugs and equipment on the same day. The salvage company had taken a big gamble for the large amount of salvage money that would have been paid out — and lost.

The Government realised that the only possible action it could take to prevent

Below:
The *Torrey Canyon* after breaking her back. *Press Association*

more oil spilling out was to set it alight whilst it was still confined in the tanks onboard the *Torrey Canyon*. Mr Foley surveyed the tanker from a helicopter for two hours and realised that rescuing any part of the ship's hull was out of the question. An experiment had been carried out of firing oil on a pond in Sussex, with 1,000gal of crude oil spread about 1in thick. The pond was agitated by air blown by a jet engine to simulate rough seas and the oil was set alight by a device known as an 'oxygen tile' and was almost completely destroyed. This greatly encouraged the Government and it ordered the Navy to start bombing the tanker on Tuesday afternoon once the salvage teams were clear. It was hoped to drop bombs into the open tanks onboard the ship; however, in the event, precision bombing was thought to be too difficult so mass bombing to blast the decks open was decided upon, followed by the dropping of fuel tanks to feed the fires and make sure the oil ignited.

Royal Navy Buccaneers carried out the first attack, working in pairs. Forty-one bombs were dropped and 30 hits were estimated. This was followed by RAF Hunters dropping fuel tanks. A total of 5,400gal of aviation fuel were used and the resultant fires burned for two hours, but little of the oil in the long slick was ignited. The Navy then tried the 'oxygen tile', which had been so successful in the Sussex pond. This is a device shaped like a tile, plastic coated and filled with sodium chlorate and towed by a helicopter on top of the water. It is ignited by passing an electric current through it. The Navy's idea was to ignite the oil in the slick from the far end, back towards the *Torrey Canyon*. Unfortunately it failed to ignite the oil, probably because it had been churned up by the movement of the sea and had lost its inflammable elements.

The bombing of the wreck resumed on Wednesday 29th, but this time the Hunters also fired rockets and 6,200gal of aviation fuel was used. Napalm too was tried. No oil was ignited. On Thursday Royal Naval Vixens and Buccaneers and RAF Hunters again attacked and some hundred thousand pounds of explosive were dropped, but still no fires were started. The authorities came to the conclusion that all the oil that had been in the wreck had been consumed in the first attack and decided against any further bombing. This was not entirely so as occasional blobs of oil appeared on the surface from time to time. A submerged inspection by Royal Navy divers was ordered and continued under very hazardous conditions right up until 8 January. They found no liquid oil.

By this time the bow had slid down a steep gully and had folded up along its centre line and split in places. A great deal of the ship had completely disappeared and other parts had been so heavily bombed that they were unrecognisable. No unexploded bombs were found and reports by pilots of bombs failing to explode must have been because they missed. The source of the oil spill had been successfully dealt with but what of the oil already spilled?

We last left the oil just coming ashore at Land's End. It soon spread to beaches and coves either side of Land's End to a final total distance of 145 miles, all of which were polluted to some extent. Fears arose that it would spread eastwards along the Channel to Dover and even further, but fortunately these fears were not realised.

One of the worst pollutions occurred at Sennen Cove, just north of Land's End. On Easter Monday the highest spring tide for many years had covered Sennen Cove completely with oil, and Whitsand Bay was little better. It soon spread to

Newquay, a large holiday resort some 36 miles further up the north coast of Cornwall. Its beaches were badly affected but were dealt with very effectively by the Urban District Council which mobilised a four-wheel drive fertiliser sprayer, 12 crop sprayers, 30 hand sprayers, stirrup pumps, 300 barrels of detergent, tractors, a wrecker, 12 boats, 35 petrol driven pumps and a crane. An efficient system of voice radio communications was established and one engineer or technical officer was put in charge of each beach and one in charge of the sea operation. It took them a week to clear all the local beaches and rocks using detergent and the action of the sea. However, no sooner had they finished than, on Sunday 2 April, another tide brought in a heavier wave of contamination to seven beaches. Newquay had only 50 barrels of detergent left and made urgent appeals to the Army, the county authorities and even the Government, only to be told that there was no more to be had. However, some was found four days later and Newquay buckled down again. Eventually all the beaches were cleared. It was a good example of how a local authority could manage to help itself given good management and determination.

On 24 March the Government put a member of the Cabinet — Anthony Greenwood, Minister of Housing and Local Government — in charge of anti-pollution efforts on land and close to the shore, but Foley remained in overall charge. The Army deployed 1,300 men at first, but most of the troops were on Easter leave. A Marine Commando of 1,000 men was mobilised to spray detergent on the beaches and the sea from small boats. It was obvious that there were insufficient men and on Easter Sunday telegrams were sent to 1,000 additional men recalling them. By Tuesday 28 March they were deployed. Apart from the infantry, other branches of the Royal Corps of Transport moved detergent and brought up food for the troops, while the Army Ordnance Corps provided pumps and spraying apparatus. The Royal Engineers made and deployed booms for the protection of river estuaries and operated bulldozers to plough up beaches heavily contaminated with oil and detergent. A particularly hazardous job was spraying rocks at the bottom of steep cliffs. Some troops approached in boats, others climbed down ropes. The US Air Force offered the help of 86 men and 34 vehicles from its bases in Britain, and they spent three weeks in Cornwall at a cost to the United States of nearly $50,000. They worked very closely with the British troops and were most welcome.

Rumours abounded and the press was inclined to make the pollution situation worse than it really was. In fact it extended from about Newquay on the north Cornish coast, round Land's End to about the Lizard on the south coast. Mr Greenwood said publicly that 'we are winning the battle', and added that he would bring his wife to Cornwall in the summer for a holiday weekend. He kept his word and he and his wife toured the beaches in June. He pronounced that the beaches were much cleaner than ever before and that they surpassed all the beaches in England for cleanliness. It was true: the detergent had so cleaned the beaches that they all sparkled in the sunlight.

We must leave the oil in Cornwall for a short time with the 2,000 troops and almost as many civilian volunteers all busy cleaning it up, and turn our attention to France. At first the French paid little attention to what was going on in Cornwall. The French Prime Minister approved a Committee, under the leadership of Frances Raoul, the Director of the National Civil Protection Service in the Ministry of the Interior, whose job it was to protect the civil population in the event of a catastrophe, such as flood, explosion, fire and now oil pollution. In addition the French Navy flew reconnaissance missions over the oil slick, which was reckoned to be about 30 miles long by five miles wide.

It was thought at first that the slick would miss the Brittany coast and go further up Channel. However, on 9 April the oil arrived on the north Brittany coast helped by a northwesterly wind. Brittany was unprepared. Initially all the Bretons could do was to dump sawdust on the floating oil out to sea. Detergent was on its way and the French Government withdrew its ban on its use, but at sea only. It was not allowed to be used on land. Four days after the oil first appeared an emergency plan, designed for use in time of nuclear disaster, was put in force. Under the plan a military type organisation of naval, military, police and civilians were mobilised to fight the oil. Troops were brought in from the 41st Infantry Regiment and 3,000 marines were mobilised. Volunteer civilians were called for, but not so many turned up as had been hoped for. The oil had turned into thick sludge, called 'Mousse', and they had to shovel it into buckets and other containers and carry them to trucks above the high water mark which then took them to previously arranged dumping sites.

By 14 April dozens of beaches along nearly 100 miles of the holiday coast and the oyster beds were reported to be spoilt. The oyster and fish markets collapsed through fear of contamination, which subsequently was found to be largely unfounded. The Breton oyster market was heavily hit, considerably more than the oyster market in Britain.

The Channel Isles did not escape. Guernsey was particularly hard hit. Pollution there was so bad that a military style operation had to be mounted to deal with it.

The task of cleaning continued for weeks, but eventually by mid-summer all the beaches were cleaned in time for the French holiday period of August. Cornwall fared better than Brittany and by the beginning of June all the beaches were clean and waiting to receive the summer visitors.

Inevitably in both Britain and France there was widespread destruction of birds which, covered in oil, were unable to fly. The Zuckerman committee estimated that some 25,000 birds perished in Cornwall alone, despite the noble work done by the RSPCA Bird Hospital at Mousehole.

There were many lessons learnt from the disaster, but perhaps the principal one was that the use of detergent on land is *not* a good idea. The Zuckerman committee said in its report that mechanical means should be used instead of detergents whenever possible. There are two reasons: in the first place detergents are very harmful to wildlife, crops, trees and hedgerows. In the second, when detergents are mixed with oil they tend to bind the oil into the well-known mousse which is difficult to clear.

Other major lessons were that: tankers, particularly large ones, should keep well clear of the shore whenever possible; that floating oil tends to follow the prevailing wind at about 3.3% of the wind's velocity; and that there is never sufficient detergent immediately available. Stocks need to be kept on the coast and not miles inland.

The *Torrey Canyon*, major disaster though it was, did not cause anything like the pollution caused by the *Amoco Cadiz*. With the increasing size of tankers now at sea, the next maritime disaster may be even worse, and it was.

18

Amoco Cadiz

The *Amoco Cadiz* was what is known as a VLCC (Very Large Crude Carrier) of 230,000 tons, with a length of 334m (1,095ft) — over six times the length of Nelson's monument. Built in 1972, she was owned by the American-owned Amoco International Oil Co. Her Captain was an Italian called Pasquale Bardari and most of the crew were Italians. She was registered in Liberia and flew the Liberian flag.

Capt Bardari was educated at the nautical college at Pisa, Italy, and first went to sea in a passenger liner, later transferring to oil tankers in which he served for the rest of his career. He had onboard an Englishman, named Lesley Maynard of the Marine Safety Services, ostensibly to give a series of lectures on safety measures. Maynard had been in the Royal Navy as a mine countermeasures officer and a deep sea diver. He was to be of considerable assistance to Capt Bardari when the accident occurred and he kept a meticulous log of the events.

On what was to be her final voyage the *Amoco Cadiz* left the Persian Gulf, fully laden, for Rotterdam, but she was to meet a smaller tanker in Lyme Bay in southern England and discharge some of her cargo to the smaller vessel, thus reducing her draught which was too great to enable her to navigate the shallow water at the eastern end of the English Channel.

Dawn on 16 March 1978 found the *Amoco Cadiz* about 30 miles off Ushant on a course of 032°. The voyage so far had been uneventful, but the Bay had been rough and the weather had now developed into a westerly gale and was even rougher. At 04.00 Second Mate Ralmedo Salvezzi noted in the bridge log 'low visibility, wind WSW force 7, sea very rough, sea breaking over deck, radar on'.

The forecasts from the British Met Office at 05.39 for sea area Biscay was 'Wind SW to W, force 7 to severe gale 9, locally Storm Force 10, rain or showers, vis Mod to Good'. For sea area Plymouth, towards which the *Cadiz* was making, it read 'Wind NW rising to severe gale 9, decreasing force 5. Showers, good visibility'. The rocky coast of Brittany was to leeward of her and at the time the *Cadiz* was in the delineated channel for north-going traffic. Bardari's present course would eventually have taken him into the separation zone, a sort of no-man's-land in which ships were not allowed to navigate. So he had made up his mind that as soon as he had rounded Ushant he would alter course to 037°, the specified course after Ushant, and would then make for Lyme Bay where he was to meet the other tanker.

This he did, but very soon afterwards he was unable to maintain the course because a particularly heavy wave broke over the poop deck and carried away a number of lubricating oil drums which had been stowed there. He therefore turned the ship into the wind and eased down to 8kt from the 15kt he had been maintaining. It took an hour and a half to secure the oil drums, so he finished up much closer to the separation zone than he had intended, but with more sea room off Ushant. He set off on the correct course, but had to alter to starboard for about 10 minutes to recover two empty oil drums and a fire hose, but this made little significant difference. Again at about 09.30 he had to alter course to starboard to avoid a small unidentified tanker heading south in the north-going lane, where she certainly should not have been. Further, a number of other ships heading south appeared and Bardari had to maintain his more easterly course for longer than he wanted to, so when the ship's steering gear broke down, he was about a mile closer to shore than he should have been. His position in fact was about 8½ miles north of Ushant and some 15 miles from the French coast.

His ship was now completely unmanoeuvrable with the rudder jammed hard-a-port. To add to his troubles the wind started to veer to the northwest and was blowing him dead on to the shore. Had it remained in the southwest he might have drifted clear of the coast.

He stopped engines and hoisted the 'not under control' signal of two black balls. He also put out a VHF broadcast to warn other shipping. The rudder had jammed hard-a-port, and since VLCCs carry their way for some 2½ miles, the ship slowly turned to port and came to rest. The time was then 10.05 and the Cadiz had come to rest to the northeast of the separation zone and right in the path of outward bound vessels making for the westerly channel. With no way on her she slewed round to a southeasterly direction, towards the shore, and was rolling heavily.

The steering gear consisted of the immense rudder, pivoted at the forward end. Across the pivot of the rudder was a horizontal bar which, whilst the rudder was amidships, lay across the beam of the ship. When the wheel was put to starboard, the starboard electric motor caused a hydraulic ram to extend which pushed the bar on the starboard side away from it, ie in a forward direction, thus causing the rudder to turn to starboard. The bar was then lying diagonally across the ship with its starboard portion further forward than was its port portion. This turned the rudder to starboard and the ship altered course to starboard. When it was desired to turn to port, the reverse procedure took place. What had happened was that a pipe between the port side electric motor and the hydraulic ram became loose, due to five bolts securing it shearing. This allowed the hydraulic pressure in the ram to leak at the joint between it and the pipe. Efforts to bleed the system failed, largely because the rudder was banging from side to side and forcing a mixture of air and fluid violently round the system. Another pipe then failed and this time there was no simple way of isolating it. The engineers next tried to secure the rudder in the amidships position using a chain tackle, but the rudder snapped the tackle immediately. The rudder then started swinging from side to side in the heavy seas running and nothing more could be done.

At about 11.00 Capt Bardari called up Brest coastal radio station to ask where the nearest tugs were. They replied promptly that there was one — the German tug Pacific — in the area and Brest would order it to the ship's assistance. Not long after, the bridge informed Bardari that it had made VHF contact with the tug and it was only 15 miles away. The Cadiz then broadcast a VHF radio message addressed to all ships which read, 'Our position eight miles North of Ushant. We have complete failure of gear. Please keep clear'. The German Captain of the Pacific told his radio operator to call the Amoco Cadiz and offer salvage under

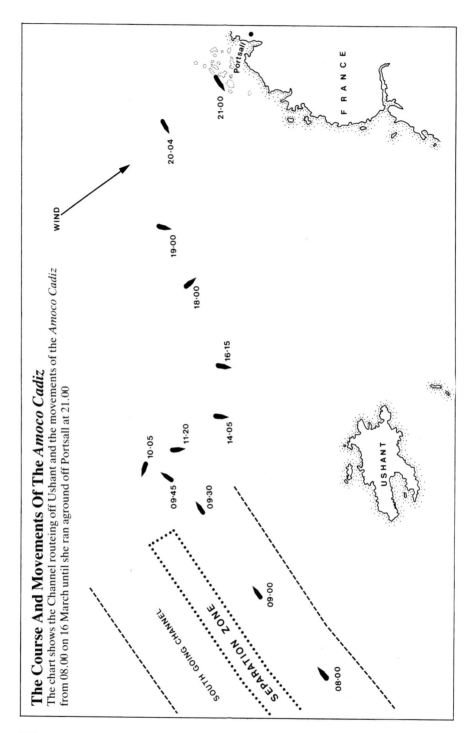

The Course And Movements Of The Amoco Cadiz

The chart shows the Channel routeing off Ushant and the movements of the Amoco Cadiz from 08.00 on 16 March until she ran aground off Portsall at 21.00

Lloyds Open Form Agreement and made for the *Cadiz*'s position as fast as he could.

Bardari did not like this at all. He did not consider his ship needed salvaging: all he wanted was a tow, and a towing agreement to, say, the UK would of course be very much cheaper than a salvage agreement. He replied to the tug that he wanted a tow mileage rate to Lyme Bay. The reply from the tug was 'OK'. It was obvious, however, that in the first instance the tug must take the *Cadiz* in tow and both Captains agreed to stop arguing until the tow had been passed.

Passing the tow was extremely difficult in the heavy sea running and with the bulky gear required, but eventually the large towing cable was passed. The time was 13.36. The Captain of the *Pacific* was an experienced German called Weinert. He sensibly headed straight into the wind paying out the towing cable behind him. At about 14.00 when the *Cadiz* was only 5.7 miles from the shore at Ushant, some progress was observed. Not for long though: the *Cadiz* turned a few degrees into the wind, and began to swing back again. The officers onboard the *Cadiz* thought that the tug was not trying hard enough, and the following was entered into her log. '14.35. It was observed that the tug had stopped pulling. Tug requested Lloyds Open Agreement. Agreement refused. Tug told to contact Chicago [where Amoco's head office was situated]. Tug threatened to release tow.'

The argument continued on VHF voice, but using intermediaries at both ends because Bardari could not speak German and Weinert little Italian, so the communication was in English as both ships had English speaking personnel onboard. However, after 20 minutes the two Captains did manage to speak a few words to each other. Weinert said he must have a Lloyds Open Agreement to which Bardari apparently still said no. Meanwhile Bardari was trying to get in touch with his head office in Chicago. At about 15.25 he was finally put through and spoke to a Capt Phillips, the Manager of Marine Operations. He at once approved an Open Agreement and Bardari informed Weinert that it was agreed. Unfortunately both Captains were not prepared to accept the other's spoken word and Weinert demanded an official signal. Bardari then sent a signal via Brest radio which read 'We agree. Lloyds Open Salvage Agreement "No cure, no pay".' The point about a Lloyds Open Agreement is that the Captain of the stricken vessel gives the Captain of the salvage vessel his agreement to go ahead and endeavour to effect a salvage. However, if the salvage fails to save the ship, no payment is made by the owners to the salvage company. The words 'No cure, no pay' appear at the head of the agreement form.

An hour and a half had been wasted by this stupid argument, but at least the *Cadiz* had not got any nearer to the shore. In fact Weinert was pulling all the time with 80% power, which he later asserted was the maximum he dared use without risking parting the tow. Soon after the argument had been settled, the tow parted. Nobody knew why it had parted: Weinert thought that the edge of the fairlead through which the tow was rove was wrongly shaped. The towing cable was growing out on the beam as the tug was struggling to get the *Cadiz*'s bows into the wind. He thought the edge of the fairlead must have nipped the cable. Bardari on the other hand thought that the cable had become twisted due to the heavy rolling of the ship and this had caused it to part.

The *Pacific* began hauling in the cable for a second attempt. Meanwhile Bardari, looking at the ever menacing shore, decided to try and gain sea room by going astern, but once stern way was gathered the swinging rudder jammed hard over which had the effect of turning the stern into the wind so that her bows swung round to about 130°, in other words pointing directly at the shore.

A second tug, the *Simson*, was approaching down Channel. She was far more powerful than the *Pacific*, and if the *Cadiz* could be held off for a few hours there was still a chance. Weinert informed Bardari and added that he would try to tow her stern first, but Bardari was against the idea as the only means of holding her off the shore was by her engines still going astern and he knew when the tow was being passed he would have to stop, as the propeller might foul the tow. However, he had no choice and at 19.01 the tug requested him to stop and to prepare for a tow aft.

By this time the nearest rocks off the Breton coast were only five miles distant, added to which some submerged rocks were less than four miles away. Time was not on Bardari's side and his state of mind was not helped by a signal from the tug telling him that he was drifting towards the shore — a fact that he well knew. Two attempts to get a line onboard the *Cadiz* failed, so at 20.00 Bardari decided to anchor. By this time, with the swinging of the ship, the tug was off the *Cadiz*'s stern and still trying to pass a line. However, the anchor, although dragging, was having some effect and the ship's bow was pointing into the wind. At that point the capstan broke a steam pipe. On investigating, the Chief Engineer found that the entire steam cylinder had been blown off the port side of the capstan. Nothing could be done to effect a repair and it soon became impossible to work on the forecastle at all.

At 20.55 the tow was secured aft and Weinert requested Bardari to go slow astern. With his stern only minutes from the rocks Bardari could not risk getting stern way on, and he informed the tug that he must go ahead and asked Weinert to pull the stern to port in order to keep his bows into the wind, which was veering to the northwest. However, he was unable to go ahead as there was a possibility that he might capsize the tug as the tow aft was growing out on the latter's beam.

At exactly 21.00, while he hesitated, the *Cadiz* grounded aft. It was almost precisely high water, the worst possible time to run aground, and the ship started to grind heavily on the rocks, causing more damage to the hull. The tug *Simson* had not arrived and it was obvious that the *Pacific* was not powerful enough to be of any use. In addition, Bardari had another problem: a mixture of gas and air filled the engine room and some of the accommodation. He had anticipated this and had already warned all departments to be ready to close down all machinery and switch off all lights for fear of a spark igniting the highly explosive mixture. When he gave the order it was obeyed instantly and the ship was plunged into darkness.

Lesley Maynard, the ex-Naval officer turned security officer, then carried out some sterling work letting off flares from the bridge which, he hoped, would not set the gas/oil mixture alight. The ship's radar could not be used, due to the lack of electrical power, but there were some walkie-talkies and some of the crew used them to call for help; it is doubtful if they were on the correct frequencies. Then at 21.30 the *Cadiz* grounded again aft. It appeared that she had initially grounded on a pinnacle of rock, but with the heavy seas running was floating off and bumping back again. This time, however, she came clear, only to be washed further inshore and grounded again. The Captain was fearful of boiler explosions; although they were turned off, they were still hot. In fact there was an explosion and flames came out of the top of the funnel, but nothing else occurred.

Although no order to abandon ship was given, the port lifeboat was got ready, but as the ship began to settle, a huge wave came over the boat and broke her into three pieces. The wave also flooded the engine room. The entry in the log read: '22.00, engine room flooded and ship settled aft. Pollution observed. Rockets fired at intervals. All crew on bridge.'

At 22.00 the second tow parted. The *Pacific* recovered what was left of the tow and she stood by illuminating the scene with her searchlight. The *Cadiz* was firmly aground in a position about 12 miles north of the small fishing port of Portsall and about 15 miles northeast of Ushant.

At midnight a helicopter arrived to take off the crew. They started with an injured man and the Chief Mate's wife, the only woman onboard, and by 01.45 all the crew had been lifted off, except for Bardari and Maynard who had volunteered to stay and help.

They took up position in the wheelhouse, waiting in case some other tug arrived to try and tow the ship off. They gradually began to get gassed, so they had to take spells in the fresh air on the windward side of the bridge. At one time when Maynard was outside, he thought he saw lightning, but on looking at the sky he saw only stars and no signs of any storm clouds. He looked around the ship and, on facing forward, he could see flashes of light. Closer inspection revealed that the ship was breaking in two and the metal was emitting sparks. He and the Captain decided that if the ship finally did break right across and their bit sank, they had better gather together some life rafts.

Maynard went off to find some, but they had all been washed away, as had the life belts. He did, however, find three flares which he fired. The tug *Simson* had arrived, but it was obvious that there was little that could be done to salvage the ship. Finally at 05.10 another helicopter arrived and winched them both to safety.

The scene was thus set for the greatest oil tanker pollution disaster at sea that the world had ever known.

The French coast in that area is liberally sprinkled with look-out posts and coastal radar stations, some manned by the Navy and some by civilians. The Navy's operation centre was at the Naval Headquarters at Brest. It had 23 observation posts under its control. They kept a visual watch, but many also had radar and they formed part of a contingency plan for an oil disaster at sea, called Plan 'Polmar'.

'Polmar' was an old plan, first drawn up in 1970 and did not envisage a spill of more than 30,000 tonnes, equivalent to about one tankful from a super tanker. It had never been tested. To make things more difficult the plan had been revised only three months before the *Cadiz* went aground, and the local authorities were not familiar with it or any amendments that had been made. In addition, it had one grave error — no one organisation had been appointed in overall control. It was soon realised that the plan was quite inadequate: instead of 30,000 tonnes of oil spilling, the chances were that the *Cadiz* would lose all her oil, some 200,000 tonnes.

The local authorities decided that their first priority must be to stop more oil escaping and to protect the more important parts of the coast, particularly the oyster beds. The burning of the wreck was discussed, but with the unsuccessful

British example of setting alight the oil from the *Torrey Canyon*, they decided that it would not be advisable.

To protect the coastline a large number of barges would be required. A rapid count showed that there were insufficient barges in the whole of France, and even those available were often situated hundreds of miles away. Dispersants were also hard to find, and in the whole of Brittany there was only enough dispersant to treat 500 tonnes of oil. The Shell Co of France had offered a number of smaller tankers into which the oil remaining onboard the *Cadiz* could be pumped. At first the idea seemed sound, but it was found that there was no suitable chart of the area (even the reef on which the *Cadiz* was stranded was not marked on any chart) and it would have been too risky to attempt to send in small tankers. The idea was abandoned and efforts were concentrated on fighting the oil already spilt. It was spreading very rapidly and was being pushed ashore by strong northwesterly winds.

The French Navy got together a flotilla of small craft and they were told to dump chalk on to the oil to sink it and to try to spray chemical dispersant in the hope of breaking up the oil before it could travel very far. They did what they could, but it had little effect and by 18 March (the day after the *Cadiz* struck) the oil slick had almost trebled in size. It stretched 18.5 miles south to beyond Le Touquet and then northeastward across the mouth of the barrage protecting Aber Bengit and Alser Winch to the Isle de Vierge. The thickest part of the slick was around the wreck and the coast and harbour of Portsall.

The local population was soon up in arms and accused the Government of not doing enough. In fact the Government had decided that with the equinoctial high tide due on 26 March, there was little point in trying to clean up the beaches when each succeeding high water washed the oil back again every few hours. Meanwhile the wind had backed to the southeast, sending the oil slick more to the north and starting to threaten the coast as far as the English Channel.

The French people's anger towards their Government grew. There were more demonstrations in Brittany, letters and leading articles in the newspapers and the Government came increasingly under attack. The main cause of all the anger was that although Plan 'Polmar' had been in use for 10 days and offers of help had been received from many other countries, the Government had failed to achieve its objective of controlling the oil spill and avoid the fouling of the beaches and, more importantly, the oyster beds.

Public opinion boiled over in a large scale demonstration in Brest on Maundy Thursday 23 March and the bombing of the Shell headquarters in Brittany on Easter Sunday. It was obvious that something must be done. A new man, M. Marc Becam, a deputy from Brittany, had been appointed by the Prime Minister, M. Barre, to head up all the pollution measures. He also advocated strongly that, as most of the oil had already spilled out of the *Cadiz*, she should be blown up and the authorities would have to face a further spillage. Measures were at once put in hand to increase the mopping up by all possible means. Thousands of civilian volunteers were recruited, and would get paid. A date was set, 28 March, for the operation of blowing up the wreck by demolition frogmen teams. In the event the divers were unable to place the charges due to the continuing rough seas.

On the morning of Wednesday 29 March the Navy decided that the only thing to do was to blow up the wreck using depth charges dropped by Super Frelon helicopters. At 15.00 therefore, three Super Frelons armed with anti-submarine depth charges carried out the attack which lasted 45min. Each charge contained 350lb of explosives and was set to explode 24ft under the water. Ten out of the 12 charges dropped exploded.

The *Cadiz* was inspected next day by frogmen. There was no fresh oil around the wreck, but the authorities were uncertain whether the bunker fuel in the rear portion of the ship had escaped or not. Another flight of Frelons was therefore despatched to bomb the rear section again. Sure enough a large spout of oil arose out of it from an apparently undamaged tank.

The *Cadiz*, or what remained of her, stayed in position for a further 11 months and finally disappeared in another storm very similar to the one in which she had stranded. In all, 223,000 tonnes of crude oil had escaped from her by 30 March 1978.

Although no more oil escaped from the wreck, the oil had done its worst. When the final analysis was made it was found that the entire coast from about 50 miles south of Brest to just short of Dinard was covered in a thick black mass of oil, and slicks out to sea extended nearly 100 miles, although, strangely enough, there were clear areas of sea up to 80 miles from the coast. To deal with the coastal pollution the French then introduced what they called Operation 'Teaspoon'.

At the start, the operation was bedevilled by the variable winds which now had periods of blowing from the east and pushing the oil out to sea, followed by periods of blowing from the west and pushing it all back again. Although only about 130 miles of coast was affected, in fact the oil covered 245 miles of the actual shoreline because of the many inlets along the coast.

At first a great deal of the oil washed ashore was more or less liquid in form and could be piped away into vehicles, but once it had been washed out to sea and back again and remained drying on the shore, it became the horrid, black, sticky and thick mess known as mousse. It became impossible to pipe it away, so the French decided that every bit of it must be scraped off the rocks and beaches into buckets and thence into trucks and wagons. The task was extremely onerous and required a colossal amount of manpower. The cleaners were literally scraping it away teaspoon by teaspoon, hence the name, Operation 'Teaspoon'.

By the beginning of April there were 5,000 soldiers on the scene, 2,000 sailors, a flight of Super Frelons and a squadron of Alouette helicopters, a flight of Alize light aircraft, 750 Commandos and 250 Marines. The Navy had 21 ships at sea with 735 men. In addition there were 3,000 civil volunteers, firemen and civil defence forces. The civil volunteers came not only from France but from Belgium and Holland and there were even some from Scandinavia. Over 1,000 vehicles were deployed, consisting of military and fire brigade vehicles, tankers, 'honeywagons', public works vehicles, skip lorries and various trucks and tippers.

Up until the end of the project, the official enquiry stated that the average manpower employed was 5,500, made up into 72 teams of roughly between 50 and 80 men, but the numbers varied considerably and at 'Teaspoon's' peak period they were probably as high as 8,000.

The management of these large numbers of men presented a considerable problem. Military personnel were little or no problem, but a great many civilian volunteers arrived from many countries and had to be accommodated and fed.

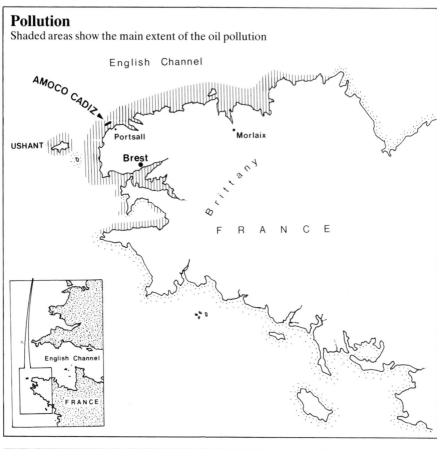

Pollution
Shaded areas show the main extent of the oil pollution

English Channel

AMOCO CADIZ

USHANT

Portsall

Morlaix

Brest

Brittany

FRANCE

English Channel

FRANCE

Left:
The *Amoco Cadiz*.

Invariably, the management was unable to cope and there were many cases of hardship. In the end the number of volunteers had to be considerably restricted.

Another problem was that there were strict orders that the various detergents were not to be used ashore because of the damage they caused to the tourist amenities, the crops and the oyster beds. Thus every drop of oil on the beaches had to be removed physically. The cleaning of the rocks was the most onerous task. To get the mousse out of the crevices and holes, long suction hoses were used where possible, but when this was not practicable teams of soldiers had to scrape the mousse off into buckets which had to be emptied into large containers and eventually into trucks, which dumped the sticky stuff into pits specially dug for the purpose. Alternatively, 30gal drums were used and were eventually emptied by vacuum trucks.

Offshore, small islands and rocks proved a problem all of their own. Most of them were accessible by boat, but it proved impossible to clean them because they were covered not only with the mousse, but with oily seaweed which made it impossible to climb on to them. Eventually, they had to be left for the sea to wash them down, but they exuded particles of oil which polluted areas that had already been dealt with.

When the major cleaning areas had been completed it was necessary to finish them with another process, particularly the jetties and prominent rocks. They were sprayed with steam, hot water, water sprinklers and high pressure hoses. Some individual rocks had to be picked up, cleaned and thrown back into the sea, which often returned them as polluted as they were before.

Another difficulty was caused by vehicles working on the beaches churning up the sand and mixing it with uncontaminated sand. The vehicles often got contaminated themselves and then ran over uncontaminated sand and polluted it.

As the days wore on, a new problem appeared almost daily. Congestion of transport, caused by delays, got worse and worse. One newspaper report stated that 569 railway tankers were waiting at or around Roscoff. The roads got overcrowded and many traffic blocks occurred.

Disposal of the oil was a constant problem. The fluid oil at the beginning of the operation was taken to Brest in road tankers and transferred to barges which took it to Le Havre for recycling. Before long there was too much for Le Havre to handle and recycling plants at Nantes, St Nazaire and La Pallice had to be commandeered, the oil being sent to them by rail. For the more solid mousse, the plan was to put it into specially dug pits, but before long trouble arose in finding the land on which to dig them; complaints came pouring in from farmers and local residents. Pits were being dug further and further away from the operational area. Overhanging it all was the constant problem of transport — not because there was not enough of it, but of getting it to the right place at the right time. A number of ships were chartered and filled with oil and mousse to be discharged right out to sea. The idea was not a success because it was easy enough to put the mousse in the ships, but getting it out again proved a tremendous task.

As time went on the French found solutions to all their problems. The transport situation eased greatly as the work proceeded and less and less transport was required. The sea proved itself a great ally and was hard at work scouring the rocks and eroding the beaches to expose clean, fresh sand. By the end of May the crisis had almost passed: a few stubborn places remained to be cleaned, but as the summer began Brittany started to take on its normal beautiful appearance, the smell had dispersed, the oyster beds recovered and the fishermen, the tour operators and the summer holiday makers all resumed their normal lives again. The worst oil pollution the world had yet known was over.

As usual in pollution disasters the bird life suffered severely. A total of 4,572 oiled birds were picked up dead, but estimates put the number of birds killed by the oil at around 22,000. The figure represented 0.1 bird per tonne of oil. The *Torrey Canyon* disaster was estimated to have killed 30,000 birds, but only 117,000 tonnes of oil was spilled, which works out at 0.2 birds per tonne of oil spilt.

All reports spoke of the natural cleansing power of the sea. Offshore currents managed to disperse a considerable amount of the oil, and the constant movement of the sea certainly helped to clean the rocks and the beaches. Compared to other pollution disasters it would seem that Brittany suffered rather less damage to the marine environment than might have been expected. In general it was thought that this was due to the massive human clean-up of the beaches, natural dispersion by the sea, and above all the limited use of chemical dispersants on shore.

The fishermen were of course affected, but were able to start fishing again about a month after the *Cadiz* struck. The worst hit was undoubtedly the oyster industry, particularly in the bay and estuary of Morlaix, just south of Roscoff. Many of the oysters died and those that were left were so contaminated with oil that they were unsaleable. Added to this, a customer resistance arose which persisted for months afterwards. The French, who love their oysters, refused to believe that when they reappeared again they were not contaminated. The same thing applied to the fish, lobsters and vegetables. The tourist trade was also badly hit by the reluctance of visitors to come to Brittany, with the obvious knock-on effect to the hotels, boarding houses, landlords and the shops.

The Government was generous in its payments of compensation to all industries affected. By December 1978 a total of £3.67 million had been paid out. This was in addition to the many charitable gifts from all over the world which poured in. It was estimated that over £1 million was received in gifts.

After such a catastrophe it was perhaps natural that the French reacted very strongly. Capt Bardari was arrested, as was Capt Weinert of the *Pacific* and the firm Bugsier, the owner of the tugs *Atlantic* and *Pacific*. Claims and counter-claims flew across the Atlantic as the Amoco Transport & Oil Co soon filed claims against Bugsier saying that the *Pacific* was unseaworthy at the time of the accident.

When they had time, the French realised that damages should be claimed from the tanker owners. Indeed, in any case, the International Convention of Civil Liability for Oil Pollution states that the owner of a ship shall be liable for any pollution damage caused by oil which has escaped or been discharged from the ship as a result of an incident. In fact Standard Oil instructed its insurers to pay $16.7 million into the French courts, which then had the task of distributing it among the many approved claimants in proportion to the amount they had claimed.

The Liberian Board of Enquiry, held in London a year later, put the primary cause of the disaster on the design of the steering gear, but it also blamed Capt

Bardari for the 'inexcusable delay' in calling for assistance. The members argued that Bardari should have called for help as soon as he had inspected the steering compartment at 10.05 and seen that the steering gear could never be repaired in time. He actually first called for help about an hour later, but the Board argued that had he called for assistance at 10.05, he would have had more sea room, and the tug *Simson* might have arrived earlier when, together with the *Pacific*, they might have been able to tow the *Cadiz* away from the rocks.

Many lessons were learnt from the whole affair, but perhaps the most important were:

(a) A VLCC must have exceptionally strong steering gear and great power so that she has an ample margin in the event of an accident or really bad weather.
(b) It is never too early to call for assistance.
(c) Plans to deal with pollution must envisage a major disaster where a VLCC loses all its cargo. Plan 'Polmar' was only meant to deal with 30,000 tonnes of oil, not nearly 230,000 tonnes.
(d) There must be one man, and one only, responsible for implementing any pollution plan.
(e) Even if every available man and all possible equipment is deployed on shore, it is likely that, if the oil reaches the shore, the neighbouring coastline will be polluted for up to four months.
(f) The sea in the end is the best possible cleanser.
(g) Finally, perhaps the most important lesson, was that a Master of a tanker must be the judge of the danger. He cannot rely on communication with his head office as to whether he should accept a tow.

On this latter lesson — which was an obvious criticism of Bardari's frequent calls to his Marine Superintendent in America — Shell put it very clearly in a letter to all its Masters of tankers.

'It must remain within the sole judgement of the Master as to the degree of danger to which his vessel is exposed as the result of any breakdown; that judgement must take into account a number of considerations, including proximity to danger, weather and other conditions which may affect the situation, but ultimately the objective must be to preserve life and property, and to make the optimum use of any assistance which may be available to secure that end.

'In these circumstances, after appraisal, an element of real risk is judged to be present, you should not hesitate to accept assistance offered under Lloyds Open Form of Salvage Agreement. Acceptance of these terms does not connote substantial or inflated settlements, but in fact normally results in an objective analysis of the circumstances, leading to an acceptable settlement.'

Such major disasters do not occur very frequently, but occur they do and regrettably will inevitably result in some pollution. Each nation is responsible for its own coastline and it is to be hoped that the lessons learnt from the *Amoco Cadiz* disaster will enable the seafaring nations to contain any spill so far as it is possible.

19

The Fastnet Race 1979

The well-known Fastnet Race for sailing yachts has been a biennial event since 1925. It is sailed from Cowes in the Isle of Wight, round the Fastnet Rock off the south coast of Ireland and back again to Plymouth, a total of 605 miles. On the outward leg the yachts may pass north or south of the Scilly Isles as desired, but on the homeward leg they must pass south of the Scillies.

In all its years the race had only recorded one death amongst the competitors, which took place in 1931 when one man was swept overboard. All this was to change in the fateful 1979 race when 15 persons lost their lives in the stormiest race ever run. The same race had the greatest number of competitors — 303 yachts, the previous record being in 1977 with 286 competitors. In fact the number of competitors had increased since the race was first run. In 1955 there were in all 47 competitors of which 44 finished the course. In 1977, 229 finished out of 288, but in 1979 only 85 finished out of 303.

The weather, over all the years, has generally been quite good for the three to four days of the race, which is always held in the first fortnight of August. There have however been years when gales have developed, notably in 1957, 1958 and 1961. Gales of course tend to increase the average speed of all yachts, except the smallest, but apart from that, yachts have become more streamlined and are generally faster these days. For example, in 1957 the average speed of the fifth boat to finish was 5½kt, but in 1979 the average speed of the fifth boat was 8kt. The fifth boat is taken as representing the average of the largest class.

The yachts are divided into classes by rating bands. The rating of a yacht is a measure of her effective sailing length, with certain allowances for factors such as engine weight and propeller drag, and also including factors such as very light displacement and excessive sail area. The yachts vary in size from about 28ft in length to about 85ft. It is interesting to note that, in the 1979 race, of the larger yachts (55ft and over), 14 boats started, 13 finished and one retired. No loss of life occurred in this class. Of the next size down (44-54ft), 36 started, 16 finished, 19 retired and one was abandoned but subsequently recovered. Loss of life occurred exclusively in boats of under 39ft, and when it came to the smaller boats of around 28-33ft, out of 55 entries, only one finished: 45 retired, seven were abandoned (but the craft were subsequently recovered) and two were sunk. In all, out of 303 entries, 194 boats retired, 19 boats were abandoned but subsequently recovered, and five were sunk — a sorry tale indeed.

The race was organised, as usual, by the Royal Ocean Racing Club which had its own yacht, the *Mornington*, at sea with the race and acting as a rescue ship and a communications link. The race started on the afternoon of Saturday 11 August in fine calm weather which held until Monday the 13th, but the weather-wise were worried by a depression coming across the Atlantic. It had started in Minnesota in the south of North America on 10 August and moved steadily eastward. As it approached, the British Meteorological Office labelled it Low Y. By Monday the

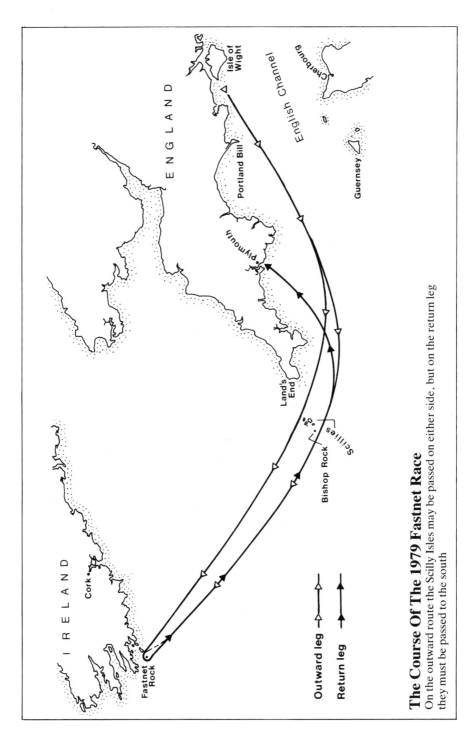

The Course Of The 1979 Fastnet Race
On the outward route the Scilly Isles may be passed on either side, but on the return leg they must be passed to the south

Outward leg
Return leg

13th it was in mid-Atlantic and moving fast, and it also altered course from due east to northeast. By Monday evening it seemed that it was going to sweep across Ireland and drive on to Scotland. Unfortunately though, it slowed right down to nearly stationary and remained over Ireland until noon on Wednesday the 14th when it gathered speed and swept over Scotland.

At 15.05 on the Monday the BBC broadcast the following gale warning: 'Sole, Fastnet, Shannon. Southwesterly gale force 9 imminent'. At 18.30 this was changed to: 'Finisterre, Sole, Fastnet. Southwesterly gale force 8 imminent'. Again at 23.00 the BBC broadcast: 'Sole. Severe gale force 9 increasing storm force 10 imminent. Fastnet. Southwesterly gale force 9 imminent, increasing storm force 10 imminent. Shannon. Northwesterly gale force 9 increasing storm force 10 imminent'. 'Imminent' generally means within six hours, but the depression was moving so fast that the gale warnings were hardly warnings but more indications of the weather being experienced at that moment. The height of the waves increased with the wind and the sea became very confused, waves seeming to appear from any direction between south and northwest.

By Monday night the Fastnet fleet was scattered between the Scillies and the Fastnet Rock with perhaps the majority of the yachts slightly to the north of a line drawn between the two points. By 03.00 (BST) on the morning of Tuesday a number of 'Maydays' had been received and already four lifeboats (three Irish and one English) were pounding through the heavy seas in answer to them. It was obvious that the situation was deteriorating rapidly and a full-scale disaster seemed imminent. At 03.16 Land's End Coastguard station requested help from the Southern Rescue Co-ordinating Centre at Plymouth. This is manned by the Royal Naval and Royal Air Force officers and it swung into action without delay.

The Centre knew that the Fastnet Race was taking place, but it did not know how many yachts were taking part. However, the Centre ordered a search and rescue Nimrod maritime patrol aircraft and helicopters from Culdrose Naval Air Station in Cornwall to be prepared to take off at first light. At 05.35 the first helicopter took off from Culdrose, followed 15 minutes later by another. These two were followed by six more from other Naval Air Stations. A Nimrod and a RAF helicopter took off from Kinross in Scotland and by 06.30 were over the Western Approaches. At sea were the Dutch frigate *Overijssel* and the British fishery protection ship *Anglesea*, which had been diverted from her normal duties. The Dutch frigate was in fact acting as the guard ship for the race as the British had no ship to spare. The Nimrod, with its many sophisticated sensors, took over the duties of the 'on the scene' commander and directed the helicopter movements. So crowded were the air waves with distress traffic that the Nimrod found it extremely difficult to get through to anybody, particularly as the yachts were scattered over nearly 20,000sq miles.

For the rest of Monday night, all Tuesday and part of Wednesday the rescue work continued and it was not until 14.00 on Thursday that all the yachts had been accounted for. Lifeboats all along the English south and west coasts were alerted and the Irish lifeboats in southwest Ireland also played a large part in the rescue. In all, lifeboats from no less than 13 stations were called out, some of the boats being called two or three times. Most of them were employed in searching, but nine boats towed yachts to safety, nine escorted yachts into harbour and others took survivors off ships which had rescued them.

Table of Helicopter Rescues

14 August

Time	Yacht/Dinghy	Event	Remarks
08.15	*Tarantula*	Sinking	1 airlifted off
09.46	*Trophy*	Abandoned	2 airlifted off, 5 missing
09.46	*Grimalkin*	Abandoned	3 airlifted off
09.48	*Magic*	Abandoned	All airlifted off
10.25	*Camargue*	Abandoned	All airlifted off
11.30	*Ariadne*	Abandoned	One body (Ferris) recovered
11.39	*Skullbladner*	Abandoned	All airlifted from dinghy
?	*Gan*	Abandoned	All airlifted off
12.19	*Hestral*	Abandoned	All airlifted off
14.00	*Gringo*	Abandoned	All airlifted off
15.12	*Festina Tertia*	—	1 hypothermia case airlifted off
16.30	*Gunslinger*	Abandoned	All airlifted off
16.55	*Golden Apple*	Abandoned	All airlifted off
17.27	*Flash Light*	Abandoned	Found abandoned, no sign of crew
18.30	*Allamande*	Abandoned	All airlifted off
?	*Billy Bones*	Abandoned	All airlifted off
19.30	*Grimalkin*	Abandoned	1 injured man and 1 dead man airlifted off

15 August

01.30	Helicopters completed last sortie of 14/15 August, but remained on 15 minutes notice

16 August

15.33	Recovered one body, flown to Trelissick hospital

17 August

?	Recovered one body

Times given are approximate only. A total of 74 people were recovered of which three were dead.

Helicopters played a major role in both search and rescue. Some crews had to be recalled from leave and others went out on mission after mission, sometimes with only half an hour between them. All the survivors agreed that had it not been for the helicopters, many more lives would have been lost. The table accompanying this chapter shows the work done by mostly, the Wessex helicopters.

There were numerous stories told by survivors of their own adventures, of the quite incredible endurance shown by many, of the wounds and of the deaths. It would be quite impossible to cover all of them, but here are the stories of two yachts and their crews, chosen not because the crews were particularly heroic, not because all the crew survived, but to illustrate what terrible hardships were endured by all who took part in this never-to-be-forgotten race.

The *Grimalkin*

The story of *Grimalkin* is not one of heroism or of selflessness, but it is one of hardship beyond belief. The yacht was owned by David Sheahan, an accountant and an Englishman who had done a great deal of sailing in small boats but had only recently acquired a large ocean-going yacht. For all that, she was not a very large boat, being only 30ft long and built of glassfibre by Camper Nicholson.

Sheahan set sail for the Fastnet Race with a crew of six (including himself), which was quite a large number considering the boat was one of the smallest in the race. His navigator was Gerry Winks, who was also second in command. The remainder of the crew were made up of his son, Mathew, aged 17, Mike Doyle, Nick Ward and Dick Wheeler. Winks was an arthritic and Ward was an epileptic — perhaps not the fittest of crews to take part in such a gruelling race as the Fastnet.

Saturday and Sunday were calm days and on Sunday they were in fog for much of the time, but they had an uncomfortable ride in the heavy southwesterly swell. The BBC weather forecast on Sunday afternoon gave them some idea of bad weather to come and they took various precautions. By late Monday afternoon the wind shifted to the southwest and increased and at 20.00 they picked up a French forecast which predicted a force 8 to 10 gale gusting to storm force 11. By 23.00 *Grimalkin* was in a full gale and sailing under a storm jib only. To add to their troubles heavy rain started falling. The crew sealed off the cabin as best they could but the rain and the sea soaked everything inside it and equipment, food, clothing and bedding was flying all over the place with the heavy rolling.

They were on the port tack still making for the Fastnet Rock and entering the dangerous quadrant of the depression, although they did not know it. Gerry Winks was at the helm, but at 03.00 on Tuesday morning he was exhausted and had lost a great deal of body heat — in fact he was well on the way to hypothermia. Nick Ward relieved him at the helm and Winks went below to try and get some sleep.

The seas increased alarmingly and eventually David Sheahan decided to abandon the race and run before the wind. They streamed a sea anchor (made out of a length of rope) behind them to try and steady their movements, but even then the yacht was nearly out of control, surfing badly down the slopes of the following waves and tending to somersault over the bow. They had given up using the cabin and all six of them were in the cockpit, their safety harnesses hooked to the lifelines that David Sheahan had rigged before they sailed.

Ward was now at the helm but he could not prevent the boat broaching-to no less than six times between 03.00 and 05.00. Broaching-to means that the boat gets out of control and becomes broadside on to the waves. She rolled over so far that her masts touched the top of the waves and each time it happened all six of the crew were thrown out of the cockpit into the sea, but their harness tethered them to the boat and they were able to scramble back though they suffered badly from bruising and immersion. On the fifth 'knockdown' Ward was thrown out of the cockpit as usual, but his left leg was caught in the harness tethering him to the boat. The Sheahans, father and son, dragged him back but he had badly damaged his left leg and he thought he must have broken it. He remained in the cockpit, bracing himself against the waves, each movement causing him intense agony.

David Sheahan opened up the hatch to the cabin to go below and radio for help on his VHF transmitter. He raised the yacht *Mornington*, the Royal Ocean Racing Club's escorting yacht, and it agreed to pass his distress signal to Land's End. On returning to the cockpit the yacht was once again knocked down and David Sheahan had his head badly cut. His son attempted to spray antiseptic into the open wound and they fixed him up as best they could.

The position then was that the Captain (and owner) was dazed and in great pain and frequently lapsed into periods of unconsciousness, Ward, the navigator, was in terrible pain with his leg, Winks was suffering from hypothermia, was hurt and was also lapsing into unconsciousness from time to time. There was little they could do and when, for the sixth time, *Grimalkin* was knocked down and lay upside down, David Sheahan was trapped under the cockpit. To free him the crew cut his safety harness tether and when the boat finally righted herself a minute or two later, he drifted away in spite of the crew's efforts to hold on to him. He was never seen again.

The capsize dismasted the yacht and the rigging and the boom clattered on to the deck. The five men now remaining managed to drag themselves back into the

Below:
The yacht *Camargue*, whose crew were all lifted off her by RN Wessex helicopters. The last man is seen about to leave. *RNAS Culdrose*

cockpit through the rigging. Ward collapsed on to the floor and Winks rolled unconscious on top of him. Mathew Sheahan, Doyle and Wheeler did not take long to decide that the yacht was completely unsafe; she was half full of water and wallowing uneasily in the waves, which now seemed higher than ever. Ward and Winks appeared to be dead. They therefore decided to abandon ship. They pulled the inflatable dinghy from its storage space in the cockpit and pulled the line which triggered the CO_2 bottle and the dinghy inflated itself quite well. They then began the difficult task of getting into the dinghy and disposing of their harness. They pushed themselves away down wind, leaving the bodies of Ward and Winks onboard the *Grimalkin*.

The dinghy did not prove to be any more reassuring than the yacht, but they covered themselves with the built-in canopy and waited. About an hour later they saw a Sea King helicopter: they waved to it and it hovered over them. A rescue airman was lowered and he secured each one in turn to the webbing harness and one by one they were winched up into the helicopter. After picking up two more survivors from another yacht, the *Trophy*, the helicopter took them to Culdrose and safety.

The *Grimalkin* was still afloat, but once more capsized. Ward regained consciousness under water and found his head was being banged on the inside of the hull and his arms and legs were caught up in the rigging. With great difficulty he extricated himself and climbed back into the cockpit as the yacht once again righted herself. Then he saw Winks being dragged through the water by his tether harness. He managed to wrap it round a winch and hauled him onboard. He was very done in but, amazingly, still alive. Ward started to administer artificial respiration, but it was too late. His last words were 'If you see Margaret again [his wife] tell her that I love her', and he died a few seconds later.

Ward was now alone with a badly damaged leg and a dead man beside him. The gale was blowing as badly as ever. He went back into the cabin, but as he tried to bail, the sea came in again. He was worried because he had not taken his four hourly dose of medicine for his epilepsy, but he could not find the bottle. His watch had stopped but he thought that the waves were now not quite so steep and the clouds were definitely clearing away. He also noted that the wind had shifted to the northwest. The time was, in fact, about 16.00 on Tuesday afternoon.

Some hours later he heard an aircraft passing overhead, but by the time he had scrambled into the cockpit it had gone. He decided to remain in the cockpit, alongside the corpse of his dead friend, in case the aircraft came back. Shortly afterwards a yacht appeared and Ward was able to attract its attention by the use of a hand operated foghorn. The yacht had no radio transmitter but fired off several flares which attracted the attention of a third yacht, which radioed a request for assistance. At last the long awaited helicopter appeared. A man descended on a line and landed right on *Grimalkin's* deck. He soon secured Winks' body in the harness and signalled to the helicopter to haul it up. The harness was lowered again and Ward was similarly secured into it and winched to safety.

Ward ended up in Trelissick hospital in Truro and the doctors told him that the leg he thought was broken was badly bruised, but no actual fracture had occurred. Mrs Winks visited him in hospital and he was able to give her the last message from her husband.

Shortly after his release from hospital he went, with Mathew Sheahan, to the small town of Baltimore in southern Ireland where *Grimalkin* had been towed by a fishing boat. She was in quite a reasonable condition, and Ward and Sheahan got to work to clean her up for future races.

The *Ariadne*

Ariadne was a 30ft boat, owned and skippered by a 61-year old American named Frank Ferris who lived in the UK. His crew consisted of Robert Robie, aged 63 and also an American. A friend of his, Kingman Brewster, the US ambassador to the Court of St James, was to have sailed in the race with them, but at the last minute had to cry off due to being recalled to Washington for a meeting. The rest of the crew were all English: Matthew Hunt, 19-years old and a medical student; Rob Gilders, a sail maker from the Caribbean; David Crisp and Bill LeFevre.

During Monday afternoon they endured the long Atlantic swell experienced by all the boats. At about 22.00 the wind increased and they had to shorten sail, but unfortunately the mainsail split and had to be discarded as useless. This was a grievous blow as they could hardly be expected to race effectively without it. However, they carried on using only a small jib in the rapidly deteriorating weather. At midnight they heard the BBC's shipping forecast which predicted a force 8 or 9 gale, gusting force 10. Already their anemometer was showing 60mph.

Ferris decided that it was not worth continuing and the others agreed, but by now the Irish coast was to leeward of them and they decided that they must beat out to sea. They also discussed whether they could make for Crosshaven harbour for shelter, but for the moment they could only run before the wind. Their jib split, so they formed it into a sea anchor and towed it astern of them to slow the boat down.

Some time later they got caught under the curl of a wave and rolled right over. Gilders was thrown overboard to the limit of his tether attached to his harness. Crisp was trapped under the boat but managed to get free and pull himself back onboard. Whilst the rest of the crew recovered Gilders, with considerable difficulty, LeFevre received a bad head wound and was bleeding profusely. Hunt, with his limited medical knowledge, thought that the wound might prove fatal. Water in the cabin now came up to their waists, so they set to, to try and bail it out and generally clean the boat up a bit. To add to their troubles the mast had broken in two.

At about 05.30 daylight arrived and they had got the water level in the cabin under control. Their spirits were just starting to rise when, once again, the yacht was rolled over right through 360°. Crisp and Robie, who were in the cockpit, got washed overboard. Crisp's harness held and he was towed along by it for a short time before the others could get him onboard again. Robie, however, had disappeared and they could only presume that his harness had snapped. They searched the sea with their eyes and to their delight he appeared some 50yd away on the crest of a wave, but there was no way they could manoeuvre the yacht to pick him up. He waved to them and disappeared again in the trough of a wave. He was never seen again.

This was too much for them and Ferris suggested abandoning the ship. They all agreed and wasted no time in getting the rubber dinghy out. It inflated perfectly and they dropped the dinghy into the sea and gingerly climbed into it. The dinghy proved much more comfortable than had the yacht and its canopy provided a little shelter. LeFevre was obviously in pain and still bleeding profusely. Water kept coming in and they were forced to bail with a small bucket they found in the dinghy.

Two hours later they saw a small freighter so they lit a red flare. The freighter, which proved to be German, altered course towards them. At that moment the dinghy capsized again. Gilders was thrown several feet away, but managed to scramble back. Crisp ended up under the dinghy, but also managed to get back into it. The other three had their harness still hooked to the dinghy, but they still had to board the ship which was rolling frantically in the rough seas. However they managed to right the dinghy.

The German master brought the ship alongside the dinghy with great skill and they were invited to jump for the rope ladder which was dangling over her side. Gilders jumped first and just caught the ladder. He pulled himself up and was dragged onboard and to safety. Ferris went next. He jumped for the bottom rung of the ladder, but missed and to their horror he was swept away — a helicopter subsequently recovered his body. The coaster made a second attempt to get alongside them and Hunt was chosen to go, but he was unable to reach the ladder. The ship went round again. This left Hunt, LeFevre, badly injured, and Crisp, now very weak. Hunt told them both to hook their harnesses to a strap in the bottom of the dinghy to prevent being swept away again and they did so. As the German ship came round again for the third time, Hunt unhooked his harness and rememberde to warn the other two not to forget to do the same when their turn came. Then he jumped for a high rung and a moment later, Crisp jumped for a lower rung. The dinghy jerked away from the ship's side, but Crisp had forgotten to unhook his harness and was pulled off the ladder when he was half way up it. He was washed under the stern of the ship, taking with him the dinghy with LeFevre still in it. They probably got caught by the propeller and they too were never seen again. The German ship searched for a short time, but realising that they could not have survived, she gave up and proceeded on her course up Channel. The Lizard lifeboat was alerted and met them at 01.00 on the Wednesday and took off Hunt and Gilders, the only survivors of a crew of six.

Ariadne was recovered some time later and was towed to Penzance where she lay for three months in the care of the Receiver of Wrecks. She was eventually sold in Plymouth.

These are but two examples of the terrible dangers faced by so many. Others had similar experiences, some more lucky, managing to save their lives, but others had equally terrifying deaths. In all 15 lives were lost and as many had escaped death by inches. A total of 85 boats completed the race, and for the record the overall winner was Ted Turner — a wealthy American — in the 61ft *Tenacious*.

So ended one of the worst disasters ever known in the history of yacht racing. It may have been that some of the crews were not as experienced as they might have been. It may have been the exceptional ferocity of the storm, or it may have been sheer bad luck. Whatever the cause, it has led to the safety rules and regulations for the race being revised in an effort to prevent it ever happening again, but, as every sailor knows, safety of life at sea in bad weather can never be guaranteed.